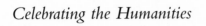
Celebrating the Humanities

Celebrating the Humanities

A HALF-CENTURY OF THE
SEARCH COURSE AT RHODES COLLEGE

Michael Nelson, *Editor*

VANDERBILT UNIVERSITY PRESS • *Nashville and London*

Copyright © 1996 by Vanderbilt University Press
All Rights Reserved
First Edition 1996
96 97 98 99 00   5 4 3 2 1

This publication is made from recycled paper and meets the minimum
requirements of American National Standard for Information Sciences—
Permanence of Paper for Printed Library Materials. ∞

Library of Congress Cataloging-in-Publication Data

Celebrating the humanities : a half-century of the search course at
Rhodes College / Michael Nelson, editor.
        p.   cm.
Includes bibliographical references and index.
ISBN 0-8265-1282-8 (alk. paper)
1. Civilization, Western—Study and teaching—Tennessee—
Memphis—History. 2. Rhodes College—Curricula—History.
I. Nelson, Michael, 1949–
CB245.C38 1996
909'.09812—dc20   96-33546
                                                          CIP

Manufactured in the United States of America

S . D . G .

Contents

Foreword

When I matriculated at age eighteen into the local Agricultural and Mechanical College, shortly before it became the rather more grand-sounding "Colorado State University," I was eager to learn. I wanted to read and to think, to break out of everything small and parochial about my way of seeing the world. As a freshman, I took a course in Western Civilization and fell in love with the Middle Ages, in part because of my enthusiastic instructor, one of that remarkable group of American men who had fought World War II, who had gone to college on the GI Bill, and who were then beginning to fill the ranks of the professoriat. These were men who, at one time, could have conjured no such possibility for themselves. Many of those who survived the war were liberated by the aspiration for higher learning, and many went for it with gusto.

I became enamored of all things medieval. This, I learned, was part of my world as the daughter of a great civilization, but a part that was alien as well—strange, foreign, "other," as we now say. I read Helen Waddell's wonderful book on *The Goliardi*, wandering student poets and trouble-makers. Charles Homer Haskins's *Renaissance of the Twelfth Century* gripped me altogether. It seemed that those lofty souls who later saw themselves leap-frogging over a thousand years of monkish superstition, as if all had been dark before they brought in the light, were making rather too much of themselves. Others had been there before them.

What must it have been like to follow Peter Lombard around Paris? (Of course, women were not then able to matriculate in the great centers of scholastic learning, but one's imagination and aspirations are not thus constrained!) To engage in disputation with Abelard? Or perhaps to wander to Bologna to attend its famous law school? James Westfall Thompson's labor of love on *The Medieval Library* offered an enthralling account of the growth of libraries—what sorts of libraries emerged, where, and how many. Medieval Germany had at least a thousand libraries. I was touched by a poignant discussion of "The Wanderings of Manuscripts," documents found, then lost, then found again miraculously, resurfacing in some other library in a place thousands of miles away. Codices told fascinating tales of cultural transmission and, sadly, of cultural loss as manuscripts disappeared never to be found again. Westphall concludes that it ill becomes those who came later to cast stones at the Middle Ages, "for the destruction of precious books that was most appalling came later when secular power made war against the church, dissolving monasteries, scattering and destroying tens of thousands of medieval books—the accumulation of eight hundred years of intellectual life." The process of modern state making was particularly destructive in this regard. And yet so much remains, warranting so many centuries later St. Bernard of Clairvaux's poignant reminder that we "stand on the shoulders of giants."

But we have arrived at a time and a place—our own—where we do not want to be reminded of this indebtedness, of the gifts others have given us. Hubristic arrogance toward the past thrives in many quarters. We have become puffed up with self-pride and have fallen low as a result. Michael Nelson and his Rhodes College colleagues, by contrast, work from a stance of gratitude for much that has gone before, for brave men and women dedicated to life and learning, to letters and theology, to philosophy and the arts. They remain dedicated—in a lively, not a dour way—to what John Henry Cardinal Newman called "the university as an ethical idea."

To all, like myself, who worry that we may be squandering much of our rich inheritance rather than nurturing it, contesting it, and thereby adding to it as a deposit of cultural faith to pass on to generations to follow, the complex story of the Search course at Rhodes College offers an example of the way a robust but resilient engagement with the past in the present can be sustained. Nelson and his colleagues remind us that a critical education helps students to engage in debate with interlocutors long dead or protagonists who never lived save on the page and, in that engagement, to elaborate rich concepts through which to understand our world. That is the way a living culture, and the education continuously defined and imperfectly realized within it, works.

In his great work, *The Idea of the University*, Newman warned against any single-minded approach to education, any reductionist account of human meaning, purpose, and motivation. He knew things were more complicated. He understood that if you begin from impoverished assumptions, your view of education is itself bound to be impoverished—it cannot help but be—and you lose thereby education as "action upon our mental nature...the formation of character." In *Celebrating the Humanities,* a wonderfully conceived and engagingly executed book, the dedicated keepers of the Search course flame at Rhodes College accomplish something remarkable. They offer solid grounds for hope—not, to be sure, giddy optimism, but hope, nonetheless—that our culture may yet have the resources with which to renew itself and to go on creating generations of scholars, seekers, and citizens.

Jean Bethke Elshtain

Preface

I had a good idea in 1992 and a better one two years later. The good idea was to write a book marking the fiftieth anniversary of the "Search" course (formally titled The Search for Values in the Light of Western History and Religion) at Rhodes College, a Presbyterian-affiliated college in Memphis. The course, which was created for entering freshmen in 1945–1946 under the name Man in the Light of History and Religion, is a two-year, colloquium-intensive study of the literature, philosophy, religion, and history of the West from *Gilgamesh* to the present. Its catalog listings are Humanities 101, 102, 201, and 202, and it constitutes more than 10 percent of a student's total credits toward graduation.

My motivation for writing such a book in the early 1990s was that, at a time when similar courses were being attacked at some colleges and universities as the dark vestiges of "Eurocentric patriarchy," arrogantly presented at others under the banner of "our Judeo-Christian heritage," and, at all too many institutions of higher education, indifferently taught in large lecture sections by resentful junior faculty, the Search course at Rhodes seemed evergreen. Its faculty were united in their commitment to the course but diverse in almost every other way, ranging from staunch traditionalists to feminists and postmodernists and including representatives from nearly a dozen academic departments. Its students comprised a substantial majority of the first-year class, and almost all of them elected to enroll in the course's second year. Faculty and students alike took pride in how the students' writing, critical thinking, verbal expression, and general education improved because of the course. Clearly the story of the Search course—how it began, how it developed, and how it has continued to thrive in a constantly changing intellectual and cultural environment—was worth recovering and recording.

If telling the Search story was the good idea, the better one was to share the research and writing of the book with several other participants in the course, including longtime faculty, recent faculty, men, women, historians, philosophers, political scientists, linguists, classicists, religious studies scholars, even (or perhaps especially) students. Bringing in others made the book better in ways that for half a century have made the course better, augmenting it with a large number of excellent voices, talents, and perspectives, all of them working together with just the right mix of individuality and collaboration.

The opening chapters of *Celebrating the Humanities* tell the history of the Search course from its origins at the end of World War II through its fiftieth year. In chapter 1, I introduce the course's founders—John Henry Davis, Alexander P. Kelso, Laurence F. Kinney, W. Raymond Cooper, and John Osman—and describe how they and President Charles E. Diehl influenced and were influenced by prevailing currents in humanistic and Christian higher education in the 1940s and 1950s. Douglas W. Hatfield picks up the narrative torch in chapter 2 and carries it through the 1960s, when the course was beset by many of the challenges of that tumultuous decade, up to 1975. In chapter 3, Robert R. Llewellyn chronicles the course from 1975 to 1985, equally stormy years because of obstacles that arose within the college itself. Then, in chapter 4, James M. Vest and Daniel E. Cullen bring the story of the Search course into the present, describing a decade in which the change in name from "Man" to "Search" neatly symbolized the turbulent academic waters that the course, like "Western civ" and "great books" courses everywhere, had to navigate. Vest and Cullen also analyze how Search has been able to survive and flourish, undamaged but not unaltered by the experience.

The remaining chapters offer a more eclectic mix of perspectives on the Search course. In chapter 5, Vest describes the spread of the course, or variants of it, from Rhodes to Davidson, Millsaps, Eckerd, Hampden-Sydney, the University of the South, and other distinguished liberal arts colleges. Chapter 6, written by Rhodes students David Welch Suggs, Jr., and James W. Turner, with assistance from a number of other student reporters, presents Search as a living institution by recording a week in the life of the course during the spring 1995 semester. Finally, in chapter 7, I speculate on the future of the Search course at Rhodes and of similar courses at other colleges and universities. In doing so, I take into account numerous trends in the humanities and higher education, ranging from the ongoing war over the "canon" to changes in educational technology.

Sprinkled throughout the book are a number of brief "perspectives" essays, each written by a member of the Search faculty: Ellen T. Armour, Daniel Cullen, James Jobes, Larry Lacy, Kenneth Morrell, Fred W. Neal, Gail Corrington Streete, and me. These essays vary widely, in keeping with the spirit of the course. As its name implies, one of Search's purposes is to encourage students in their personal quests for meaning. Students differ greatly in the destinations to which their searches carry them. Why should it surprise anyone that professors do, too?

My colleagues and I have written *Celebrating the Humanities* in the hope that it will interest a wide range of readers. To those in the humanities and in higher education generally, the issue of how to treat the intellectual and moral legacy of the West within the college curriculum is a constant, significant, and often stormy one. There has been no shortage of books and essays on this subject in recent years. Nearly all of them, however, have been polemics of one sort or another. My colleagues and I hope that our book will offer a reflective, devoted, yet critical account of what one college actually has been doing for the past half-century. Perhaps others will see something of their own experiences and aspirations in this account.

Of course, another important audience for this book is the Rhodes community, wonderfully enumerated in all its diversity by Robert Llewellyn as comprising "housekeepers, teachers and coaches, students, alumni, parents, secretaries and staff assistants, retirees and saints, chaplains and counselors, benefactors, administrators and executives and deans, groundskeepers, trustees, librarians, maintenance technicians, friends." To all of them—past, present, and future—*Celebrating the Humanities* is our lovesong for the college and the course with which we have cast our lot.

Many hands, hearts, and heads have helped me and my colleagues in the writing, editing, and publishing of this book. Several of the authors have used the notes to their chapters to thank individuals who were of particular assistance to them. But all of us are grateful to Elizabeth Gates Kesler, the college archivist, for her tireless and able help in gathering primary documents, to Jean Bethke Elshtain for her gracious foreword, and to all of the good people at Vanderbilt University Press who worked so hard and well to make our manuscript a book: Bard Young, for copy editing and composition; Gary Gore, for the book's design; and the director and staff of the press for the enormous care lavished on our book at every stage of its existence. My own debt, in this as in all things, is to my wife Linda Ezell Nelson (a 1993 adult alumnus of the Search course) and my sons Michael and Sam.

Michael Nelson

Celebrating the Humanities

1

The Founding Era
1945–1958

MICHAEL NELSON

The headline in the August 1, 1945, edition of the Memphis *Commercial Appeal* must have intrigued careful readers:

SOUTHWESTERN TO TURN BACK
TO GREAT BASIC BOOKS
ADOPTING REVOLUTIONARY PLAN, MEMPHIS COLLEGE
WILL FOUND TEACHING ON ROCK OF CLASSICISM

Their attention caught by the incongruous idea of "turning back" to a "revolutionary plan," readers would have learned that Southwestern at Memphis was about to begin its fall 1945 semester by doing something that Harvard University was only talking about—namely, offering "a course designed to acquaint students with the sources of the civilization they live in, and to make them familiar with the great writings which have influenced Western culture."[1]

The twelve-credit-hour course (six hours per semester) would be offered to all freshmen, the article continued, under the name Man in the Light of History and Religion. According to Southwestern President Charles E. Diehl, five professors would teach in the course—two historians, two philosophers, and a biblical scholar. They would take turns lecturing to the students ("all five professors will be present at all formal

3

lectures, four listening while the other speaks," the reporter marveled), then break up the class into small groups for discussions of the week's reading assignments.

Those assignments, drawn overwhelmingly from primary sources, would span the millennia of recorded Western history and thought. During the first semester, students would read widely in the literature of the ancient and early medieval world: the *Epic of Gilgamesh*, most of the Bible, Homer, Hesiod, Herodotus, Plato, Aristotle, Aristophanes, Aeschylus, Sophocles, Euripides, Josephus, Livy, Sallust, Tacitus, Suetonius, Polybius, Plutarch, Terence, Plautus, Juvenal, Horace, Ovid, Lucretius, Epictetus, Seneca, Cicero, Tertullian, Augustine, Dante, Maimonides, Anselm, and Aquinas. The second semester would carry them forward to the present, concluding in a unit called The Two World Wars: Dictatorship and Democracy. The spring reading list included Chaucer, Machiavelli, Petrarch, More, Erasmus, Montaigne, Rabelais, Calvin, Luther, Shakespeare, Marlowe, Sidney, Bacon, Galileo, Newton, Hobbes, Molière, Racine, Donne, Descartes, Spinoza, Leibnitz, Locke, Bunyan, Milton, Voltaire, Hume, Rousseau, Montesquieu, Goethe, Swift, Burke, Smith, Franklin, Malthus, Ricardo, Mill, Metternich, Kant, Marx, Emerson, Byron, Shelley, Wordsworth, Goethe, de Tocqueville, Nietzsche, Darwin, Spencer, Huxley, James, Einstein, Planck—even Stalin, Mussolini, and Hitler.

The *Commercial Appeal* quoted one of the new course's instructors, philosophy professor John Osman, as admitting that the reading load would be difficult for anyone to manage, much less a student fresh from high school. "But," Osman added, "the benefits from such a course will vastly outweigh the effort required to complete it." Osman's confidence in the importance of the endeavor was shared by his faculty colleagues: philosopher Alexander P. Kelso, biblical scholar Laurence F. Kinney, and historians W. Raymond Cooper and John Henry Davis. One of their main goals, they told the newspaper, was to overcome the growing "tendency of education to divide the body of human knowledge into many different fields. . . . Such a program has led to the fragmentation which marks our thinking. The consequence has been that students majoring in particular fields have learned their subject in isolation from the rest of that body of knowledge which is our Western cultural heritage." Another important goal of the course was to recover the understanding, exemplified by Socrates' "know thyself" and Jesus' "perfect thyself," that man "is a rational animal with a spark of the divine in him. Whenever Western civilization has ignored this heritage, it has fallen into low estate."

Setting the Stage

Newspaper articles give a false sense of suddenness. Readers of the August 1, 1945, *Commercial Appeal* could have been forgiven for thinking that the new Southwestern course, reported on that day, had been invented the day before. In truth, the "Man" course, as people instantly began to call it, had been carefully constructed by Southwestern's president and faculty at the confluence of three major streams, each of which had been flowing through higher education for some time. The first was the general education, or "Great Books," movement. The second was World War II. The third was the almost three-decade long presidency of Charles Diehl.

Great Books

Diehl and the Man faculty at Southwestern were not alone in decrying the fragmenting tendencies at work in contemporary higher education; nor were they the first. As the historian George Marsden has noted, in the 1920s the massive industrial and organizational effort required by the U.S. involvement in World War I had generated "the idea that an increasingly complex society demanded trained experts and specialists. The growth of higher education therefore took directions that would fill practical needs."[2] Heeding the call that Harvard President Charles William Eliot issued around the turn of the century, colleges and universities accelerated the trend away from the traditional common undergraduate curriculum to the free electives system. They began to offer an increasing number of technical and professional programs and, so that students could specialize in these programs, to loosen long-standing requirements that undergraduates take a significant number of liberal arts courses.[3]

Others learned a very different lesson from World War I.[4] The war had threatened the heritage of the West and laid bare the human capacity for evil, they believed, in ways that made urgent the task of educating Americans about the ideals on which Western civilization had been built. Toward the end of the war, at the prodding of the federal government, colleges and universities across the country had begun "war-issues courses" for student-soldiers in the Students' Army Training Corps. The purpose of these courses, which were jointly designed and taught by the historians, literary scholars, philosophers, political scientists, and economists on each campus, was to explore the deep roots of the war in the belligerent nations' history, literature, and philosophy. "Beyond its appeal to professors as an outlet for their patriotism," the historian Carol Gruber found, "the War Issues Course was praised for having demonstrated the desirability and feasibility of educational reform to breach the walls separating the disciplines, to introduce some order in the chaos of the elective system."[5] Some scholars, notably Columbia University English professor John Erskine, President Robert M. Hutchins of the University of Chicago, and Mortimer Adler, who was Erskine's student at Columbia and, later, Hutchins's assistant at Chicago—were inspired to promote a broadly liberal general-education curriculum that was grounded in the great books of the West.

The General Honors course that Adler took from Erskine in the early 1920s was the prototype for general education—it had grown indirectly out of Columbia's War Issues Course.[6] General Honors consisted of sixty two-hour seminars spread over two years, each seminar devoted to a great book. Erskine believed that the mark of a great book was that it continued to speak to successive generations of readers. A number of curricular innovations flowed from this understanding. Because great books were timeless, students would read only primary texts, unencumbered by criticism or scholarship that would ground each work in its historical and cultural context. Because the books would shed light on the students' own lives (or so Erskine hoped), the class would discuss them, not hear lectures from the professor. And because the books were universally illuminating, leadership of the class would not rotate from specialist to specialist in literature, philosophy, classics, and so on, but would remain with one instructor, an amateur in the best sense of the word, who would be the students' fellow seeker as well as their docent in the search for truth.

Adler was evangelistic in his zeal for the great books approach. His most important convert was Hutchins, who in 1929, at age thirty, became president of the University of Chicago. Hutchins hired Adler as his assistant in 1930, and for the next twelve years they worked to infuse the university's undergraduate curriculum with great-books courses. (They even taught one together, modeled almost exactly on the course that Adler had taken from Erskine at Columbia.) In 1936, Hutchins published *The Higher Education in America*, which decried the trend toward specialization and professionalization in the curricula of most colleges and universities and urged that students be offered only general education courses during their freshman and sophomore years.[7] Hutchins's book was the most widely read and discussed work on higher education in the country for at least the next decade.

The great books approach to learning spread. Some colleges adopted the approach in its pure Erskine-Adler-Hutchins form. St. John's College in Annapolis, Maryland, for example, was founded in 1937 with a curriculum that consisted entirely of general education courses—its students read and discussed the great books and the great books only. (The president of St. John's, Stringfellow Barr, was a friend of Adler's.) Most colleges that incorporated such courses into the curriculum did so partially, however, and with more of a historical and cultural approach to the study of texts than the purists approved. But even they soon adopted the amateur over the professional ideal of instruction. "One institution after another," a contemporary observer found, "has concluded that a better humanities course could be developed when a single instructor took the same group of students through the whole program than when specialists were allowed to handle their own fields." As one instructor said, "I attribute [my success in the course] partly to my own ignorance. If I had felt really competent to teach such a course, pride would have prevented me from taking the frank attitude of the learner and sharing with the students fresh discoveries."[8]

A 1949 survey of the progress of general education in college humanities programs found that the approach had caught on mostly in private institutions outside the South, the majority of them church affiliated.[9] Curiously, however, the Bible found its way onto the reading list of few great books courses. Metaphysics—the rational search for first principles—was at the heart of general education, Hutchins argued in *The Higher Education*. As to theology, "we are a faithless generation and take no stock in revelation. . . . To look to theology to unify the modern university is futile and vain."[10] The influential *Harvard Report on General Education*, published in 1945 by a committee that President James B. Conant had appointed to reverse the trend toward specialization at his institution, was similarly nonbiblical and atheological in its recommendations for general education.

The general education movement was not without its critics. Virginia Woolf, deriding "middlebrow" culture as "betwixt and between . . . neither art itself nor life itself," singled out Adler's Great Books discussion groups as an especially egregious example of prosperous and complacent people seeking to add no more than a patina of intellectual respectability to their thoroughly bourgeois lives.[11] Stronger resistance came from within the colleges and universities themselves, which had been thriving on the trend toward specialization and professionalization. Faculty members typically were resistant; as one study found, younger professors, anxious about their careers, "often feel that promotion can be better secured by faithfully discharging departmental duties than those in a course which has no administrative status."[12]

World War II

The academic soul-searching that World War I had provoked was as nothing compared with that inspired by World War II. The rise of fascism in Hitler's Germany and Mussolini's Italy, and its early alliance with Soviet communism, both rekindled fears that Western civilization's noblest traditions were imperiled and awakened hopes that a more widespread study of those traditions would be a safeguard for the future. When, on December 17, 1942, Secretary of War Henry L. Stimson and Secretary of the Navy Frank Knox announced that colleges and universities must set aside liberal education for military training, Hutchins responded that the government was wrong to believe that "the only education useful in wartime is education designed to produce large quantities of low-grade mechanics and small quantities of high-grade ones. . . . I do not believe the technically-trained robots will be effective in time of war. I am certain that they will be a full-grown menace to their fellow citizens in time of peace."[13]

Some shared Hutchins's concern, asking, should not America cling all the more strongly to the liberal traditions that had so far spared it from a European-style collapse of democracy? As Wendell Willkie said in a January 14, 1943, address at Duke University, "The destruction of the tradition of the liberal arts, at this crisis in our history, when freedom is more than ever at stake . . . would be a crime, comparable, in my opinion, with the burning of books by the Nazis. And it would have approximately the same results. Burn your books—or, what amounts to the same thing, neglect your books—and you will lose freedom, as surely as if you were to invite Hitler and his henchmen to rule over you."[14] Hutchins's book on higher education received a new round of attention in the wartime environment.

Charles Diehl's Southwestern

More, perhaps, than any other person in the South, Charles Diehl was absorbed by the national debate about general education.[15] But initially his ability to act on his interest was confined to a remote precinct of academe. The college whose presidency Diehl assumed in 1917 was not

Southwestern at Memphis but Southwestern Presbyterian University in Clarksville, Tennessee. The school's history had been turbulent since its founding in 1848—three name changes (from Masonic College to Montgomery Masonic College in 1851, then to Stewart College in honor of its president and major patron, William M. Stewart, in 1855, and to Southwestern Presbyterian University in 1874) and four corresponding changes in affiliation (from the Masonic Grand Lodge of Tennessee to the Masonic Lodge of Clarksville to the southern Presbyterian Church's Nashville synod to several southern synods). Of more immediate concern, the college's buildings were deteriorating, its endowment was shrinking, and its enrollment consisted of only fifty full-time students.

Diehl, a native of Charles Town, West Virginia, was the forty-two-year-old pastor of Clarksville's First Presbyterian Church when the college's board of directors recruited him to become president. His life had been much influenced by Woodrow Wilson, whose father, Joseph R. Wilson, had by coincidence headed Southwestern Presbyterian's divinity school in the 1880s. Like Woodrow Wilson, Diehl had studied at Johns Hopkins University, earning his B.A. in 1896. He went on to Princeton, where he took classes from Professor Wilson and earned an M.A.; he also graduated from the university's seminary (by then he was wearing Wilson-style pince-nez) and was ordained as a Presbyterian minister. When Wilson became president of Princeton in 1902, he offered a new vision

Charles E. Diehl, oil portrait by John Henry Davis.

for the university that Diehl heartily endorsed: an Oxford–Cambridge style of education, grounded in the preceptorial method of small–group instruction, and an Oxford–Cambridge style of architecture. Indeed, Wilson decreed that thenceforth all new buildings constructed at Princeton would be in the Gothic style.

Reviving a dying college, not improving a strong one, was Diehl's immediate challenge in Clarksville. But he innovated as boldly as he could: an honor code for students in 1918, the admission of women in 1920, and a strategy of recruiting Oxford-trained scholars, including one of the founders of the Man course, W. Raymond Cooper, to the faculty. Cooper was a widely-traveled historian—he had grown up on a plantation in Alabama, earned degrees at Washington and Lee, Harvard, Oxford, and the University of Alabama law school, and served in the British army in Egypt, Mesopotamia, and India. Most significant, after Diehl and his board concluded that they could not fulfill their ambitions for the college in Clarksville, which had not developed into the large metropolis the college's founders had envisioned, they decided to move the institution to Memphis. The state's largest city rolled out not just the red carpet for Diehl, his faculty, and his students but also a green one: Memphians raised $500,000 for their new college.

Memphis proved to be a blank canvas on which Diehl could paint his portrait of an excellent college. He was thwarted in his effort to rename it the College of the Mississippi Valley; the board of directors preferred Southwestern at Memphis. But in every other way Diehl succeeded. "Determined to fashion the most beautiful campus in the South, if not the entire United States," he purchased a wooded, 100-acre site near Overton Park in the city's growing eastern residential area.[16] He secured the services of Charles Z. Klauder of Philadelphia, the leading Gothic architect in the country and the designer of several Princeton buildings, and of a Klauder protégé, the Nashvillian Harry C. Hibbs, who had designed Scarritt College and Vanderbilt University's Alumni Memorial Hall and Neely Auditorium, to plan Southwestern's campus and buildings. He even bought a limestone quarry in Bald Knob, Arkansas, so that the college could fashion all of its buildings from the same stone. During the summer before the college opened its doors in September 1925, Diehl sent Cooper, who was the dean of men, ahead to Memphis to oversee final preparations. For two months, Cooper was the only person living on campus.

Diehl instituted an Oxbridge-style tutorial system of education, in which students would study certain subjects in individual sessions with their professors. (Southwestern and Harvard were the only two colleges in the United States then employing such a system.) In addition, he redoubled his efforts to recruit faculty from the ranks of Oxford-educated Rhodes Scholars. More than a dozen Rhodes and other Oxford scholars joined the faculty during the Memphis phase of Diehl's tenure as president, including John Henry Davis and Alexander Kelso, two of the other founders of the Man course.

Kelso, the son of missionaries who were serving in India when he was born, was a philosopher and a Presbyterian minister. His two degrees from Oxford were a B.A. in ethics and an M.A. in theology, and at Southwestern he held the R. A. Webb Chair of Philosophy and Christian Ethics. Kelso was the sort of crusty, dramatic, impassioned, inspiring, unpredictable teacher whom students discuss constantly while they are in school and swap stories about at class reunions. One student penned a three-word tribute: "Socrates, Erasmus, Kelso." Another, Anne Howard Bailey, later wrote a National Christopher Award-winning television play about him for a 1951 episode of the "Armstrong Circle Theatre." The Kelso character in the play (Professor Kelsey) keeps students constantly off balance—he says things like "Exams are farcical....And I enjoy farce!" and provokes a senior to describe him as someone who "loves to hang you on tenterhooks. Says it strengthens moral fibre!" But, as with the real Kelso, Kelsey's wisdom is what proves to be of enduring influence on his students. After an honor student cheats on an exam, he guiltily remembers Kelsey's discussion of Socrates: "Professor Kelsey put it this way. He said failure is sometimes worth more than success—and a man's got to know his true worth."[17]

Davis was equally fabled for his force of personality. A Kentuckian, he absorbed Oxford through every pore as a Rhodes Scholar studying history at Exeter College—by the time Davis returned home to teach at Davenport College in Lenoir, North Carolina, he wrote, "My English clothes, and accent, were quite a curiosity." After leaving Davenport to earn his doctorate at the University of Chicago, Davis turned down an offer from Vanderbilt and accepted one from Southwestern, whose faculty he joined in 1926. Davis got on wonderfully with Kelso—indeed, he lived with the Kelsos during his first year in Memphis—and tolerably with his fellow historian Cooper, "a misogynist . . . who always took the 'brighter' boys sections and left me the girls section and the 'dumb' section of boys." Davis was a famously affable and energetic professor; a colleague described him as "Leonardo-like" in his breadth of talents and interests. He founded the Nitist Club at Southwestern, a group of faculty and students who wrote and read philosophical papers to each other. (Abraham Fortas, Class of 1930, was an early president). He also painted, including portraits of Robert Penn Warren and Allen Tate, each of whom taught briefly at Southwestern; played second bassoon in the Memphis Symphony Orchestra; and served as an ordained deacon at St. Mary's Episcopal Cathedral, whose centennial history he wrote. Davis was as Democratic as Kelso was Republican. Once, after losing an election bet over which party would carry Tennessee in a presidential election, Davis rolled a peanut down a campus sidewalk with his nose. Grandly (Davis was "a Falstaff without the vice or volume," one friend observed), he put the peanut in a little wagon, taped a band-aid to his nose, and briskly pushed it along.[18]

The mainline Protestant commitments that Cooper, Kelso, and Davis shared were no less important to Diehl than their Oxford pedigrees. Diehl's educational philosophy was Christian as well as British but in a way that resisted both of the leading educational trends of his time. Many colleges and universities, originally established as religious institutions, were abandoning their explicitly Christian identity for one grounded in science and professionalism.[19] Vanderbilt, for example, founded by Bishop Holland N. McTyeire in 1875, had cast off its Methodism in 1914. In response, a fundamentalist counteroffensive was underway. Conservative Christians founded hundreds of Bible colleges, mostly in the South, to offer students an alternative to the increasingly secular established colleges and universities. The 1925 Scopes trial in Dayton, Tennessee, accelerated this development.

Diehl wanted Southwestern to open a third way: education that was liberal and general, not professional and specialized, and avowedly Christian, but not narrow or sectarian. With regard to liberal education, his main goals were to produce a "self-reliant and physically sound individual, with a high sense of honor, and an appreciation of *real* values; a responsible human being; . . . one who is mentally alert, has a disciplined intelligence, who has the capacity for critical analysis, ability to recognize and organize sets of facts, and to interpret them correctly; . . . one who has a cultivated taste, the ability to understand and appreciate the great documents of art, morals, and religion, and to evaluate them wisely; . . . one who is socially enlightened—kindly and courteous."[20]

As to Christian education, Diehl often bragged (inaccurately) that Southwestern was the first college in the country to require study of the

Bible in English. Freshmen had to take a two-semester sequence of Old and New Testament, then complete their education with the yearlong Senior Bible course designed to tie the entire college experience together. Diehl never doubted that every faculty member should be "a Christian gentleman with a love for the Christian Church and possessing the Christian graces that would make his influence felt among the students entrusted to his care; this, of course, in addition to his training as a thorough scholar in his chosen field of study."[21] But Christian faculty, especially those who taught religion, also had to be highly intellectual in their faith and in their teaching, drawing on the scientific method, archeological studies, and modern biblical scholarship, not imparting rigid dogma based on isolated passages of scripture. Although Southwestern would offer Christianity to its students as a serious alternative, it would not indoctrinate them.[22]

Diehl had to defend his commitment to Christian liberal education against critics on more than one front. Some felt that his approach was outdated and unrealistic. Diehl's "refusal to substitute the more popular vocational studies of the day for Mathematics, the Classics, and History was deemed old-fashioned," notes Cooper in his centennial history of Southwestern.[23] (Students had to choose from a limited range of courses in mathematics, Latin or Greek, English, a modern language, history, philosophy, and science, in addition to Bible.) Diehl did not dispute the accuracy of the label. The curriculum he admired most was the one that had prevailed in American higher education from the seventeenth century through the late nineteenth: a fixed course of study resting on the twin pillars of Christianity and the classics.[24] In a biographical statement written around 1950, Diehl trumpeted, "The program of religious studies has steadily increased [at Southwestern]; in the 1920s there was strenuous opposition to it by the Babbits of the day, who wanted more rah-rah and revenue for the college, but Dr. D. held his ground stoutly."[25]

Fundamentalists took a different tack in criticizing Diehl. In September 1930, at the instigation of W. S. Lacy, who had just resigned unhappily as Southwestern's executive secretary, a group of local Presbyterian ministers filed charges with the college's board that Diehl "is not what may be called Sound in the Faith," in part because "he did not believe in the historical or scientific accuracy of the first part of Genesis" and held unorthodox views concerning hell. On February 3, 1931, at a public hearing of the board presided over by Memphis mayor Watkins Overton, Diehl responded, "With regard to the first chapter of Genesis, I said I did not think it was a scientific treatise." He added that "it was hard for me to think about [Plato] in an undying hell." But the burden of Diehl's testimony was to affirm his faith that "Christ alone is '*the* Word of God,' that He alone is the perfect revelation of God, and that everything is to be judged and measured by His teachings and life." The board exonerated Diehl completely, to the joy of a widely supportive student body and faculty; so did his home presbytery in Nashville, where conservative Presbyterians had filed similar charges.[26]

World War II only confirmed Diehl in his commitment to Christian liberal education. In a 1943 speech to the Egyptians, a Memphis philosophical society, he argued that "one of the prime causes" of the current world crisis is the joining of the professionalization of education to

the secularization of education that has brought us to our present plight. . . . The religious aim was supplanted by the modern god efficiency, and the emphasis came to be laid on means rather than ends. . . . Technology, whether in the creation of new explosives or a new method of super-salesmanship, stands outside and disclaims the moral results of its acts. This war shows that the education of the past few decades has trained a fine group of technicians. It shows also that we might well turn back to the older theory of a liberal education for free men, which is concerned with convictions and consciences, with ultimate values.[27]

Early Efforts

As concerned as Diehl was about what secularization and professionalism had been doing to higher education before World War II, he was even more concerned about the future. "The question we want to ask is, what about the postwar period as it relates to liberal education?" he said in his 1943 speech. "Are the humanities outmoded, or are they—philosophy, history, literature, and the arts—still to be depended upon to give perspective, poise, insights, conviction and a right sense of values? . . . Will there be a renewed effort to make our young men and women familiar with our history, more appreciative of our heritage, and more responsible for carrying forward our democratic way of life? . . . Will those in authority realize that education cannot be divorced from religion except at the peril of both, and the consequent impairment of our civilization?"[28]

Diehl's first effort to have Southwestern address these questions ended in disappointment. On October 28, 1943, he appointed the twelve-faculty-member Committee on Post-War Liberal Education, with political scientist David M. Amacker as chair, and charged it to discover ways "of imparting a sense of the uses of knowledge in the lives of our students." "Great Books" were to be a part of this effort, Diehl added—"reading not about them, but reading the books themselves."[29] In addition, "It is probably wise to consider breaking down hard and fast departmental lines." The committee held many meetings, and eventually came up with a new program of comprehensive examinations in each senior's major field of study. But as to liberal education, "it produced only a host of conflicting definitions arranged in the fashion of Abelard's *Sic et Non*," according to John Henry Davis.[30]

John Osman and "The Great Centuries"

Frustrated by the difficulties of generating reform within the college, Diehl turned outside for help. In July 1944, he sent a faculty delegation to a conference on the humanities at Vanderbilt. Several of them, including Kelso, came back fired with a stronger commitment to general education than when they left. Diehl also invited Theodore M. Greene, a philosopher and the chair of Princeton University's humanities division, and George A. Works, the former dean of the University of Chicago, to visit Southwestern as consultants on curriculum. Both were, like Diehl, Christians with a strong commitment to liberal education. Works came in February 1944, met with the faculty, and stimulated an inconclusive discussion about whether "a required survey of the humanities, consisting of a careful study of great books selected from various fields of thought" would be a good way to reduce the prevailing lack of "coordination or synchronization of the courses" taken by freshmen and sophomores.[31] Greene, whose contribution to the development of the Man course later would turn out to be substantial, was too tied down by war-intensified responsibilities at Princeton to visit Southwestern in 1944.

Greater success came when Diehl converted an outsider into an insider. John Osman was a young professor of philosophy at Presbyterian College in Clinton, South Carolina, during the war, but he was spending most of his time as physical-training director for the Army Air Forces Training Detachment that was based on campus. (Osman had been a champion sprinter for Presbyterian College as a student, making it to the finals of the 1932 U.S. Olympic tryouts.) Diehl invited Osman to speak at Southwestern's spring vesper service on April 2, 1944. Osman, who had an M.A. in philosophy from the University of Richmond and an M.Th. from Richmond's Union Theological Seminary, accepted the invitation, and his visit was a great success. As a speaker he was, in the words of one observer, "limber and nice"—the front-page headline in the *Sou'wester* after his vesper talk was a mildly astonished, "Dr. Osman Proves to Be Interesting." (His theme was that the students should be worthy of the sacrifice made once and for all time by Jesus Christ and those made currently by American soldiers.) More important, Diehl discovered that Osman's views on Christian liberal education resembled his own— Osman believed strongly that one should study the great books and that the Bible was "the classic of classics."[32] Soon after Osman's visit, Diehl invited him to join the Southwestern faculty. He accepted with alacrity and arrived on campus in July 1944. Osman's position required him to teach philosophy, to serve as a wide-ranging assistant to Diehl, and, above all, to create the new adult education program that the college wanted to offer in anticipation of large numbers of returning veterans.

Osman's first act as adult education director was to organize a symposium for the Memphis and campus communities on The Great Centuries during the 1944–1945 academic year. Every Friday night for sixteen weeks, townspeople and students were invited to Southwestern's Hardie Auditorium to hear ninety minutes of lectures from various faculty members and (if the lecturers finished in time—they often did not) to ask thirty minutes of questions. The titles of each week's programs tended toward the celebratory—The Greek Miracle (5th Century B.C.), The Greatness That Was Rome (1st Century A.D.), The Century of Hope (19th Century), and so on. As the program booklet indicated, two of the main premises of the symposium were that, intellectually and spiritually, the past was better than the present and that the way to make things better in the future would be to recover the best ideas and beliefs of the past:

The world is intellectually and spiritually adrift. Long established standards of life and conduct are being swept away in a torrent of fluid history. There are absence of direction and confusion everywhere. . . . Perhaps if we can trace our heritage back to Israel, Greece, and Rome, we shall find those "first principles" which order our lives.[33]

One additional premise underlay the Great Centuries symposium: the importance of Christianity in sorting out the wheat in the Western tradition from the chaff. As Osman wrote, "The cultural materials of a Nazi, a Dane, or an American do not essentially differ. It is in the arrangement of these materials and the emphasis placed upon certain ones of them that the great difference lies. The Symposium strives to work the materials of our Western cultural heritage into an organic whole under a single integrating principle. Such an arrangement will give us an approach to knowledge in the light of the highest truth—the sovereignty of God."[34]

The public's response to the Great Centuries was enthusiastic. Both Memphis newspapers, the *Commercial Appeal* and the *Press-Scimitar*, assigned reporters to write day-of and day-after stories each week. Chairs lined the aisles to accommodate the overflow crowds. Occasional interruptions—flickering lights on one occasion, a panicked, crowd-buzzing bird on another—were taken in stride. A student reporter for the *Sou'wester*, impressed by all that he had heard, proclaimed: "Southwestern has one of the best faculties in the United States."[35]

As a window opening on the Southwestern faculty of the day, the Great Centuries series revealed not just the faculty's excellence but also its evolving appreciation for Diehl's vision of Christian general education. Nineteen of the college's thirty faculty members took part, including all of the humanities faculty except for two Romance language professors. Two of the five natural scientists (one of them was Peyton Nalle Rhodes, a physicist and the future president of Southwestern) but only one social scientist, David Amacker, participated. Those who later would found the Man course were especially active, including Osman and his fellow newcomer and Union Theological Seminary alumnus, Laurence Kinney, a Presbyterian minister with a Ph.D. in philosophy from the University of Virginia who had joined the Southwestern faculty in January 1944 as the Albert Bruce Curry Professor of Bible. Kinney and Kelso spoke at eight sessions each, on topics ranging from, in Kelso's case, Virgil to twentieth-century pragmatism, and, in Kinney's, from Jesus to the nineteenth-century philosophy of progress. Osman, in addition to being the symposium's organizer, appeared five times, treating the Stoics and Epicureans, Kierkegaard, and a variety of other topics. Davis and Cooper spoke almost as frequently, and with equal range. Together, the five gave nearly half the lectures in the series.

The tone of the lectures was, as promised in the program, celebratory about the past, deeply concerned about the present (especially the American present), and urgent about the future. "The problem which faced the old Romans is similar to one which faces us today," said Cooper in a representative peroration. "Will we at the end of this war insist that laws and institutions peculiar to the American system are more enlightened than those of the rest of the world, and therefore must be adopted by the 'One World' of the future; or will we be willing to study the laws and institutions of all nations, and assist in developing legal institutions and a legal system based on the ideas of justice and equality common to all nations?"[36]

The Great Centuries symposium crystallized some of the faculty participants' thinking about the kind of higher education that must follow the war if the future was to be better than the present. "The fate of the world is in the hands of the Democracies," Kelso said in one lecture, "and, in the last resort, of the people of the United States. . . . The fate of democracy in this land depends on education which reaches deep into a man's soul, leading to spiritual growth and development and, ultimately, spiritual freedom."[37] Osman drew the issue more plainly: "We tried to sell the boys the war on a materialistic basis . . . and it didn't work. No man is willing to go out and die for a mechanical refrigerator. But a man is willing to die for an ideal or a great spiritual concept, and the only way we can judge what is worth dying for is by using the yardstick of time."[38] Diehl, impressed by all that he had heard during the preceding fifteen sessions, ended the symposium approvingly on April 6, 1945. "Our only hope for the future is to return to the life of the spirit," he urged; "to realize that the problems we face today and in the future can be solved only by those who are intellectually disciplined and morally enlightened, that that which is economic and social and political must be subordinated to that which is spiritual."[39]

Consultants and Planning

The Great Centuries symposium laid a strong foundation on which to build the kind of curriculum innovations for the postwar period that Diehl had been wanting. Because the lectures had been so successful, faculty participants such as Cooper and Davis made the obvious suggestion: Why not do something like this for our students? Kinney and Osman, before coming to Southwestern, had already spent many hours together in Richmond sharing their passion for interdisciplinary education.[40] They and some other faculty members, including Kelso, were especially eager to bring a version of the symposium into the curriculum: they had invested a great deal of time preparing lectures and had enjoyed the experience of working and teaching together in a common endeavor. The combination of Osman's energy, Kinney's irenic calmness ("He had a way of being a kind of central spirit without exercising any kind of authority," said one observer),[41] Kelso's dramatic flair, Davis's breadth, courtliness, and confidence, and Cooper's commitment to the college gave the group team-like coherence. All stood, unselfconsciously, on the traditional liberal arts side of the prevailing divide in the humanities that separated wide-ranging "men of letters" from the specialized philologists who had come to dominate the universities. As the literary scholar Gerald Graff has observed, "Literature for them was about spiritual and social values, not the pedantic etymologies, linguistic laws, and antiquarian facts that seemed to be the only thing the research scholars could find in it."[42] Most important, the five of them had developed whatever inchoate ideas they previously may have had about the importance of Christian general education into a mature educational philosophy.

Diehl was excited about the prospects for curriculum reform. On January 15, 1945, he praised the Great Centuries series at a faculty meeting and, according to the minutes, "raised the question of whether or not such a course should be required of all Southwestern freshmen."[43] The next day he wrote to Theodore Greene, who finally had been able to take time off from Princeton and was scheduled to visit Southwestern on January 27. In his letter, Diehl mentioned the idea (which he attributed to Cooper) of introducing a Great Centuries-style course into the curriculum, then asked Greene to broach the following topics when he met with Southwestern's faculty: "Indoctrination in ideals and values, religious, moral, esthetic, social, of Western World for citizenship and international mindedness. General reading of great books to be required of all students?"[44]

Greene was more than receptive to Diehl's suggestion. A Christian philosopher—"one of the few Christian philosophers in the country," Diehl had said of Greene when seeking the directors' approval to invite him[45]—and a passionate advocate of liberal education, Greene was a friend of Diehl's and an old friend of Cooper's. (While Cooper was with the British army in India during World War I, Greene was serving as secretary of India's YMCA and teaching at Forman Christian College of the University of Punjab.) In 1940, the American Council of Learned Societies had commissioned Greene to study how liberal education was faring in the increasingly hostile environment of specialization and professionalization in higher education. In the course of his research, Greene had visited forty-five colleges around the country, including Southwestern, where he gave the 1941 commencement address. The theme of his address—that World War II had come about because "the acids of modernity have eaten away, or at least gravely weakened, our cultural and spiritual foundations" and that "[t]he cure, and the only one, is liberal education"—was music to Diehl's ears.[46] When Green's ACLS report, *Liberal Education Re-Examined: Its Role in a Democracy*, was published as a book in 1943, Diehl sang its praises in a review for the *Commercial Appeal*.[47]

Greene's book contained, among other things, his proposal for the ideal humanities curriculum. This curriculum set history and philosophy apart from and, implicitly, above the rest of the humanities: arts, letters, and religion. According to Greene, "The primary function of both [history and philosophy] . . . is to provide integration and synoptic interpretation. So conceived, they have no distinct subject matter. Their primary task is to relate the specialized activities of the less comprehensive disciplines. . . . Parts acquire new meaning when they are set in a larger context."[48]

During Greene's visit, Southwestern's faculty seemed to embrace his vision of the humanities curriculum and considered how to adapt it to the college's distinctly Christian view of liberal education. They discussed with him, in an evening session, the "desirability of a course combining religion/Bible, philosophy, history in freshman year." After Greene's departure, in the section of the report on their conference with him that dealt with the goal of infusing values and coherence into the curriculum, the faculty secretary wrote, "History, philosophy, religion are synthesizing disciplines touching all. These are basic axes of all knowledge."[49] The three disciplinary building blocks of what soon would become the Man course—not just history and philosophy, but also religion—were now in place.

The Man Course, 1945–1958

Institutional inertia and departmental narrowness are powerful forces in academe. The momentum behind Diehl's ideas for, in general, a renewal of Christian liberal education in the postwar era, and, in particular, an interdisciplinary humanities course for Southwestern's freshmen that would serve as the basis for such an education seemed to slacken as soon as the glow of Greene's visit wore off. On March 3, 1945, Diehl proposed at a faculty meeting that the college "consider the idea of giving the Great Centuries course next year to freshmen and sophomores." No response is recorded in the minutes.[50] When he renewed his plea two days later, the faculty "moved and passed that this suggestion be tabled."[51]

Diehl quickly arranged for Greene to return to Southwestern on May 21. He preceded Greene's arrival with a May 14 letter that revealed his frustration:

As you well know it is very difficult to get members of a faculty, nearly all of whom are individualists, who think well of themselves and their departments, to be openminded about the matter of making changes. The idea of paying less attention to departments than to fields or divisions is not heartily welcomed, and yet this is one matter that must be seriously faced. I wish that you would exercise your persuasive ingenuity in connection with the problem.[52]

Diehl was not alone in wanting to bring about change, however. After the faculty voted to table his March 5 motion, the proposal for a Great Centuries-style course ended up in the hands of a committee that was dominated by Davis, Kelso, Cooper, and, as chair, Osman. One week before Greene returned to Southwestern, the committee issued a report whose stated purpose was "To construct a course in Western Civilization offering a new intellectual adventure to the student who seeks a liberal education." Tentatively titled Humanities or The Cultural Heritage, the course was "proposed for next year and constructed around the general plan set forth in 'The Great Centuries Lectures.'" It would be two semesters long, interdepartmental ("or nondepartmental"), chronologically arranged, and "concerned with the effects of events upon human attitudes and relationships." The readings would come from primary sources, and nonliterary "great works of art" also would be included. One-fourth of the course would be spent on each of four units: The Classical Heritage (to 500 A.D.), The Medieval Scene (500–1550), The Culture of Modern Europe (1550–1815), and Our American Heritage (1815-present).[53]

Greene's May visit, joined to Diehl's steady pressure and the committee's recommendation, turned the faculty tide in favor of the new freshman humanities course. On May 21 and 22, Greene and the committee worked to refine the proposal, addressing questions such as: How many people would be involved in teaching the course?; how many credit hours would it receive?; would it be a required or an elective course?; how would religion, history, and philosophy be intermixed? The next evening, with Greene present as a "special guest," the faculty voted to approve the still unnamed course and charged the committee to spend the summer getting it ready for the freshman class that would arrive in September.[54]

The First Year, 1945–1946

With Osman as chair, Davis, Kelso, Kinney, and Cooper as members, and Diehl frequently in attendance, the Committee on the Course—now the staff of the course—met frequently during the late spring and early summer of 1945. Because they were people who generally liked and respected each other, shared a common educational philosophy, and had worked together before, they resolved the major issues of the course with remarkable speed and congeniality. They chose the name Man in the Light of History and Religion because it embodied the course's union of history, religion, and philosophy. The purposes they defined for the course, as stated in their jointly authored introduction to the bound syllabus (actually a full-blown study guide) that they distributed to all students, were threefold: first, to learn about "our cultural heritage by study of the historical movements and institutions and the philosophical and religious ideas which have produced Western man"; second, to help students grow personally ("Students need such an historic-religious framework into which they can fit their own lives and times"); and third, to lay an intellectual foundation for college study. Ruing "the tendency of education to divide the body of human knowledge into many different fields, such as history, art, economics, politics, religion, philosophy, and

Founders of the Search course. (Left to right): W. Raymond Cooper (inset), Lawrence F. Kinney, John Osman, John Henry Davis, Alexander P. Kelso.

the various physical sciences," as well as the consequent "fragmentation which marks our thinking," the Man staff committed itself to offering students a "cultural synthesis" so that their entire college education "will be fashioned into an organic whole."[55]

Not all the challenges of constructing the course were so stimulating; many were simply logistical. The staff needed a large lecture hall with maps, a slide projector, a screen, and windows that could be darkened— room 101 in Science Hall (now Kennedy Hall) was secured. A daily hour, six days a week, on the schedule needed to be cleared—the registrar pushed aside other freshman classes so that the new course could meet at nine o'clock in the morning. A massive amount of assigned reading material had to be gathered and made available to students—the library provided a room (soon dubbed the "Man room") on the third floor of Palmer Hall, and Mary Osman, the assistant librarian, placed thirty or more copies of each text on reserve, along with works of visual art and music. (A $10 fee was assessed students in the course to help pay for the purchase of these materials, a substantial sum considering that the college's annual tuition was $300.) In addition, the staff strongly advised students to purchase Helen Gardner's *Art Through the Ages* and required them to buy *Western Civilizations: Their History and Culture*, a 1941 text by the Rutgers University historian Edward McNail Burns that avowed to embody "the New History," in which "factual material" is mostly "presented as the groundwork of great cultural movements."[56]

The major question that faced the staff during the summer of 1945 was pedagogical: How best to organize and teach the course? They decided to arrange the academic year into thirty weekly units: the first semester would cover the Hebrews, Greeks, Romans, early Christians, and part of the Middle Ages; the second semester would move forward from the medieval period to the present. Each week would begin with four days of lectures by some combination of Cooper, Davis, Kelso, Kinney, and Osman (the load was distributed fairly evenly among them), then end on Friday and Saturday in small-group discussions of the week's reading assignments, with each group led by a member of the course staff. Every staff member pledged to attend every lecture. Davis described one good effect of this practice in a 1949 progress report on the course— namely, that "the lecturer is [thus] put on his mettle and is less inclined to trust to inspiration or to the digressions or diversions which are sometimes indulged in when one is not under the critical scrutiny of confreres."[57]

The Man course embodied the general-education ideal that the best instruction is by broadly curious, fiercely dedicated amateurs. Although the lecture assignments tended to accommodate each instructor's area of specialization, the comprehensiveness of the course meant that each also had to stretch beyond his discipline. The philosophers Kelso and Osman lectured on Homeric Greece and Canaanite Culture, respectively. Kinney, a biblical scholar, handled Dante. The historian Cooper talked about The Jew in the Roman Empire and his colleague Davis about Copernicus and Galileo. The requirements of leading discussion sections were even more demanding. "The historian or the philosopher must be prepared to discuss with his section the assigned books of the Bible," Davis noted, "and on predominantly historical or philosophical readings the Bible instructors must be prepared to conduct discussions in what formerly may have been considered alien subjects."[58] To assure that every student would have every professor for part of the year, each group of students rotated periodically from professor to professor.

The load on the students was formidable. One hundred five freshmen, or 40 percent of the entering class, enrolled in the Man course in September 1945, attracted in part by the publicity the course had received in the local press (most Southwestern students at this time were from Memphis or its environs) and in part by the college's willingness to accept the Man course as a substitute for freshman Bible and history in the list of degree requirements. The shock that many of them felt during their first week in the course, which was also their first week in college, must have been acute. Lectures on subjects like The Nature and Origins of Civilization and The Hebrew Cosmogony, a list of discussion topics that included "What is the origin of art?" "Creation: ultimate explanation and proximate causes," and "The meaning of history" were complemented by reading assignments that covered 98 pages in the Burns textbook, 101 pages in Gardner, all of Genesis, the *Epic of Gilgamesh*, selections from Herodotus, and a variety of other primary texts.

The pace never slackened, especially because each week brought either a paper or a quiz. A weeklong spring semester unit on The Puritans, for example, required students to read Bunyan's *Pilgrim's Progress*, Milton's *Areopagitica*, and selections from Locke, Harrington, Jonathan Edwards, and others. Sometimes the course's assignments were farfetched, as when the staff told the students to read Buddha and Lao-Tse alongside several Hebrew prophets but gave no guidance about how to connect them with each other. Often the assignments were brilliant, as when the Old Testament book of Esther was paired with Homer and "The ancient woman: Helen, Penelope, and Esther" was offered for discussion.

During the summer, Diehl had warned the staff that it was wildly overestimating the amount of work that freshman students could handle, but "John Davis and one or two others thought I was a pessimist."[59] Midway through the fall semester, however, even as class attendance remained so reliable that the staff did not bother to take roll, many students were floundering. One student quipped to Cooper, "If it takes five learned professors to teach this course, I don't see how one poor freshman can be expected to pass it."[60] Gloria Ash Minor later recalled, "I could not read all the assignments, much less understand them all—I was so at sea in the freshman year."[61] The staff, which met weekly over lunch to discuss how things were going in the course and how they could be improved, began editing assignments out of the syllabus even as the course proceeded.

The Course Evolves, 1946–1958

After a relentlessly busy first year, the summer of 1946 offered Cooper, Davis, Diehl, Kelso, Kinney, and Osman an occasion to assess what had worked in the Man course and what needed repair or replacement. Davis's notes from that summer's deliberations, scribbled on a copy of the 1945–1946 syllabus, are revealing. The basic structure of the course—the thirty weekly units, the chronological design, most of the readings, the blending of history, religion, and philosophy, the emphasis on primary sources, and other essential elements—was to remain unaltered in the 1946–1947 version. But incremental changes (noted by Davis in pencil in the margins) and deletions (boldly crossed out) were to be made in nearly every unit.

Moderating the load on the students "from unimaginable to merely impossible" (as one professor put it) was one reform. The Gardner textbook on art was abandoned, along with most references in the course to architecture, music, painting, and sculpture. (The thinking seemed to be that since they could not do art well, it would be better not to do it at all.) Nips and tucks were made in the remaining weekly reading assignments—Herodotus was removed from the first week's list, for example, and Edwards and much of Bunyan were excised from the unit on the Puritans. Wednesdays now offered, in place of a fourth lecture, a third discussion session to consider the week's reading assignments—the result of another "I told you so" from Diehl, who had thought from the beginning that the course was lecture heavy.[62] Finally, the weekly discussion ques-

tions listed in the syllabus were focused directly on the reading assignments themselves, instead of on broad and abstract topics.[63]

More dramatic than the changes in the syllabus were the changes that
were taking place in Southwestern's student body. Wartime enrollments
had been small (382 in 1944–1945), overwhelmingly female (80 percent),
and of traditional college age. Now, as the armed services demobilized,
older male veterans flooded back to college; indeed, the 801-member
freshman class that enrolled in September 1946 consisted mostly of men.
Initially, Southwestern greeted the veterans with some trepidation—the
relieved tone of a 1947 report by Peyton Rhodes, the chair of the Faculty Committee on Veterans' Counseling and Education, is revealing in this
regard: "I think most of the fears we had about the adjustment of ex-ser-
vice personnel to college life were groundless. In general, and in fact almost without exception, I have found them pleasant, cooperative, and
uniformly courteous."[64] Tom Jolly, an early student in the Man course and
later a classics professor at Rhodes, recalls, "All of us were living in the
shadows of the depression and the war and were serious about our education. Then when the veterans came it intensified. They were dead serious about getting an education."[65] Another fear—that the veterans
would reject the liberal arts and demand professional and vocational programs—also was quickly allayed: they embraced the college's curriculum
and impressed the faculty as more intellectually curious than most of the
younger students. In fact, the only significant change that Southwestern
had to make to accommodate the newcomers was to purchase thirty-six
trailers from a wartime base in Oak Ridge, Tennessee, and establish a small
village north of the football field to house the married veterans and their
families. Soon "diapers waving like banners among the veterans' trailers"
became a familiar sight.[66]

Other veterans and their spouses were among the intended audience
for the new Division of Adult Education that Osman had been hired to
create at Southwestern. During the Man course's first year, Osman offered a noncredit course called The Great Tradition, in which adults met
weekly for a two-hour evening discussion of twenty classic works from
East and West. In 1946–1947, the adult education division offered a full-
blown great-books program—a new version of The Great Tradition; The
Great Books Theatre (professional readings of plays by Aeschylus, Sophocles, Euripides, and others); and The Soul of Russia, a study of Russian
literature. Osman previewed these offerings in a manifesto that embodied

the same mix of crisis warnings and exhortations for general education that had produced the Man course:

We waged a war with fear and in victory find defeat. . . .

Everywhere there is fear—fear of the atomic bomb, fear of Russia, fear of the Negro, fear of seemingly impossible economic problems, fear that the world of men has at last reached the end of a cycle and that civilization is on the wane. . . .

We have arrived at a time when man must fulfill his nature as a rational being. Ignorance is a crime against the state. . . .

The materials for this education are found today, as they were in Plato's day, in the Great Books.[67]

Planning the third year of the Man course brought further revisions in the syllabus. In September 1947 Osman took a leave of absence to pursue a doctorate at the University of Chicago, leaving Kinney, Davis, Cooper, and Kelso, the new chair of the course, to carry the load by themselves. (Kinney took over the adult education program.) The effort that had begun the previous year to tie the students' reading assignments to what was actually covered in class was intensified: the staff jettisoned the Burns textbook in favor of staff-authored one- to two-thousand-word essays that introduced each of the thirty units by setting the historical stage and previewing the assigned readings. The essays were uniformly literate and erudite. As one would expect from this group of writers, the tone of the introductions was respectful of Western civilization and, in particular, of the assigned authors and their works—not iconoclastic but not gushy either. The Christian perspective did not dominate the essays, nor was it concealed. For example, Kinney's introduction to the first of two units on Jesus began, "The lines of the Bible converge in the person of Jesus," and the final unit's essay (by Kelso) claimed that "only the spirit that makes man conscious of God as his Father can create [democracy]." In addition, the postwar domestic and international turmoil that Osman had described in his adult education brochure replaced the war itself as the dark force that was seen to be shadowing the times. Kelso's preface to the third edition of the syllabus asserted, "Today we are in what may well prove to be the greatest of world crises." Two new concluding units to the course were devoted to Our American Heritage and Our American Destiny.[68]

Southwestern's Class of 1950 was the first to approach graduation with the Man course under many of its members' belts, and Dean A. Theodore Johnson used the occasion to survey student reaction to the course. He asked 139 students from all four classes to fill out a questionnaire. The results were encouraging. Ninety percent said that the Man course was "more valuable" than "other elementary courses, and as a basic orientation for college work;" only one student checked "less valuable." Sixty-three percent answered "much more meaningful" when asked, "Did it succeed in making clearer your concept of the role of religion in life?"; again, only one dissented. Sixty-four percent liked the balance of lectures and discussions, and of those who did not, almost as many wanted more lectures as more discussions. Yet seventy-one percent said that "the discussion sections aided [me] in understanding the reading material," far outnumbering the two students who said that the colloquia had been of no help.[69] Summarizing the results, Johnson wrote, "A number of students said it was the best course they had ever taken."[70]

To be sure, Johnson had surveyed a select group—namely, those who chose the Man course instead of going the traditional freshman-Bible, freshman-history route. As Davis noted a few years later, because Man "has the reputation of being more difficult than the separated study of Bible and history, I must report that enrollment has tended to diminish rather than expand." (The course bottomed out at eighty students.) The staff consoled itself with the thought that "like Gideon, we are attracting a larger proportion of the brave and the strong."[71] Indeed, students who enrolled in the Man course were widely regarded—by fellow students as well as by themselves—as an elite band. Richard C. Wood, who later joined the Southwestern faculty as an English professor and taught in the Man course, recalls that as a student, "Those of us who took the alternative program sometimes felt benighted, such was the reputation of 'Man.'"[72] An annual award, named for retired Bible professor William O. Shewmaker, was established by donors to honor the freshman who attained the "highest distinction" in the Man course. And it is the barely concealed pride of the boot camp survivor, not the overt complaints, that shines through this Sou'wester column by Eugene Botsford:

And that Man course! Imagine my joy when I open the syllabus and find that the professors have neatly arranged for me to read for tomorrow's lecture the following: 1) The Old Testament, 2) Ancient Hebrew Relics and their Origins, pages 10–898, and 3) The Encyclopedia Britannica, Volumes A–M.[73]

The word of mouth among students about the Man course consisted of more than just "great course, real hard." Some of those who had been raised in conservative Christian homes and churches also spread the alarm that the course was a threat to students' faith. To be sure, all of the faculty members were avowed Christians—a student's notes from the course, for example, record the title of one lecture ("The Risen Lord") and the professor's conclusion that there are "more facts for than against the resurrection." But they were clustered in the liberal Protestant band of the theological spectrum, and students also could expect to hear in lecture statements like this from Professor (and Reverend) Kinney about the first two chapters of Genesis: "If the object of the writers of these chapters was to convey physical information, then certainly it is imperfectly fulfilled." Kinney went on to say, quoting Marcus Dods, that "if their object was to give an intelligible account of God's relation to the world and to man, then it must be owned that they have been successful in the highest degree." He and his colleagues no doubt hoped that students would focus on the second of these two sentences. But conservative Christians often found the first, with its suggestions that the six-day chronology of creation is inaccurate and that "imperfectly" is a word one can properly use in connection with the Bible, to be the more arresting.[74]

The 1950s maintained the pattern of change within a basic framework of continuity in the Man course. The syllabus continued to be revised, but less frequently than during the first few years. The major change—to reduce the thirty weekly units to ten longer ones, each with the word *man* somehow infused into the unit titles in the 1956 sixth edition of the syllabus—was more organizational than substantive, although science-laden lectures on the origins of the universe and the origins of life were added to the opening unit. As for the faculty, Cooper had dropped out to concentrate on his history courses in the late 1940s, and Osman left Southwestern in 1952 to accept a position with the Ford Foundation. But Kinney, Kelso, and Davis continued to teach in the course, along with new colleagues who shared their and Diehl's commitment to Christian general education. In 1952, W. Taylor Reveley, a Presbyterian minister who had been the college's chaplain from 1946 to 1949, returned from doctoral studies at Duke University to join the faculty as a professor of Bible and teach in the Man course. Daniel D. Rhodes, also a Presbyterian minister with a Duke Ph.D., began teaching philosophy and Man at Southwestern in 1956. Although neither remained at the college—Rhodes accepted a teaching position at Davidson in 1960 and Reveley was named president of his alma mater, Hampden-Sydney College, in 1963—each took the Man course to his new institution. Indeed, Rhodes was recruited for the specific purpose of creating a Man-style program at Davidson (see chapter 5.)

The logistical challenges of the 1950s proved to be more substantial than the curricular ones. To accommodate its swelling postwar enrollment, Southwestern had purchased some old army hospital buildings from Camp Forrest in Tullahoma, Tennessee, and replanted them on the north side of the campus. One of these thinly-walled, erratically heated "G.I. shacks," as they came to be called, became the Man building, the home of the course's reading room, lecture hall, and faculty offices. "The heater was old and rickety," recalls Marcia Calmer Beard, a student in the course, "and when it was on, the fan would drown out the lecturer's voice. We usually asked for the heater to be turned off, preferring to hear the lecturer even though freezing with our coats on."[75]

Conclusion

By 1958, Man in the Light of History and Religion had evolved from a glimmer in Charles Diehl's eye to the flagship course of Southwestern at Memphis. Enrollment had climbed to 150 students—more than two-thirds of the freshman class—as the course's "reputation spread from graduates to entering freshmen."[76] Diehl had distributed the syllabus widely among his fellow educators, and to good effect. Theodore Greene spoke for many when he hailed the course as "one of the most significant educational projects in America."[77] In 1949, U.S. Commissioner of Education Earl J. McGrath, who was compiling a national study of general education in the humanities, invited John Henry Davis to submit a chapter about the Man course, joining authors from Harvard, Haverford, Wisconsin, Cal Tech, Chicago, Reed, Wesleyan, and other distinguished colleges and universities. Davis was later invited to write a similar chapter for a subsequent volume in 1960.[78]

For a number of reasons, the 1960s would usher in an era of controversy about "great books" education in general and the Man course in particular. But on the eve of that decade, the main challenge at Southwestern seemed to be to spread the concept more widely across the curriculum. Kelso, in his preface to the 1947–1948 Man syllabus, had thrown down the gauntlet to the disciplines of psychology and sociology, which he and his colleagues regarded as the humanities'"academic competitors" in the effort "of awakening the mind of the scholar." The social sciences, Kelso charged, are ahistorical and prone "to the folly of a purely secular, that is, contemporary view of man." Similarly, Peyton Rhodes, who became Southwestern's president when Diehl stepped down in 1949, affirmed Diehl's commitment to Christian liberal education in his inaugural address; in 1958, he renewed efforts, first undertaken by Diehl in 1947, to persuade the college's social science and natural science faculties to develop general-education courses in their divisions that would be comparable to the Man course.[79] Those efforts failed, leaving Man's primacy in the Southwestern curriculum unchallenged.

On Faith and the Critical Method

L A R R Y   L A C Y

As best I can tell, I am the only person to have both taken the Search course and taught in it. As both student and instructor, I have sensed a strong relationship between my involvement in the course and my Christian faith.

What was it like for me to be a student in the Search course (then the "Man" course) in the late 1950s and, a few years later, fresh from three years of graduate study in philosophy at the University of Virginia, to become a member of the course staff, working with most of the professors under whom I had studied? In one way nothing changed—it seemed to me when I was a student, when I was a new faculty member, and now, as someone looking back more than thirty years later, that in those days "there were giants in the land." Two of these giants especially stand out in my mind—Charlie Bigger and Larry Kinney. Both were philosophers; Kinney was also a New Testament scholar. Both were committed to philosophical reflection but also open to the claims of revealed truth. Both were grounded in Greek philosophy, especially Plato, but they were also passionately interested in every area of the life of the mind, such as the latest scientific theory about the origin of the universe and of life. Although they delighted in the dialectic of philosophical reflection, they loved literature, music, and art. Because of their breadth of interest, Bigger could easily relate Plato's *Republic* to Veblen's *Theory of the Leisure Class* to Koestler's *Darkness at Noon*; and Kinney could draw illuminating con-

nections between Augustine and Kierkegaard and between each of these
and the Gospel of John or Paul's Epistle to the Romans.

Working with these men as colleagues on the Search staff was, therefore, both exciting and vastly intimidating. Among the most valuable aspects of teaching in the course in those early years, and one that gradually
helped me to feel comfortable in my new role, was the weekly staff luncheon. These were not just administrative meetings, but gatherings at
which the staff probed the issues in the assigned readings from many different angles.

If the subject for the week was the *Epic of Gilgamesh*, a meeting might
go as follows—Granville Davis would suggest a question like, "How did
realizing that he was not immortal influence the behavior of Gilgamesh?"
to open the class discussion; he called them his "sparkplug" questions.
Charlie Bigger would then show how the myth at the end of the *Republic* reveals some implications of a belief in immortality for the way one
lives one's life; Fred Neal would explain how the concern for immortality in *Gilgamesh* is similar to, yet in important ways different from, the significance of resurrection to Paul; and Larry Kinney would probe the
existential meaning of the idea of immortality, perhaps drawing on
Kierkegaard. Generous of spirit, my former teachers would bring me into
such discussions. Their interest in and response to my halting contributions created the kind of atmosphere in which I could grow both in understanding of the issues and in confidence as a teacher and colleague.
Such meetings were not only exhilarating, but also a great preparation for
a novice Search teacher anxious about the next colloquium meeting with
his students and about his place at the table.

Because the course has always included so much biblical, theological,
and philosophical material, it has called on its participants, students and
faculty alike, to consider issues of personal religious belief and conviction.
When I enrolled in the course in 1957 as a junior transfer student, I was
in the process of reexamining my Christian faith, which had been called
into question during my freshmen and sophomore years at Georgia Tech
by a worldview shaped primarily by science and technology. Although I
never completely lost faith in the reality of God, I was plagued by questions and doubts. After that fundamental issue was settled in my mind, I
then had to wrestle with issues specific to Christianity: Was Jesus God incarnate? How should one understand the atonement? What is the nature
of biblical inspiration? One of the things that strengthened my faith and

34 CELEBRATING THE HUMANITIES

encouraged me to continue grappling with such issues was to see people like Bigger and Kinney, with their intellectual gifts and their erudition, taking the Bible seriously.

When I returned to the college as an instructor, one of my concerns was to help students work through struggles they might be having relating their faith to the new ideas they were encountering. I was happy to be asked to teach in the Search course in part because that gave me an opportunity to read the Bible from a critical perspective *with* my students. I found in doing so that I was still in the process of forming and reforming my own theology, a process that continues to this day.

One of the great challenges in teaching Search to first-year students is helping them come to grips with the critical method of studying the Bible without assaulting their faith. Many people experience a tension between belief in the divine inspiration of the Bible and acceptance of the critical approach to biblical studies. Through teaching in the Search course, I found that the attempt to resolve this tension sometimes required that I be as critical of the critical method as of the Bible itself. For example, some New Testament critics proceed from the naturalistic assumption that miracles do not occur—or at least that miracles cannot be acknowledged by the critical method. Here the instructor's task is the philosophical one of examining the reasonableness of this version of the critical stance. On the other hand, sometimes it was my preconceived theory of inspiration that needed to be modified in light of the Bible as it is revealed by critical study. I have found myself working back and forth between these two strategies, seeking what one philosopher (in a different context) has called a position of "reflective equilibrium." Perhaps one of the best things we can do for our students is to allow them to see us wrestling with such issues as we engage with them in the critical study of the Bible.

In all, my involvement with the first-year units on the Old Testament and the New Testament, both as student and as teacher, has strengthened my faith as well as challenged it. Perhaps, however, the contrast between strengthening and challenging is misleading. One of the important ways in which I have found my faith strengthened is precisely through my attempt to respond to the challenges my faith has faced. An important facilitator of this challenging and strengthening has been the Search course.

2

Curriculum Innovation
1958–1975

DOUGLAS W. HATFIELD

By the mid-1950s, a decade after its creation, the Man course had been established both as a central feature in Southwestern's curriculum and as a measure of the school's identity as a liberal arts college. The evidence of this centrality may be seen in the college catalogues of this era, in which descriptions of the course were included in three different places. First, in the section that extolled the ideals and objectives of the college, the Man course was listed, along with the tutorial plan and honors courses, as one of the three distinctive marks of Southwestern's commitment to the ideals of liberal education. Man was described as "an integrating course," one that would "help the student see the relations among his various college courses and to make unified understanding possible." The course also "harmonizes with Southwestern's tradition as a Christian college" concerned with understanding "[h]uman experiences . . . in the light of history and Christian truth." As a twelve-hour course, it offered three credits in Bible and three in humanities each semester.[1]

A second, more extensive, description of the Man course appeared in the listings of the Bible department as Bible 3—4. It defined the course as "[a] study of the origins and development of Christianity and its role in world affairs integrated with a study of the history of Western Civilization." This description also noted a twofold academic aim: "(1) to train a student in handling the primary sources; (2) to create a realization of the role of the Christian world community in solving modern problems."[2]

The third description appeared not in the listing of history courses but rather under a heading of "Special Interdepartmental Courses," of which, in the mid–1950s, the Man course was the only one. This description duplicated the one in the Bible listings.[3]

These descriptions show how the Man course had become central to the college's understanding of its primary mission and also how the course fit into the curriculum. The general degree requirements specified that each student must take either Bible 1—2 (introductions to the Old Testament and the New Testament) or Bible 3—4 (the Man course), as well as Bible 51—52 (Senior Bible). In addition, every student was required to take one year of history courses or Humanities 3—4 (the Man course). Alongside the Bible-history-humanities component, the college required all students to take a year of English composition, a year of English literature, two years of either Greek, Latin, or mathematics, one year of social sciences, one year of either philosophy or psychology, and one year of a laboratory science. Each student was also required to demonstrate proficiency in a modern foreign language. (Proficiency was equated with two years of college study in the language.) Except for Senior Bible, the student was expected to finish all of these requirements by the end of the sophomore year, before becoming heavily engaged in the work of the major.[4]

The Standardization of the Man Course

Out of the experience of the Man course's first ten years, the staff had developed a standard body of topics and supporting texts. This standardization of the course was formalized in the sixth edition of the syllabus, published by the college in 1956, and it remained substantially unaltered until 1965.[5]

Although Granville Davis, a historian who had come to Southwestern in 1954, and other new members of the faculty had been added to the teaching staff of the course, the 1956 syllabus was the work of the Committee of the Man Course, made up of the remaining founders (Alexander P. Kelso, John Henry Davis, and Laurence I. Kinney) along with W. Taylor Reveley and Daniel D. Rhodes, who had replaced the now departed John Osman and W. Raymond Cooper. Thus, the syllabus essentially reflected the experience of those professors who had been in the course from the beginning. They divided the course into ten units of study, with five to be covered each semester. The typical unit contained alternating sets of lectures and discussions, with the class for the final dis-

cussion given over to a unit test (dubbed "collection"). This nearly equal
division between lectures and discussions (over the whole year, there were
only eight more lectures than discussions) reflected the staff's conviction
about the importance of discussion as a means of teaching and learning.[6]
The Man course's commitment to discussion was especially remarkable
in a time when nearly every other course in the curriculum was essentially a lecture course.

The first semester began with an introductory unit that explored the
great questions of origin (of the universe, of humans, of history, and of religion). A substantial body of material, the introduction constituted about
7 percent of the whole course. It was followed by units on the Old Testament and the Hebrews, the Greeks, the Romans, and the New Testament and the rise of Christianity. In terms of balance among these topics,
the biblical units comprised 27 percent of the course (12 percent for the
Old Testament and 15 percent for the New), while the two classical units
made up about 16 percent.

In the second semester, the units emphasized the Middle Ages (10
percent), the Renaissance and Reformation (10 percent), the seventeenth
and eighteenth centuries (16 percent), the nineteenth century (9 percent), and modern America (6 percent).

To each of the units of study the course committee gave titles, which
may be seen as devices for interpreting the distinctive contributions each
of these eras made to the development of human society and human self-
consciousness. The unit on the Old Testament was called God and the
Meaning of Human Life: Hebraism. The readings, drawn from the
Deuteronomistic history of Israel, selected prophets, and the Psalms, were
all designed to show how a national community developed that defined
itself by its relationship with a universal God. The unit also drew the contrast between this view and that of Israel's Canaanite neighbors.

The unit on the Greeks, Man's Discovery of Man: Hellenism, introduced the origin of a second major stream of influence in the development of Western civilization. In progressive steps, the students traced the
contributions of the Greeks to human self-understanding through the
heroic tradition of the epics (the *Odyssey*), the historical works of
Herodotus and Thucydides, the philosophical concern for living a worthy life (Plato and Aristotle), and the tragic vision of human experience
in Sophocles' *Antigone*.

The consideration of the classical influence concluded with a much
briefer unit on the Romans. Under the title Man's Domination of Man:
Rome and Imperialism, this unit concentrated on the mythic origins (the

Aeneid) and historical development of the Roman Republic (Polybius) and Empire (Plutarch). The focus on the establishment of the Roman Empire set the stage for the unit on the New Testament, called Christianity in Roman History: Its Concept of Man and God. In readings from the four gospels, Acts, the letters of Paul, the catholic epistles, and other documents drawn from early church history, the unit traced the rise of Christianity from its initially contentious position within the Roman world to its ultimate fusion with Roman culture on the eve of Rome's collapse in the West.

The second semester of the course opened with a unit called The Hierarchy of Man and Society: The Middle Ages. Beginning with Augustine and concluding with Dante, this unit emphasized the interplay between religious sensibility and political developments, especially as this interplay was reflected in historical documents (on Charlemagne, Magna Carta, and the crusades) and in works of literature (*Song of Roland* and *Aucaussin and Nicolette*). Curiously missing, however, was any consideration of the works of Thomas Aquinas.

The age of the Renaissance and Reformation was called The Emergence of Modern Man. In this unit, the emphases were on the rise of humanism, illustrated in the works of Pico and Erasmus, the ambiguities of the new political realism, as seen in Machiavelli's *The Prince* and Shakespeare's *Richard II*, and the Protestant Reformation, studied through the writings of Luther and Calvin.

Unit VIII, which was called The Emergence of the Modern Mind, centered on the intellectual flowering of the seventeenth century. The readings ranged from the works of the scientific revolution (Bacon, Galileo, and Descartes) to the diverse puritanisms of Milton and Bunyan, the neoclassicism of the French theater (Molière), and the rival contractual theories of government proposed by Hobbes, Bossuet, and Locke.

The increasingly political character of modern life, as it developed in the eighteenth and nineteenth centuries, was the focus of Unit IX: Modern Man in Quest of Freedom and Democracy. Beginning in the Enlightenment with the origins of the quest (Voltaire, Swift, Rousseau, and Kant), the unit traced its development through the French Revolution and into the nineteenth century, when the original ideas were challenged by the rise of romanticism (Coleridge), reinvigorated by the development of nineteenth-century liberalism (Smith and Mill), and then challenged again by the emergence of virulent nationalism (Treitschke), Marxian socialism, and the philosophy of Nietzsche.

The final unit, Man and Society in Crisis, turned the course's focus to the development of human experience in the United States since the eighteenth century. Beginning with the political ideals of the Declaration of Independence, the Constitution, and Madison's *Federalist* No. 10, the unit then traced the historical challenges to those ideals through the sectional conflicts of the nineteenth century (Calhoun and Lincoln), the closing of the frontier (Turner), and the emergence of the United States in the twentieth century as a contestant for world power (Wilson's Fourteen Points and the Atlantic Charter). The course concluded with a consideration of the challenges modern technology posed to human existence and well being.

The Changing of the Guard: The Revision Of 1965

Although a seventh edition of the syllabus was brought out in 1961, it introduced virtually no changes to either the organization or the content of the Man course.[7] In several ways, however, changes were taking place in the course, and also in the college, which led in 1965 to the first significant revision in the course (the eighth edition), and then, five years later, to the fundamental revision of 1970 (the tenth edition).

New Faculty Members

For the Man course, the drive toward change was fueled by an increase in enrollments, an increase that reflected both Man's appeal and the steady growth in the college's student body, which expanded from 640 students in 1958–1959 to 916 in 1964–1965.[8] Correspondingly, enrollments in Man increased steadily through the early 1960s, reaching a peak of 182 in 1964–1965.[9] To keep pace with these increases, by 1965 the teaching staff had expanded to ten, among whom only Davis and Kinney, of the founders, remained active in the course.

The newcomers arrived in two main waves. The first, coming in the mid- and late 1950s, included Granville Davis and Fred W. Neal, both of whom helped to create the seventh edition of the syllabus in 1961. The second wave, which came in the early to mid-1960s, included biblical scholars Milton P. Brown and Richard A. Batey, as well as philosophers Larry Lacy and James Jobes. All of these newcomers brought to the course a range of perspectives and interests that differed significantly from those of the founders.

The key figures in the 1965 revision were Neal and Lacy, who served as coeditors of the eighth edition of the syllabus. Neal had come to Southwestern in 1958, with an appointment in philosophy and religion, to replace the retiring Kelso. Educated at Lewis and Clark College in Oregon, and with a B.D. from the Chicago Theological Seminary and a Ph.D. in church history from the University of Chicago, Neal had been teaching for several years at Mississippi State College.[10] Bringing with him a wide range of academic interests and a contagious enthusiasm for everything he undertook, Neal was the perfect addition to the Man course staff. Although he was committed to the ideals and traditions on which the course had been founded, he believed that for the course to remain a vital part of the curriculum, it must be sensitive to changing times and conditions and, especially, to the interests and ideas of the newer members of the staff. He also believed that the Man course should be a central road by which students were helped to make the transition from high school to college. The course would aid in this transition by confronting first-year students with a variety of viewpoints from a diverse group of instructors, by pushing them to read primary sources reflectively and critically, and by leading them from the kind of thinking that focuses concretely on things to the kind of thinking that centers abstractly on ideas.

Larry Lacy was the first member of the Man staff who had also been a student in the course. As a transfer student to Southwestern from Georgia Tech, in 1957 he had the unusual experience of taking the course as a junior. After graduating in 1959, he went to the University of Virginia, where he earned the Ph.D. in philosophy. He returned to Southwestern in 1962 as a member of the philosophy department and began teaching in the Man course, which was using essentially the same syllabus he had studied as a student. Lacy shared with Neal the desire to incorporate a more philosophical and reflective perspective into the course, a desire that arose both from his experience as an undergraduate and from his graduate training in philosophy.[11]

The Course Revision of 1965

On the surface, the changes that were introduced in the 1965 eighth edition of the syllabus appear relatively minor. The number of units was reduced from ten to nine by combining the Greeks and Romans into a single unit. In addition, staff-edited readings for the course were included for the first time as a second volume of the syllabus, providing students with short selections from a variety of works that were not available in the published anthologies. Otherwise, the course appeared to be unchanged: the same topics were covered in the same order, and the regular alternation of lecture and discussion days continued.[12]

A closer examination, however, reveals several fundamental innovations in the content of the course. One of these, a more conscious and concentrated emphasis on philosophical issues, is apparent in the introductory unit on origins, in which the emphasis was turned from an examination of primitive texts to abstract questions about the nature or essence of things: "What is history?" "What is religion?" and even "What is man?" These questions were raised in secondary works by modern scholars such as R. L. Calhoun's *What Is Man?* S. M. Thompson's *A Modern Philosophy of Religion,* and the novel by Vercors, *You Shall Know Them.*[13]

The new emphasis on abstract questions was incorporated into subsequent units as well, even though the editors generally retained the unit names of the seventh edition. A new reading assigned in the Old Testament unit was the Book of Job, which raised fundamental questions about the meaning of life. In the Greek and Roman unit, students were introduced to Aristotle's analysis of tragedy in the *Poetics* and Sophocles' *Oedipus Rex* was substituted for *Antigone,* in part because it provided a more coherent example of Aristotle's tragic principles. The material on Roman philosophies was much expanded with the addition of selections from Marcus Aurelius, Epicurus, and Cicero. In the second semester, other significant new material was introduced, including selections from Thomas Aquinas, the empiricism of Locke's *Essay Concerning Human Understanding,* the rationalistic treatment of religion by Voltaire and of education by Lessing, and the philosophical essays *On Religion* by Schleiermacher.

A second fundamental innovation in the 1965 syllabus was the greater emphasis on historical-critical methods of biblical study. This emphasis reflected the influence and interest of one of the new members of the staff, Milton Brown. After earning a Ph.D. in biblical literature and languages from Duke University and teaching for three years at Washington and Lee, Brown came to Southwestern in 1960 to replace Daniel Rhodes, who had been recruited by Davidson College to help develop its own version of the Man course.[14] Brown was the Man course's first staff member to be trained in the methods of biblical critical studies. As evidence of his influence, background reading for the lectures was assigned from two scholarly texts: Bernard Anderson's *Understanding the Old Testament* and *Understanding the New Testament,* by Howard Clark Kee and Franklin W. Young.[15]

The third significant innovation in the content of the course involved the expansion of the final unit, Man and Society in Crisis. This increase in the number of sessions devoted to the twentieth century was made possible by cutting back the material covered in the early modern era. As before, the focus was on the United States, but the range of topics was broadened to include the influence of religious experience on American life and to trace some of the fundamental currents in the development of a peculiarly American intellectual history. These changes reflected the interests of Fred Neal (society and religion) and Granville Davis (intellectual history). Davis not only taught in the Man course, but also was the executive director of Southwestern's Adult Education Center. In that capacity, he had helped to create the Institute for Executive Leadership, a program to educate young Memphis business executives in the great ideas and traditions of the humanities. At the same time, Davis held an appointment in the history department, where he offered popular courses on the Civil War and on American intellectual history.[16] He brought all of these roles together in helping to redesign the final unit of the Man course. With the revision of this unit, the course for the first time gave attention to the twentieth century commensurate with the treatment afforded the earlier eras of Western history.

The Great Reform

The syllabus underwent a further, but minimal, revision in 1967. Also edited by Neal and Lacy, the ninth edition maintained the basic emphases that had been introduced in 1965. The main change was to iron out the asymmetry created in the eighth edition, in which four units were covered in the first semester and five in the second. This was done by eliminating the unit on the Renaissance and Reformation, then attaching the Renaissance material to the Middle Ages unit and the Reformation material to the unit on the seventeenth and eighteenth centuries.[17] The conceptual soundness of this reorganization would never be tested, however. Beginning in 1968–1969, the college launched a monumental curriculum reform that rendered the entire syllabus obsolete and forced the staff to undertake a far more thorough revision of the course than any that had come before.

National Trends in Higher Education

In the country as a whole, the 1960s saw the emergence of fundamental changes in higher education. The most visible source of change was the upsurge of student activism: demonstrations against both the war in Southeast Asia and the institutional ties of colleges and universities to the war-making apparatus; sit-ins in favor of "free speech"; confrontations with governing authorities about issues of student autonomy and institutional regulation of student life; and outcries against bureaucratic depersonalization and demands for wider ranges of choice in academic programs and living arrangements. All of these activities, as covered by the news media, gave many Americans the impression that "reform" in higher education was to be equated with a chaotic anarchy in which every traditional value was thrown out or turned upside down.

The highly visible phenomenon of student protest obscured other changes that were emerging at the same time concerning the curriculum, especially those involving general education, pedagogy, and institutional management. Although these changes had their origins in the quieter period before the protests, they continued to develop during the 1960s and led to a profound transformation of American higher education by the beginning of the next decade. These national trends had a substantial effect on Southwestern, influencing major alterations in the academic program in general and the Man course in particular.

At the center of the drive for change was a reaction against core programs in general education, which, like the Man course, had become entrenched almost everywhere since the 1940s.[18] The assault on these programs came simultaneously from several directions. One complaint was that general education courses tended to be wide-ranging surveys that never required students to dig beneath the surface or engage the material in any sophisticated way. The proposed solution was to provide a variety of courses that studied narrower topics in depth.[19] This approach also assumed that a wide range of such courses, coming from a number of disciplines, would be developed, and that in choosing from them students would be given great latitude to determine their individual programs. The result was, in essence, a reestablishment of the elective system that the general education movement had earlier overturned.[20]

The trend to more specialized study was justified, in part, as a means to establish a higher standard for student performance than the general surveys of the standard core could exact. That there was a need for greater rigor was validated for many by the launching of *Sputnik* in 1957, an event that was widely interpreted to mean that American higher education had fallen behind the Soviet Union in the education of scientists and scientific technicians. The trend to the proliferation of specialized courses was further promoted by the federal government, which funneled greater and greater amounts of money into higher education in the interest of closing the "missile gap" with the Soviets. The most graphic illustration of the fragmentation of core programs may be seen at Harvard, where the number of options in the core expanded from two in 1949 to four in 1950, seven in 1960, and fifteen in 1970. [21]

A second assault on the general education core was spurred by a reaction against the Western-oriented perspective of many of the core courses.[22] A unifying theme of such courses was that the rise of Western civilization embodied the political, cultural, and spiritual liberation of humanity and, as such, represented the highest achievement of human beings. When other traditions were considered at all, it was in the context of how they had been touched, and perhaps transformed, by Western civilization. The historian Gilbert Allardyce argues that such an orientation had arisen out of the emotional context in which these programs were conceived and brought to fruition: namely, the era of the two world wars and the opening stages of the cold war, when the unified nations of the Atlantic world seemed to stand in defense of civilization against a variety of brutal enemies.[23]

In opposition to that Western orientation, proponents of change now began to argue for including studies of non-Western cultures—Asian, Middle Eastern, and African. Such studies, they argued, would illuminate the accomplishments and values of these cultures in their own right, not just as variants to be measured against the Western norm. In the 1960s and 1970s, colleges and universities attempted in various ways to infuse non-Western topics into the curriculum, either by integrating such material into the existing Western civilization courses or by creating parallel courses in non-Western cultures to supplement or replace the Western orientation of the core. Such infusions proved difficult to accomplish, however, because of the shortage of qualified instructors, the lack of access to suitable reading material, and the resistance of many faculty members, who continued to view a thorough grounding in Western traditions as the fundamental requirement for a liberal education. Nonetheless, incorporating non-Western perspectives became a serious topic of discussion on most campuses, and such courses were introduced at many colleges and universities.[24]

The revolt against the required core also involved rejecting the idea that every freshman must encounter a common body of knowledge to lay the foundation for a successful academic career. In its place, advocates of reform argued that beginning students would be better served by courses of independent study,[25] directed toward topics they chose on the basis of personal interest and "relevance." If individualized projects could not be accommodated, then at least the first-year student should be involved in seminar courses that included a significant component of independent study.[26]

Associated with the drive for individualized study was the emergence of a calendar reform movement. Proponents of change argued that innovative courses could be more easily presented in an unconventional academic term, created just for that purpose, than in a more conventional semester or quarter. By the mid-1960s, many institutions, especially liberal arts colleges, were adopting unconventional calendars in order to create a framework for unconventional courses. Although many approaches were tried, the most widely adopted calendar was the "four-one-four," which involved fall and spring semesters when students took four more-or-less conventional courses per term and, in January, a winter term in which students were fully engaged in a single course of independent or small-group study.[27]

One countertrend of the 1960s reflected a backlash against the revival of highly specialized courses in the various disciplines.[28] Supporters of this effort promoted interdisciplinary courses as an antidote for overspecialization. Such courses were to be taught by two or more professors from different disciplines and offered in large enough numbers to give the students a wide range of choices.[29]

Early Responses at Southwestern

Many of these national trends were reflected in developments at Southwestern during the late 1950s and early 1960s, and one of them affected the Man course directly. In 1957–1958, the college abandoned the Humanities 3–4 alternative to the requirement for a year's study of history.[30] What earlier had counted as six hours of credit in humanities now became six hours of credit in history. (The course's other six hours still counted as six hours in Bible). This change made necessary the adaptation of the Man course as a history course with a corresponding description in the history listings in the catalogue. The long description of Bible 3–4 was abbreviated and reproduced as the description of History 3–4 as well. The more detailed description of the course was still to be found in the catalogue under "Special Interdepartmental Courses," along with a new listing for a program in American Studies. This change was more than just a change in terminology and labeling: it was a statement by the college that it did not give degree requirement credit for "humanities" courses per se and that to justify such credit the course must now be either "legitimized" within the disciplines or be offered only as electives, as was the case with American Studies.

At the same time, the college responded to the national trends toward creating interdepartmental courses and non-Western courses by drawing in part on the tradition of the Man course. A new interdepartmental course in Oriental Humanities, created as a non-Western counterpart to Man and taught by James E. Roper (English) and Robert G. Patterson (Bible), was offered for the first time in 1963–1964.[31] The faculty then initiated efforts to establish new interdepartmental courses in literature, music, and the natural sciences.[32] These ventures drew inspiration from the example of the Man course, but they also aimed at exploring possibilities for interdisciplinary study that was detached from Man's specifically Judeo-Christian foundation. Even as the new courses in the natural sciences were being created, the faculty organized itself to carry through a thorough revision of the curriculum and a radically new design of the college calendar.[33]

John David Alexander and the Work of the Task Force

The impetus for calendar and curriculum reform, which had begun in the mid-1960s, reached its climax in the final years of the decade, a period marked by conflict as well as by high expectations of growth and further development at the college. For a decade Southwestern had enjoyed a steady increase in the size of its student body[34] and a corresponding increase in the faculty. New buildings in the college's trademark collegiate gothic style had been erected, and a major grant from the Ford Foundation not only had provided the college with national recognition for the excellence of its programs but also had made possible the construction of a first-rate center for the sciences.[35] The expectations for growth and development were brought together by a young, energetic, and ambitious new president, John David Alexander. A Phi Beta Kappa graduate of Southwestern and a Rhodes Scholar, Alexander was appointed by the Board of Trustees in May 1964 and took office on July 1, 1965.[36]

Alexander was firmly committed to Southwestern's liberal arts tradition, but he argued that the tradition was one of innovation and that the college should seize the opportunity provided by the times to strengthen itself in every way.[37] He wanted the faculty to assume a major role in deciding the future of the college, and he was prepared to enter into partnership with the faculty and students to bring about change. One of his first steps as president was to create a task force, made up of faculty, students, and administrators, and charge it both to examine every aspect of the college's life and operations and to make proposals for improvements in whatever areas such improvements needed to be made. The task force, which became the driving element in the college-wide reforms of the late 1960s, was broadly representative of faculty interests—more than half of the faculty served on it at one time or another. The members of the Man staff were intimately involved in the task force's discussions and recommendations; indeed, Kinney served as the first chair. When failing health forced him to step down, the torch was passed to Dean Jameson M. Jones, a staunch supporter of the Man course who served as chair until the task force finished presenting its major reports.[38] At this point, the body was converted into a standing committee of the faculty, styled as the Committee on Educational Development, and charged with the ongoing responsibility to find and recommend improvements in the educational program. The first chair of the standing committee was another stalwart of the Man course, Granville Davis.

The Reform of the Academic Calendar

The first major reform proposed by the task force, and the one that cleared the way for all that followed, was a new college calendar for the 1968–1969 academic year. Reflecting the national trend, especially among liberal arts colleges, the traditional calendar of two semesters, with thirty weeks of classes meeting five and one-half days per week, was abandoned. Contrary to the general trend, however, the college adopted a calendar that came to be designated as "four-four-two." Under this plan, students were to continue to take ten courses per year, four courses in each of the twelve-week "long terms" and two courses in the six-week "short term." At the same time, Saturday classes were discarded, leaving an instructional week of five days.[39]

The main appeal of the new calendar lay in the short term, which was reserved for new and innovative kinds of courses, particularly those emphasizing independent study or off-campus academic experiences. Although each class was assigned a two-hour block of time for all five days of the week, faculty members were encouraged to develop courses that would minimize classroom time and maximize the time spent by students in individual and group projects. By putting the short term at the end of the academic year, rather than between the two long terms, the planners hoped that courses in that term could be linked to already existing summer instructional programs at the college and elsewhere.

In attempting to establish a niche for the Man course in this new structure of instruction, the staff was faced with several difficult problems. Although the staff initially gave some thought to the idea of extending the course through all three terms, they quickly abandoned this approach after recognizing the practical difficulties of making the last six weeks of the Man course conform to the college's expectations for short-term courses. Yet teaching the entire course in the two long terms meant fitting material that had been taught in 180 class days under the old calendar into the 120 class days provided under the new calendar. To be sure, the loss of class time was not as drastic as it may appear, since class hours were expanded from fifty-three minutes to sixty minutes on Monday, Wednesday, and Friday, and ninety minutes on Tuesday and Thursday. Counted in total hours, instructional time was thus reduced by only 10 percent. For the college as a whole, the rationale for continuing to award three hours credit for less time spent in class was that students would be able to spend more time out of class on each course, since their normal course load was reduced from five to four. It was clear, however, that for the Man course the task was more complicated than just excising one-tenth of the material that had earlier been covered. Recognizing that it would be desirable to have the lectures on the sixty-minute days, the staff saw that the tendency would be to do in those sixty minutes a slightly enriched version of what had earlier been done in fifty-three. By this computation, the number of lecture topics to be lost constituted 20 percent of those covered under the old calendar: seventy-two topics rather than ninety.

By the same token, the discussion sessions, held during the ninety-minute class periods on Tuesday and Thursday, could feature expanded readings for each topic, but the number of topics covered would necessarily be reduced by nearly half, down from about ninety to about forty-eight. Furthermore, in reducing the number of class meetings per week from six to five, the new calendar rendered obsolete the practice of coupling a Friday lecture to a Saturday discussion. This left the staff with the additional problem of determining what to do with the Friday class sessions.

From the Man faculty's point of view, the new calendar created one other major concern. Under the old calendar, the Man course constituted 40 percent (six of fifteen credit hours) of a student's schedule in both semesters of the freshman year. Under the new calendar, Man accounted for 50 percent of the course load during the two long terms (six of twelve hours). The heavy commitment required by Man meant that some students simply would not be able to elect it, especially those who planned to major in one of the natural sciences and needed to start right away the foundation courses in their majors and the requisite courses in mathematics. The nature of most of these courses, like that of the Man course itself, was such that they could not be shifted to the short term.

During the first two years of the new calendar, the staff of the Man course attempted to meet these challenges by simply removing certain lecture and discussion topics from the 1967 (ninth) edition of the syllabus. The incoherence of this approach was recognized from the beginning, and the staff resolved to redesign the course completely to make it compatible with the new structure of the academic year. In attempting to address the problem of scheduling for some students, the staff decided to open the course to sophomores.[40] Even so, the course suffered a 40 percent decline in enrollment during the first year of the new calendar,[41] a decline that could be explained only in part by a 3 percent dip in the size of the student body.[42] Before any progress could be made in dealing with this problem, however, the faculty began introducing sweeping changes to the general curriculum, and those changes also had to be accommodated in the redesign of the Man course.

The Reform of the College Curriculum

Even before the reform of the calendar was proposed, the college had taken some steps to modify its curriculum and the degree requirements that defined that curriculum. For example, the traditional liberal requirement of two years of Greek, Latin, or mathematics, which had already been reduced to one year, was abandoned altogether.[43] In an even more distinct break with past practice, the requirement for one year of Senior Bible had been loosened to include any six hours of advanced courses offered by the Bible or philosophy departments, and these could be taken at any time.[44] The latter change was made in part to relieve students of the burden of taking courses outside the major in their senior year and in part to give them more flexibility in devising their courses of study.

For 1969–1970, the second year under the new calendar, the faculty Committee on Educational Development proposed a pilot project that would allow a number of freshmen (the first fifty to apply to participate) to experiment with a program of individually designed courses of study. The key ingredient in this experiment was the creation of a series of interdisciplinary "colloquia," each limited to ten students and taught by two professors, in which the fifty students would enroll during the two long terms of their first year. As entry points for students into college, each colloquium, regardless of its subject, was to stress individual learning and nurture study skills and writing. In addition, the professors in each colloquium were to serve as the academic advisers of the ten students. The advisers, being well acquainted with their students' strengths, weaknesses, and academic goals, would be able to assist them in working out courses of study that would provide a broad grounding in the liberal arts. For these students, no particular course or body of knowledge was seen as indispensable to a liberal education. Toward the end of the sophomore year, each student was to select a major, either in one of the traditional disciplines or in an individually designed interdisciplinary program. The final two years would be spent completing that program.[45]

This experiment anticipated a radical departure from Southwestern's traditional approach to liberal education. The new curriculum envisioned a shift in emphasis from general education to education in the major field. Within general education, the shift was from a common body of knowledge to skills development. The new program reflected the national trend toward the ideas that in developing basic skills and attributes, any course could serve about as well as any other, and that it was more "relevant" for students to design their own courses of study than it was for them to plug into already existing programs.

The outcome of the fifty-student experiment was assessed by a team of Southwestern psychology professors, Herbert Smith and James Morris. They concluded that the students had done as well academically as those in the conventional curriculum and appeared to have devoted more time to their academic work than had the general student body.[46] Acting on that report, the Committee on Educational Development proposed extending a modified version of the "Freshman Program" to the entire entering class in 1970–1971. The modification involved establishing a minimal structure of area degree requirements in place of the carte blanche that had been afforded the experimental class. Under this system, in addition to the two terms of the freshman colloquia, each student was required to take four courses in the humanities, three in the social sciences, three in the natural sciences (including mathematics), and three in arts and communication. In fulfilling each of the requirements in this system, the student had literally dozens of courses from which to choose.[47]

The New Curriculum and the Man Course

The staff of the Man course faced a monumental task in finding its niche in the new curriculum. Although interdisciplinary courses such as American studies, oriental studies, and the natural science courses were awarded distinct places in the scheme of degree requirements, the Man course was reckoned more modestly as either history or religion within the humanities division. It was up to the staff to redefine the course in such a way as to include it in the set of departmental options and, at the same time, to make it appealing to students, lest it die by reason of neglect.

As if that challenge were not formidable enough, other forces were at work in the larger life of the college that also impinged on the task of redesigning the Man course. One of these forces was represented in the report of the Committee on Institutional Racism. This committee, led by Jeff Carter and composed primarily of politically active liberal and radical students, was formed in the aftermath of the sanitation workers' strike in Memphis and the subsequent assassination of Martin Luther King in April 1968. The committee investigated various aspects of the problem of racism at Southwestern and issued a report of its findings, along with specific recommendations for remediation, in January 1969. The report was sent to the faculty, the administration, and the board of trustees. The faculty then dispersed the report to its various committees for consideration, as well as to those academic departments to which the report addressed specific recommendations for course revisions.[48]

Among the recommendations for course revision were several applying specifically to the Man course. The suggestions appeared to be relatively minor, considering the overall sweep of the course, but they were highly significant in terms of rethinking the concept of "man" as it had been traditionally treated. The report called for the "use of materials that include outstanding Negro men in American history," "a lecture and/or discussion on African history" (noting that this might require the redefining of African history as Western history), and "discussion and reading of the White-black [*sic*] problem in [the] modern [U]nited S[tates]." Here certainly were issues that the staff had to consider in its efforts to revamp the course.[49]

The other force at work in the life of the college was subtle and more difficult to define, and yet its effects on the character of the Man course were profound. For want of a better term, this force may be described as a progressive secularization of the college. Although this did not involve an explicit repudiation of Southwestern's Presbyterian foundation, it did reflect a redefining of the significance of that foundation and a dramatic alteration, or even elimination, of traditional practices that were rooted in it.

The Secularization of American Higher Education

The processes of secularization at Southwestern reflected a general phenomenon in higher education that had developed during the course of several decades. As early as 1959, the theologian George Buttrick had noted the emergence of the "secular university," in which the traditional trappings of religious life, such as required chapel, were being abandoned and the concern for scientific truth denied the legitimacy of including "biblical thought" in the curriculum.[50] To the extent that religion remained an acceptable academic topic, it was as an object of inquiry within the various disciplines: philosophy, sociology, literature, and psychology.[51] At universities in which separate departments of religion retained control of the study of religion, these departments became "professionalized," being staffed by scholars who had established their academic "legitimacy in the arts and sciences through the development of a posture of analytical rigor, of disinterested objectivity, and sometimes of disinterested irreverence."[52]

Although these trends became entrenched first at the nonsectarian private universities, by the 1960s they were also manifesting themselves at church-related liberal arts colleges in the mainline denominations.[53] The changes reflected in part the need of the small colleges to broaden the base of their constituencies by moving away from narrow sectarian orientations, and in part their need to hire faculty members whose qualifications conformed to national academic standards.[54] As teaching about religion at church-related colleges became indistinguishable from religion as taught at secular universities, those colleges were forced to ask themselves hard questions about what constitutes a church-related college and how it differs from any other. George Marsden argues that the very fact that so many studies were commissioned in the 1960s to determine the meaning of church-relatedness is itself an indication that not much was left to find, at least not in the curriculum.[55]

At Southwestern the most visible manifestation of these trends was the abandonment of required daily chapel services. Although these "services" had long been largely secularized in content, by the late 1960s students and faculty had come to see the requirement as anachronistically ecclesiastical. To bring an end to the practice, the students mounted a drive that gained the support of a majority of the faculty as well as a majority of the ministers in the Memphis presbytery.[56] The attempt to maintain the services on a voluntary basis soon fizzled out, thus demonstrating the general indifference of the college community to that part of its tradition.

A more subtle but also more significant manifestation of this secularizing trend was the loosening of institutional controls on the private lives of students. Again it was the active appeal of the students that brought about the liberalization of rules regarding dormitory hours, room visitation, proper dress, alcohol consumption, and a variety of other traditional prescriptions and proscriptions for student behavior. Students eventually were empowered to establish and enforce their own social regulations in a way that paralleled student enforcement of the honor code.[57] Although the rationale for these changes was tied to the curricular trend of allowing students to assume responsibility for their own lives, the rules that were overthrown or modified were popularly associated with religious axioms of behavior.

Secularization in the life of the college was given voice in the catalogue for 1970–1971, in the section that explained Southwestern's church-relatedness:

Southwestern is a church-related college. In view of common stereotypes of what this might mean, it is useful to say what it does *not* mean. There is no "rules" approach toward cultivating student morals, there are no sectarian religion courses; nor are there any restrictions on faculty viewpoints. The religious and moral dimensions of education at Southwestern have found various expressions over the years. There is a continuing commitment to the belief that self-liberation and self-development have a greater end and a larger purpose than self-gain and simple mastery over the natural world and other men. Students and faculty are encouraged to give expression to religious and moral dimensions through concern with social and moral issues, volunteer service projects, and through practice of their faith and worship.[58]

At the academic level, the "professionalization" of the study of religion had also proceeded apace at Southwestern. In the early 1960s the Bible department was restyled as the Edwin Summers Hilliard department of Bible and religion, thereby indicating the expansion of the department to include various kinds of religious phenomena, both within and beyond the biblical tradition.[59] Milton Brown and Richard Batey were joined in the department by other scholars who were trained in critical studies.[60] Another indication of the new emphases in the study of religion may be seen in the change adopted in 1966 in the catalogue description of the Man course: from "A study of the origins and development of Christianity and its role in world affairs integrated with a study of the history of Western Civilization" to "A study of the history of Western Civilization integrated with a study of the origin and development of Christianity and its role in world affairs."[61] Although the new language implied a fundamental rethinking of the nature and the priorities of the course, at the time no change at all was made in the actual content of the course. By the end of the decade, however, it was abundantly clear that changes in "image" would not be sufficiently responsive to the substantial changes that were occurring in the college as a whole. A real question was whether the course could be maintained at all or could be maintained only by disconnecting it from its twenty-five-year emphasis on the Western tradition, biblical study, and ecclesiastical history.

The Course Revision of 1970

The great revision of the course that was embodied in the 1970 tenth edition of the syllabus was almost two years in the making. Although all of the members of the staff were involved in the process, the central figures in putting it all together were Fred Neal and Robert Patterson.

Fred Neal

Beginning with the 1965 revision, and especially with the retirement in 1969 of the last of the founders, John Henry Davis, Fred Neal had emerged as the leader of the staff and as the chief advocate for the course in the faculty. In the founding era, no one person had assumed such a role. The founders on a yearly basis had rotated the responsibility for calling staff meetings and seeing to it that decisions were implemented.[62] With the growth of the staff and the greater complexity of coordinating the business of the course, it seemed sensible for one person to take on these tasks. Because Neal had been in the program since 1958, was already assisting John Henry Davis in the operations of the course, and had a clearly articulated vision of what the Man course was about, he became the course's leader, with the consent of the staff. Although he was teaching full loads, and even overloads, Neal devoted uncounted hours and boundless energy to the task of guiding the course.

During the crucial period of reform, Neal's leadership was significant in at least three areas. First, he was committed to the fundamental concept of the course as an interdisciplinary inquiry into the development of the Western, Judeo-Christian world of thought and belief, as well as to the continuation of the basic traditions that had made the course a major force in the life of the college for more than two decades. Within the staff and among the faculty at large, Neal was quick to defend the integrity of the Man course, the rigor of its content and methodology, and the challenging demands it imposed on students and staff alike. He invited any faculty member who had doubts about the academic rigor of the course

Longtime Search director Fred W. Neal pursues a point with students following a colloquium.

to teach in it for a year before making a judgment. At the same time, however, Neal firmly believed that preserving the essence of the course did not mean standing pat and refusing to change. He argued that Man was always in the process of developing, adapting, and making itself relevant, even in radically changing situations. The course was constantly being invigorated with new staff members and by a continuing reassessment of its content and methodologies. Neal was the chief advocate of the idea that the Man course could be reformed in line with the new directions the college was taking and, at the same time, remain true to its heritage. In view of the challenges the college's new directions posed, it is likely that any approach other than the one he adopted and promoted would have doomed the course.

The second significant contribution of Neal's leadership was in recruiting staff members. Although not many professors who were hostile to the course took up his challenge to teach in it for a year, he was constantly seeking out members from many different departments, attempting to convince them to join the staff. This was a hard sell because the scope of the Man course was so broad and because the time commitment for any faculty member was far greater than in a more conventional course. At that time, every professor in the course taught it as an overload. (Although Man was, in fact, a "double course," it was reckoned, at most, as only one course of a professor's course load per semester.) Neal wanted very broad faculty representation in the Man course. He believed that a natural scientist or a social scientist could make a substantial contribution to the course. He was particularly active in seeking out the newer and younger members of the faculty, those who were most likely to be narrowly focused as a result of recent graduate training, to invite them to help make the course even better than it was by bringing into it new vitality and a greater diversity of perspectives.

Neal believed that Man would benefit from a diverse faculty that represented different points of view and even different value systems.[63] Students could learn a lot by observing and participating in reasoned debates among the faculty members. Neal described Darrell Doughty, a new member of the Bible and religion department whose degree was from the University of Göttingen and who had taught New Testament at Princeton Theological Seminary, as the first member of the Man staff who did not have a generally positive view of the effect of the biblical tradition on Western civilization. Furthermore, Doughty was more aggressive in defending his positions than had been the norm in the college's faculty.

Nonetheless, Neal believed that Doughty's perspective added something important to the mix of the course.[64] Carl Walters, also a member of the Bible and religion department, was seen by Neal as one who could relate directly to the "subculture" of the "new breed" of students, those who were rebelling against conventional standards of courtesy, decorum in dress and personal appearance, and restrictions on personal activity.[65] These professors were strong advocates of the general changes taking place in college life and could be counted as supporters for a thorough (more thorough than Neal himself was likely to support) revision of the Man course.

On the other hand, among the ten or eleven professors who now constituted the staff were other new ones who, although they supported the general curriculum reform and saw some need to revisit the Man course to bring it into line with the overall changes, were more traditional in outlook. Among these were James Jobes and Robert R. Llewellyn of the philosophy department. Jobes had studied a "great books" curriculum as an undergraduate at St. John's College and brought to the Man course a particular devotion to the project of reading and interpreting the primary texts of the traditional "canon."[66] Llewellyn, who had come to philosophy by way of mathematics, was equally committed to the course's interdisciplinary enterprise. As an undergraduate at Davidson, he had admired the version of the course that Daniel Rhodes had helped to establish there.[67] George Apperson of the history department embodied a wide variety of interests as an ordained minister with a Th.D. degree in church history, further graduate work in English ecclesiastical and cultural history, and an abiding interest in Asian cultures.[68] Another history professor, Dale E. Benson, a student of the American Revolution, was perhaps the only conservative on the Man staff and a primary supporter of the course's traditional character.[69] Richard Batey[70] and Julius Melton,[71] both of the Bible and religion department, were advocates of tradition but were equally amenable to modifying and revising the course to bring it into line with the general reorganization of the college's curriculum.

The staff that Neal had assembled was larger and more diverse than the founding faculty of the course, and its members were generally in tune with the changes taking place in the college and in higher education in general. At the same time, a majority of the staff retained confidence in the course's traditional approach and tended to see the task as one of revision and adjustment rather than complete reconstruction.[72]

Robert Patterson

Neal's third contribution during the period of reform was his success in securing Robert Patterson to serve as the principal editor for the 1970 revision of the syllabus. Although Patterson had been at the college for almost ten years, he had been a member of the Man staff for only one year when Neal approached him. The son of Presbyterian missionary parents in China, Patterson had spent his early years in Asia and maintained a life-long interest in the continent's religions, philosophies, and cultures. Trained in biblical traditions as well, Patterson had spent his first years at the college teaching Bible courses and collaborating with James Roper of the English department to create the course in Oriental Humanities. Neal's choice of Patterson presupposed that a broadening of the course to include non-Western traditions would be considered.[73]

In a February 17, 1969, memorandum to the staff, Patterson outlined what he saw as the main objectives for the 1970 revision and his own preliminary view of the structure the revised course should take. Along with the existing syllabus, this memorandum became a basic planning document for the staff.[74]

Patterson prefaced his agenda by noting the recent argument of John Perry Miller, the retiring dean of the Yale Graduate School, that because the secondary schools had taken over the task of providing students with good backgrounds in Western civilization and literature, the colleges should concentrate on areas in which the schools were doing less well: "'non-western' studies, philosophy, the social sciences and the more recent developments in the sciences."[75]

With that as his point of departure, Patterson made the case for reform in four areas. Of these, the first and most important was the introduction of a non-Western perspective to the course:

(1) *"Non-western" studies.* All parties concede that the title of our course, if it were to describe what we really do, should be "Man in the Light of Western History and Religion." And there is, after all, considerable justification for this occidental canon of selection. Still, if anything is clear in the study of man, it is that contemporary sensibility has replaced the traditional canon of the Occident by the canon of the globe. Non-westerners are no longer "natives," nor are non-Western cultures any longer peripheral or non-essential. To be sure, we may agree to what has just been said and yet hold that it does not need to affect our course, that someone else will have to do the job of globalizing perspectives in the liberal arts. But if we are so to decide, I think we would have shrunk from a frontier

in liberal arts that a course such as ours ought to face up to, and in the long run we will have lessened the significance of our course for the students who take it.[76]

Second, although Patterson conceded that Man was doing well in philosophy, he proposed to give a more conscious characterization to each unit's basic concepts of what constitutes human existence.[77] Third, he advocated adding anthropological perspectives to the introductory unit on origins, particularly in regard to the "rise of consciousness in archaic man and the biological-historical differentiation of man from the animals." He saw such an addition as the obvious place to introduce "some taste of African myth and primitive visual arts."[78] Finally, Patterson argued for beefing up elements in the course that could use "symbols and non-discursive modes of communication," especially art and music.[79]

In an attachment to his memorandum, Patterson proposed, in broad outline, a new structure for the Man course.[80] The first semester was to include five units. Unit I he designated Archaic Man as Symbol Maker. In it he proposed to retain the traditional material on cosmological origins, but to add anthropological works on prehistoric man as well as material on tribal existence, cave painting, and African sculpture.

Unit II, called Conscious Existence as Illusion and Suffering: Buddhism, would provide the main coverage of non–Western material. Earlier in the memorandum, Patterson had made the case for focusing on Buddhism:

For the glimpse into non–Western studies, why focus on Buddhism? My argument would run as follows: (i) We can't cover everything. (ii) For various reasons, the chief options to consider are Buddhism and Islam. (iii) Buddhism offers the more dramatic or striking contrast to our normal cultural assumptions. (iv) Buddhism's deliberate denial of the significance of conscious existence is an existential option that is attractive to many students today. (v) Today's student is fascinated by Buddhism but largely ignorant of it—a promising situation for an exciting educational experience.[81]

Unit III would be entitled Reflective Man: The Greeks and Unit IV, Responsible Man: The Hebrews, thus reversing the order of these two blocks of material. To accommodate the chronological implications of this change, Patterson recommended that the readings from the Old Testament be drawn primarily from the eighth century and later. The first semester would conclude with Unit V, Eschatological Existence: Early

Christianity. Among other things, this arrangement would eliminate the course's traditional consideration of the Romans as distinct from, but related to, both the Greeks and the early Christians.

For the second semester, Patterson's outline was sketchier, but he did propose two additions to the end of the course to tie back to the new material in the first semester: material on African Americans and material on the European and American "discovery" of Asia in the nineteenth and twentieth centuries.[82]

Course Revision: A Collaborative Undertaking

To deal with Patterson's proposals, the Man staff was divided into teams, with each team charged to flesh out and complete the design of a particular unit. This work went on for more than a year, from February 1969 to May 1970, before agreements were reached regarding the details of lectures, readings, themes, and assignments. In the late spring of 1970, editors were designated for each of the units to prepare the final copy for the new syllabus.[83] The result of this long process, in which every member of the staff participated extensively, was a course plan that, although introducing some of Patterson's main recommendations, was much more consistent with the earlier versions of the course than his proposal of February 17, 1969, had anticipated.[84]

The introductory material in the course was reorganized into two units, an introduction proper dealing with the concepts of history and religion, and a unit called The Emergence of Man, in which the new anthropological emphasis advocated by Patterson was introduced. This new approach occupied four fewer class sessions than the old introduction it replaced, but because of the new calendar, the introductory material was increased by about one-fourth as a percentage of the whole course.

The third unit, titled Eastern Man: The Buddhists, consisted of three lectures and three colloquia. In contrast to Patterson's recommendation, the syllabus next treated the Old Testament. This unit was severely truncated, however, with the number of lecture-discussion pairings falling from twelve to six. In particular, the staff gave up much of the historical material, skipping from the exodus to the creation of the monarchy, from David to the eighth-century prophets, and from the eighth century to the exile and restoration. The prophetic works of Hosea, Micah, Jeremiah, and Ezekiel were dropped entirely.

The next unit, Reflective Man: The Greeks and Practical Man: The Romans, also reflected a significant reduction in material. From the thirty class meetings assigned to it in the earlier syllabus, the classical tradition was now to be covered in twelve sessions. The most consequential change was to abandon considerable Aristotelian material. Also eliminated were the readings from Polybius on the Roman Republic. The first semester then concluded with a sixth unit on Faithful Man: The Christians, which also suffered a significant decline in coverage: from twenty-four sessions to ten. Under this scheme, the only parts of the New Testament that students read were Mark's gospel, the Gospel of John, and the letters of Paul.

The second semester of the course was altered less extensively. Unit VII was called Medieval Man: Europe in the Middle Ages. The material on the Renaissance and Reformation was recaptured from its earlier dispersal into the units on the Middle Ages and the Early Modern Era and recast into two separate units: Unit VIII, Self-Sufficient Man: The Renaissance, and Unit IX, The Renewal of Contrition: The Reformation. Unit X was called Secular Man: The Modern Period, and it gathered together all the material from the seventeenth, eighteenth, and nineteenth centuries. Each of these four units occupied fewer class days than had the analogous units in the previous syllabus, but as a percentage of the entire course, each enjoyed a significant increase. Unit XI, Age of Crisis, included a new lecture-discussion pairing on racial conflict, but the total time assigned to the twentieth century declined by one-third.

One other aspect of the 1970 revision warrants attention. Because the staff wanted to retain the practice of pairing lectures and discussions (now called "colloquia"), it was necessary to develop alternate uses for the Friday class sessions that were not needed for testing. The solution it devised involved creating special topic "seminars" and "common experiences." Every semester, a seminar was offered by each of the faculty members. The topics for the seminars were all related to the course, but they involved readings that were not included in the syllabus. This device gave staff members the opportunity to discuss materials in which they were interested but that could not be included in the regular sequence of topics. Because each seminar had its own topic, the seminars marked a departure from the traditional practice of having every student study the same body of material. Students had a limited right to select the seminars in which they would participate and, in most of the seminars, were also expected to write papers on some aspect of the topic. As for the "common experiences," they provided an opportunity to salvage some of the lectures on subjects such as Greek art and architecture that had been removed from the syllabus; they also made possible the showing of films and the use of other nondiscursive materials, as Patterson had advocated in his first memorandum.

Taking the 1970 revision as a whole, one can see two kinds of adjustments being introduced simultaneously. The solution to the problems created by the new calendar's reduction in class periods was to reduce the number of days devoted to each unit. The result was a significant loss of materials covered across the whole range of the course.

The other adjustment involved reassigning the relative weight given to the different units of the course in order to accommodate the new topics Patterson had proposed: the anthropological view of human origins, the unit on Buddhism, and the material on race relations in modern America. In the first semester, these changes were made possible by disproportionately large reductions in the time assigned to the classical period, the New Testament, and, to a lesser extent, the Hebrews. In the second semester, the new lecture-colloquium pairing on contemporary race relations was incorporated into the final unit on modern America. Curiously enough, however, this unit was the only one to suffer a relative reduction. All of the other units, on the Middle Ages, the Renaissance, the Reformation, and the seventeenth through the nineteenth centuries, showed small relative increases in the time allotted to them. Thus one effect of the 1970 revision was to reverse the reform made in 1965 by curtailing the treatment of twentieth-century topics in favor of the earlier eras.

Implementing the Revision of 1970

Why was the outcome of the 1970 revision, which started out on such radical terms, so conservative? The answer has to do with how the course fit into the overall structure of the revised degree requirements. Because no niche was created for Man as an interdisciplinary course in the humanities area, it was essential that students be able to count the course as either history or religion in fulfilling degree requirements. Thus the catalogue description of the course was retained in the listings of the Bible and religion department and was given a corresponding course designation in the history listings, although the description there simply referred the reader to the longer description that appeared under Interdepartmental Courses.[85] Of the twelve credit hours assigned to Man, then, a student could count six hours as either history or religion. The other six hours fulfilled the new requirement for a freshman colloquium.[86] By tying Man to the colloquia, the staff successfully cemented the revised course to the new structure of the curriculum. But embracing the colloquia entailed two other significant changes. The first was to abandon the recently adopted practice of opening the course to sophomores. As a result, enrollments in Man, both in numbers and as a percentage of the student body, remained well below the high point that had been reached in the mid-1960s. Even so, the course continued to enroll more than one-third of the freshman class and its decline was not nearly as severe as that suffered by some other courses (History of Western Civilization, for example), which had also lost their privileged place in the arrangement of degree requirements.

The other, more significant change that occurred as a result of tying the course to the freshman colloquium program was the abandoning of the traditional practice of rotating the discussion groups from one professor to another as the course proceeded through its several units. Under the colloquium program, it became necessary for each discussion group, which was also an advising group, to remain attached to the same professor for the entire year. What was gained from this change was a more intense and intimate relationship between a professor and a group of students. What was lost was the exposing of the students to the teaching styles of the other members of the staff, although this loss was somewhat mitigated by the introduction of the special-topics seminars, in which students were encouraged to study with professors other than their own colloquium leader.

During the next few years the structure of the college's degree requirements continued to be modified, requiring constant adjustments by the Man staff to keep in step. In 1973–1974, frustrated by the perception that students' writing skills had declined under the new system, the faculty reduced the freshman colloquium requirement from two courses to one and reinstated a required writing course (English 151). At the same time, Man was extracted from the history department and the newly renamed department of religion and established as a freestanding option, along with American Studies and Oriental Humanities, in the general area of the humanities. With this change, a student could elect to take Man and have it count as freshman colloquium and as two courses in the humanities. The remaining three hours of the course were reckoned as an elective. This change was a return to the idea that the Man course was interdisciplinary and humanistic in its own right, apart from any connection it might have with particular departments. At the same time, the change reflected the desire of the humanities departments, particularly history, to strengthen their positions in the general curriculum by no longer allowing Man to "count" as history credit. To achieve that same end, the number of courses in the humanities, languages, and literature requirement was increased from four to six.[87] This increase worked to the Man course's advantage.

Although these changes enhanced Man's visibility in the curriculum, the reduction of part of its credit to elective status meant that the course was rendered less attractive as an option for students. In spite of that disadvantage, however, the course continued to enroll more than one-third of the entering class. Clearly, the Man course was once again solidly entrenched at the heart of the college's curriculum. Indeed, because Man provided the majority of the interdisciplinary colloquia for the freshman program, the course was experiencing increased enrollments.

After only one year of teaching the 1970 syllabus, the Man staff determined that it could not sustain even the modest changes that the revision had introduced. After the first year, the unit on Buddhism was dropped completely. This decision was not the result of hostility toward non-Western traditions, but rather an acknowledgment of the practical difficulties arising from time constraints and the limitations of the staff. These difficulties meant that non-Western materials could not be integrated into the course on the same level and with the same effect as the traditional materials. The "tokenism" of a brief unit was seen as more demeaning to non-Western traditions than the earlier omission of those traditions had been. Finally, the staff discovered that trying to make room for non-Western material necessarily meant eliminating some topics and readings that in earlier editions of the syllabus had seemed crucial to the overall coherence of the course. Although Patterson had left the Man staff in 1971 to become the dean of academic affairs, he acknowledged the necessity of this retreat.[88]

During the next three years, the staff also decided to abandon the anthropological emphases in the introductory unit and the lecture-colloquium pairing on American race relations. Again, it was determined that to cover these topics properly would take a much greater commitment of time, but that to make that commitment would only truncate further the main part of the course. By 1973 all that was left of the 1970 reform was the reduction in the various units made necessary by the change in the calendar, the use of the Friday class sessions for seminars and common experiences, and the attachment of the Man course to the freshman program.

Conclusion

In summing up the era of curriculum reform, it may appear that no real change in the Man course had occurred at all. A careful review of the developments from 1958 to 1975, however, will show that this was a critical era, one in which some of the main trends for the future development of the course were firmly established.

In the first place, the staff demonstrated that the Man course could be adapted to a new academic calendar as well as to radical changes in the curriculum, especially the system of degree requirements. At the same time, the staff reaffirmed the importance of a fundamental body of common study, even in a curriculum that stressed an individualized, smörgåsbord approach to education, and made that body of study an attractive option to a sizable number of students. The staff also reaffirmed, even strengthened, its commitment to the importance of interdisciplinary approaches to general education.

A second main outcome of the reform of 1970 and its aftermath, especially the experiment of adding non-Western materials to the course, was the conviction that the course ought to limit itself to the Western perspective it had presented from the beginning. Although this outcome ran counter to the national trend toward the addition of broader perspectives to general-education courses, it also reflected the discovery made at many institutions that it is difficult, if not impossible, to achieve breadth by grafting non-Western perspectives onto an existing Western course. One eventual outcome of that decision, described in chapter 4, was to rename the course to indicate its Western perspective. This was the logical alternative to changing the content, as Patterson had pointed out in his February 1969 memorandum.

A third outcome of the experiment was the decision to concentrate on traditional humanistic perspectives on the human situation, rather than to broaden the base to include the contributions of the social sciences (and of the natural sciences, for that matter). Yet this decision did not alter Fred Neal's determination to recruit a broadly based staff for the course. He continued to seek faculty members from all divisions of the college and later was successful in several cases, including Robert Amy of the department of biology, E. Llewellyn Queener of psychology, Diane Sachs from anthropology and sociology, and Diane Clark from the music department. That faculty members from the natural sciences, the social sciences, and the fine arts all began to participate in the avowedly humanistic course was itself a testimony to Neal's vision of the universal accessibility of the humanities and the fitness of the Man course in serving the needs of different kinds of students.

Finally, the great reform launched a trend that has become ever more pronounced in the development of the course since the 1970s: an increasing emphasis on the discussion of primary sources and a corresponding decrease in the role given to lectures and background reading in secondary sources. Although this trend began as an accommodation to the new weekly schedule, in which the discussions were assigned to the ninety-minute classes on Tuesdays and Thursdays, in time the staff came to regard the discussion of primary sources as a distinctive feature of the Man course.[89]

A Dialogue with Values

FRED W. NEAL

Faculty in the Man course (now the Search course) often say—and alumni often confirm—that students do not significantly realize the value of the course until ten years after graduation. Strangely enough, by then they will have forgotten most of the information that they once learned, through arduous labor, and recapitulated in full detail on the final examination.

What one does remember about the course after ten years is hard to ascertain. We are influenced by many things both during college and afterward, and we are not always aware of those influences. Moses said that one does not know what God has revealed to us during the encounter, but only after God has passed by. So do we know what has happened to us only by later reflection.

Of course, forgotten knowledge can be recalled, and past events, people, and ideas have a paradigmatic power to enrich present experiences. Yet after the knowledge of facts and information has disappeared, what remains? Habits of thought, habits of the heart, an appreciation of and devotion to significant values, maybe some great commitment? Maybe a sense of the vast sweep of western history? Maybe the recognition that basic issues of human life recur in succeeding ages and challenge us to make new responses in ways enlightened by the experience of the past? Maybe an appreciation of human beings in both their common humanity and rich diversity? Maybe a concern for responsible living in the civic community?

Sitting down to review the Search course ten years after retirement, as I do now, is illuminating. I see the course with greater objectivity than when I was its director. I am still impressed by its scope. The founders of the course—Davis, Kelso, Kinney, Osman, Cooper, and of course Diehl— left us a remarkable legacy, and although many changes have been made in the past half-century, we have profited by their judgments and been faithful to their vision.

I still remember many of my colleagues' lectures—some of them brilliant. But more significant to my mind were the study and discussion questions we gave to our students to accompany each reading assignment. I remember them as probing into vital issues of life, dealing with problems that have plagued human beings throughout Western history, asking for reactions of all sorts from the reader—personal opinions, reasoned conclusions, careful interpretations and evaluations—all as a prelude to discussion with faculty and fellow students. It was through this entrance into the life of dialogue, whether with the written word, with companions in discussion, or with oneself, that influences on personal values became effective. One didn't realize until later what a difference had been made in one's character, outlook, and self-understanding.

I remember so many of our first-year students as eager and questioning, sometimes harried and worn-down by the relentless daily assignments and the vast amounts of knowledge to assimilate, and also sometimes troubled about readings that raised questions they had not confronted before. For the first time, in many cases, they met fellow students from different locales and backgrounds who disagreed radically with them on all sorts of issues. The experience, although sometimes a rough awakening, always brought about a broadening of perspective.

Then, during the progress of the course, we began to see our students gain a new breadth of learning and depth of insight, fuller maturity in judgment, greater assurance in their own opinions and values, and augmented courage to express and defend both. To witness that growth was sheer joy. Inwardly we knew that something was happening that was not the result of teaching and learning but rather was a work of grace.

The course had a transforming effect on the teaching staff as well. Recruited across departmental lines, new members had to master material that was foreign to their expertise and to learn new methods of teaching. Any competent teacher can lead a quiz section. But how to develop a dialogue that could elicit self-discovery in students was a strange and difficult problem.

The first year of teaching in the course was painful. One could not merely read the unfamiliar material; one had to master it sufficiently to enter into significant conversation in the colloquium. To do so involved a risk not taken when one only imparts information. I was impressed by the courage of new staff members to undertake this task.

Team teaching was a great resource. Veteran teachers helped new re-cruits. In the early days of the course, the staff would meet for lunch in a private room in the refectory to discuss the assignment of the day—both the import of the reading and ways of approaching it with our students. But the newcomers helped the veterans, too. We discovered that col-leagues from different disciplines had distinctively penetrating questions to ask and perceptive interpretations to offer. New colleagues also made refreshing suggestions about the content and organization of the syllabus, helping us to keep it open and fresh.

Extended staff seminars during the summer involved a systematic re-consideration of the entire course. During the year, vehement tussles in exam preparation sessions made us reconsider what was important for our students to know. Yet we respected differences and continually learned from—and enjoyed—each other.

The course had an effect on the college community far beyond the classroom. Because it involved more than half the entering class, by the end of any four-year period the majority of the student body had gotten to know us and had shared with us a common body of learning. As such, we had fulfilled what John Henry Davis had written about the course around the time of its creation: the Man course was "not to be just an-other history of Western Civilization, but would synthesize knowledge, cut across department lines, and prepare the student for a fuller life of constructive citizenship in society."

Many of the issues we faced as a staff are described in the chapters of this book. Some of these were practical problems—drastically revising the syllabus in response to changes in the college calendar, assembling ade-quate primary source material for our students (we eventually had to publish our own volume of readings), making better use of audio-visual materials (a problem not yet satisfactorily resolved), and others.

Serious intellectual and moral problems also arose in the course. How should we respond to the upheavals of our times without becoming hostage to every new movement: fifty years of war, hot and cold, the struggles for human freedom all over the globe, the battles for racial jus-tice, equal rights for women, the student campaigns for personal liberties?

How should we face the perennial questions of students: Why limit the course to the Western world when we are entering a global society? Why waste time on ancient material when we live in a modern world?

Our best answer was, and I think remains, that the Search course is an introduction to the liberal arts curriculum, not an end to it. Knowledge and intellectual skills gained in these first years of college study are amplified, reinforced, refined, even challenged in other courses during later study. But the Search course is a provocative and seminal introduction to liberal learning and a stimulating incentive for constructive citizenship. In this process, for more than thirty years, it was my privilege to play a part.

3

ROBERT R. LLEWELLYN

The ancient Greek philosopher Protagoras expressed the essential point of his philosophy in a famous statement: "Man is the measure of all things—of things that are that they are and of the things that are not that they are not." An adaptation of this statement adorned the front cover of the syllabus for the Man course from 1980 to 1990, which was designed by Melanie Mitchum, an art major, a former student in the Man course, and a 1980 graduate of Southwestern.

The cover, the first to display anything other than the title of the course, the seal of the college, and the name Southwestern at Memphis, included a series of quotations from texts used in the course. Biblical texts, such as Genesis 1:2—"So God created man in his own image; male and female he created them"—and quotations from philosophical writers (for example, from Rousseau: "Man is born free, and everywhere he is in chains") framed the title of the course and the name of the college. The statement from Protagoras was at the top of the cover, the most visible one at first glance.

"Man is the measure" is an appropriate characterization of the Man course in the decade from 1975 to 1985. Measure suggests two dimensions of assessment, involving both standards and expectations. A *standard* defines how something is measured; in addition, a particular judgment determines whether or not something measures up to *expectations*. In both of these ways the Man course was the measure of the college's curriculum. In discussions of curriculum reform in the mid-1970s the style of instruction and learning in the Man course was cited as a standard for curriculum design. In fact, during two academic years, 1981–1982 and 1982–1983, Man was a requirement—a standard—for a degree from the college. In the process of becoming a requirement, however, the course had to measure up to expectations, in part those of agencies beyond the campus community. By the mid-1980s the Man course, although no longer required, continued to be basic to the college's degree requirements, and it remained the course with which a majority of students met one such requirement in the humanities.

A Pivotal Decade

What happened to the Man course can be appreciated by marking the boundaries of the decade 1975–1985 and noting two important contrasts.

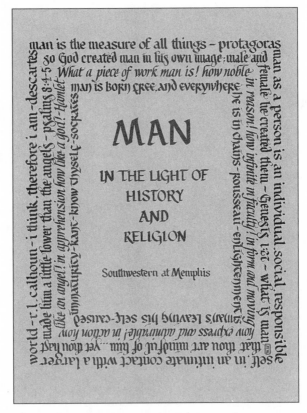

The covers of the Search study guide for 1983–84 (page 72) and 1984–85 (page 73).

In the academic year 1974–1975, Man was a one-year humanities course. Three of its twelve credit hours satisfied a degree requirement called the freshman colloquium, a program designed to emphasize interdisciplinary learning and to provide a more efficient faculty advising structure. Ten sections of the Man course were scheduled, enrolling 160 students from an incoming class of 298. By the academic year 1984–1985, the Man course was part of the Basic Requirement in Humanities. Its twelve credit hours, now distributed over two academic years, satisfied a college requirement for "two years of sound and comprehensive study of the Bible for the granting of a degree." Of the incoming class of 361 students, 245 enrolled in the first year of Man; as sophomores, 180 of them continued with the second year of the course.

This change in Man's role within the academic program was accentuated by differences in the way it was described. In the 1974–1975 catalogue Man was an "interdepartmental course," characterized simply as:

"A study of the cultural and religious history of man."[1] In the 1984–1985 catalogue the course was listed under Interdisciplinary Study, and this listing was supplemented by almost three columns of text in a new section of the catalogue called Biblical Studies at Southwestern.[2]

The decade 1975–1985 also witnessed major changes for the college. At the opening faculty meeting on September 4, 1984, James H. Daughdrill, who had become president of the college in 1973, noted that the occasion was the beginning of the academic year for "Rhodes College."[3] The new name, adopted by the college's board of trustees, honored President Emeritus Peyton Nalle Rhodes, who had served the college since 1926. For sixteen years, from 1949 to 1965, Rhodes was the president of the college, the successor to Charles E. Diehl in the office.

Along with the change of name came a new commitment by the board: "Rhodes College is committed to being a nationally outstanding college of the liberal arts and sciences." Rhodes was preparing to enter the next ten years with a sense of purpose befitting a college seeking a national reputation in higher education.

The matter of an appropriate name haunted the Man course as well. The course's revised second-year syllabus for 1984–1985 had a new cover that proclaimed "M A N" in large block letters, each letter comprised of "MAN~WOMAN~MAN~WOMAN~" printed left to right in miniature type. This design was a response to the charge of gender bias in the name of the course. In May 1986, after a yearlong study, the name of the course was changed to The Search for Values in the Light of Western History and Religion, immediately shortened by students and faculty to Search.

In 1975 it was Southwestern and the Man course. By 1985 it was Rhodes and soon would be the Search course. The changes in names are not merely coincidental. Both the course and the college faced severe challenges and, in response, substantially altered the academic program.

More Curriculum Study and the National Mood

In May 1977, two major events occurred in the life of the college, one of which occasioned shock and the other challenge. Robert G. Patterson, who had succeeded Jameson M. Jones as dean in 1971, announced his departure from the office to become Southwestern's first professor of humanities, and a report that was intended to guide curriculum reform for the college, jointly authored by Patterson and others, was published. The report, titled "Year of Challenge: Report of the Committee to Plan for the Eighties Regarding Faculty and Educational Program," made several recommendations concerning the college's curriculum, especially "general studies." Among the principles it propounded were that interdisciplinary and general studies should be a greater proportion of the curriculum and that ethical and value dimensions should be included more widely in teaching and learning.[4]

The report's call for curriculum reform was answered in May 1978 by Dean Charles O. Warren, a biologist noted for his interdisciplinary interests, and others in a subsequent report from the Ad Hoc Committee on Educational Program. The committee's recommendations concerning a general education component in the humanities and fine arts cited the Man course as a model and as one option to fulfill the humanities requirement. The committee also recommended that the component for the natural sciences and mathematics include interdisciplinary courses. Jacob Bronowski's *Ascent of Man* television series was mentioned as a possible model for a general education course in the natural sciences.[5]

In continuing its consideration of curriculum reform into the late 1970s, Southwestern did not follow in anyone else's wake. Indeed its efforts were contemporaneous with and paralleled those at Harvard University, which received national attention for its decision to reemphasize a "core curriculum." The "Redbook," as the Harvard report was called, required course work in literature and the arts, history, social and philosophical analysis, science and mathematics, and foreign languages.[6]

The Harvard report heralded a flood of publications beginning around 1980 that called for a national revitalization of the humanities.[7] Although the motives for curriculum reform ranged widely, nearly all of the participants in the discussion were convinced that the aims of general education could not be met by a collection of discrete, departmentally based courses. Charles Frankel, the president of the National Humanities Center, spoke of the national need for coherence, continuity, and direction that study of the humanities could help to address:

The modern world, almost by definition, is a world in which new knowledge and techniques produce rapidly changing social conditions, which in turn produce vertiginous changes in human beliefs and values. The coherence that people have thought they have seen in things is regularly broken; their sense of connectedness with what has gone before and of an intelligible direction in where they are going is disrupted. . . . What use are the humanities? . . . [I]t is in the

difference in people's experiences if they know the background of what is happening to them, if they can place what they are doing in a deeper and broader
context, if they have the metaphors and symbols that can give their experience
shape.[8]

The national effort to revitalize higher education pinpointed the challenge as one of reaffirming the humanities' moral role in higher education. Doing so would be the needed corrective to the overspecialization
of the academic disciplines, to an excessive emphasis on career-oriented
education, and to the public's general discontent with the loose structure
of higher education as manifested in the absence of degree requirements.
Post-Watergate assessments of national morality also underscored the
need for a greater effort within higher education to provide ethical training. Southwestern's curriculum reform studies in the late 1970s were very
much in tune with this national agenda.

Warren's 1978 report laid the groundwork for the faculty to make a
thorough reform of the curriculum during the 1978–1979 academic
year. Two events, however, slowed the momentum for reform. First, Warren and the faculty were diverted into a detailed consideration of the college's policies concerning tenure and promotion. No fewer than nine
faculty meetings during the fall 1978 term were devoted to this issue.
Then, in March 1979, Warren resigned to become vice president for academic affairs at the State University of New York at Plattsburg. President
Emeritus Rhodes was named as acting dean.

When the faculty finally did turn its attention back to the curriculum, it was in response to unexpected pressure from a long-standing beneficiary of the college.

The Bellingrath–Morse Foundation

In a May 1978 letter to Daughdrill, George Downing, who chaired
the Bellingrath-Morse Foundation in Mobile, Alabama, informed Southwestern that it was no longer in compliance with the deed of trust that
had established the foundation and that made provision for annual distri-
butions of money to five beneficiaries, including two churches and three
colleges: Southwestern at Memphis, Huntingdon College in Montgomery, Alabama, and Stillman College in Tuscaloosa, Alabama.

The Bellingrath-Morse Foundation was established by Walter D.
Bellingrath in February 1950 to carry on the work that he and his wife,

Bessie Morse Bellingrath, had begun. In part this work was the transformation of a fishing camp into what is now the Bellingrath Gardens in Mobile. In addition, the Bellingraths believed in supporting Christian higher education. As the deed of trust stated:

Our forefathers believed not only in Almighty God, but also in the Church, in the sanctity of the home, and in the responsibility of the home for religious training. They believed in teaching of the Bible, in family prayer, and in the necessity for discipline for the development of moral integrity. It was from the Bible that they learned the root principle of democracy, the dignity and worth of the human individual. Made in the image of God and accountable to Him, endowed with reason, conscience, emotions, and the power of choice, they recognized that it is of vital importance that this human being make the most of his abilities and opportunities.[9]

The foundation was directed in the deed of trust to distribute income generated by its property and securities, in excess of what was needed to perpetuate the gardens and to administer the foundation, to the beneficiaries. Southwestern was named as a 40 percent beneficiary, by far the largest of the five. Its central position echoed the friendship between Diehl and Bellingrath.[10]

The foundation's three college beneficiaries were required to meet a special curriculum provision in order to receive their share: "every regularly enrolled student for a bachelor's degree shall be required to take a sound and comprehensive course in the Holy Bible of six (6) semester hours during the first academic year and at least six (6) semester hours in one other academic year."[11] The trustees of the foundation were to determine whether each college was in substantial compliance with this provision by examining annual reports and other documents submitted by the college, including the catalogue. The deed of trust spelled out the procedures to be followed if a college beneficiary failed to measure up. Essentially, the college would have three years to reinstate an appropriate degree requirement. Failing that, the trustees were authorized to name a replacement beneficiary that did meet the curriculum provision.

Downing's letter of May 30, 1978, called Southwestern to account— the college's requirements for a bachelor's degree in 1976–1977 did not include study of the Bible. Biblical and religious study—indeed, the Man course itself—was merely an option within a general six-course humanities, languages, and literature requirement.[12] In truth, the college had been out of compliance beginning in 1970–1971. The 1969–1970 degree requirements had still included two courses in biblical studies and two courses in theology or the history of religion. The Man course at that time was reckoned as twelve credits in these areas and thus satisfied the requirement.

If the Bellingrath-Morse requirement was like a hot coal that smolders long before a fire erupts, two related events fanned the coal into an intense flame. First, in 1978 the three college beneficiaries looked more closely at the management of the foundation's assets. Its principal asset was the Coca Cola Bottling Company of Mobile. Offers to buy the company had been received but rejected by the foundation's trustees. All three colleges argued that the financial return to the foundation and hence to them would be substantially increased if the company were sold and the proceeds invested. In the case of Southwestern, the annual income to the college would jump from the approximately $28,000 anticipated for 1977 to a projected $380,000 to $714,000.

Obviously, a challenge to the management of the foundation's assets could only come from beneficiaries in compliance with the deed of trust. Downing's letter had placed Southwestern on notice that it was out of compliance. In addition, Huntingdon College and Stillman College requested that the trustees of the foundation monitor Southwestern's progress closely during the three-year period it had to requalify. In the event that Southwestern did not requalify, they asked the trustees not to substitute a new college beneficiary but to redistribute Southwestern's percentage to them.[13] This became the second event that fueled keen interest in curriculum revision at Southwestern.

The Lilly Workshop in the Liberal Arts

In a letter to Downing on January 28, 1980, Daughdrill told the Bellingrath-Morse Foundation that the faculty had already begun a thorough review of the college's curriculum, and that any changes designed to bring Southwestern into compliance with the deed of trust would be made well within the three-year limit.[14]

Earlier, at its January meeting, the faculty had been informed that the college's degree requirements were out of compliance. At this same meeting Associate Dean Robert R. Llewellyn announced that the college had accepted an invitation by the Lilly Foundation to send a team to its Workshop in the Liberal Arts at Colorado College that summer.

The Lilly invitation had been unsolicited, but its timing could not have been better. Llewellyn told the faculty that the team's purpose would be to revive the curriculum discussions that had lain dormant since Warren's spring 1978 report. He believed that the outcome might be a revised curriculum that would requalify the college as a beneficiary of the foundation. But he and other members of the administration insisted that these curriculum discussions would proceed along the same lines as earlier faculty deliberations about curriculum.

The reason Llewellyn was optimistic about requalifying was that the Man course had in 1968–1969 and 1969–1970 been reckoned as meeting the Bellingrath-Morse requirement.[15] Prior to these two years, six credit hours of the Man course had been accepted as meeting the foundation's explicit demand for two biblical studies courses in the first year of a student's undergraduate program. Since the faculty's own curriculum discussions in the mid-1970s had already seemed to position the Man course prominently in any future degree structure, it might be possible to requalify with the foundation by making the Man course a principal component in the college's degree requirements.

Although Gerald Duff, a professor of English at Kenyon College, was named in mid-January 1980 as the new dean of academic affairs, he was not scheduled to take office until July. Thus, as associate dean, Llewellyn chaired the Lilly workshop team. He asked Douglas Hatfield from the history department, Bernice White from the English department, and David Jeter from the chemistry department to join him. Hatfield had been a member of several curriculum revision committees. White had been active from the start in the freshman colloquium program, which she and Fred Neal, the director of the Man course, cochaired. Jeter had long been an outspoken proponent of a substantial natural science and mathematics component in the curriculum. Llewellyn, whose faculty appointment was in the philosophy department, had been a member of the Man staff since 1970.

The work of the Lilly team was conducted in an atmosphere made tense by the Bellingrath-Morse trustees' finding of noncompliance. In fact, from time to time during the spring of 1980, doubts about the college "selling its soul" were murmured by some faculty and students. But the team itself saw its work primarily as a continuation of the faculty's earlier curriculum discussions; in fact, the subtitle of its final report to the faculty was "A continuation of the discussions of the curriculum initiated in 1977 by the Faculty of Southwestern At Memphis."[16] Daughdrill and members of the board of trustees affirmed that the college's curriculum was not "for sale to the highest bidder."

The final report of the Lilly team was distributed to the faculty before the beginning of the 1980–1981 academic year, and the opening faculty workshop was devoted to discussing it. The most far-reaching recommendations were in the area of the General Education Program. Five courses were proposed for all students, two to be taken in the first year and three in the second year. The measure—the standard to be achieved—of the proposed program was clearly the Man course.[17] The first two of the five courses would be "[b]asically, [the] Greek-Roman/Old and New Testament units in the present Man course." The third and fourth would be either two courses that are a "continuation of the present syllabus for the 'Man' course" or two courses in a proposed new program in the history and philosophy of the natural and social sciences and mathematics. The fifth would be one of several courses addressing specific issues that emerged from the preceding four courses. Oriental Humanities, Science Fiction as Literature, and Creationism and Evolution were offered as examples.[18]

The general education program embodied the educational values that the Lilly team believed to be consistent with the fundamental purposes of Southwestern: to introduce students to the cultural and historical perspectives that have shaped Western civilization, to encourage an interdisciplinary approach to learning, and to articulate clearly that education has a moral framework. As for the Man course in particular, it

is not only continued and expanded, it is also used as the model for the general education program. It has represented the college's best efforts to accomplish the purposes of the general education program. It is firmly grounded in the Judeo-Christian and Greek-Roman traditions which shape Western Civilization; it is designed and taught by instructors from a variety of disciplines who have considerable interest in and talent for interdisciplinary teaching; it is a course of study in which value-questions and value-issues are clearly seen to be most reflective of a society's character and in which there is a determined effort to reflect on and to assess critically value commitments; it is comprehensive in its scope, providing a good humanities background for students regardless of their particular major.[19]

Two features of the Lilly team's proposal were directed to compliance with the foundation's deed of trust. First, the twelve credit hours of the

Man course were divided into two six-hour components. The first six hours, including the Old Testament and New Testament units, would be required of all freshmen. By precedent, these six hours had counted with the foundation as biblical studies and presumably would be counted that way again. Sophomores could then take either the remaining six hours of the Man course—which covered the medieval period to the present and which the foundation had previously accepted as meeting the curriculum provisions of the deed of trust—or an alternative set of courses. The alternative courses would focus on the origins and development of science, with some attention to its effects on church and society. But they were conceived of as values-oriented studies in the same spirit as the second year of the Man course; in addition, the same chronological sequence would be followed.

In all likelihood, faculty adoption of the Lilly team's recommendations would have restored the college to substantial compliance with the foundation. Southwestern's position was based on Walter Bellingrath's statement in the deed of trust that "if the Foundation Trustees are convinced that any one or more of the beneficiary institutions is not *substantially complying* with the requirements which I have stipulated . . . said Trustees shall make no distribution to said institution or institutions . . ." (emphasis added).[20] The "substantial compliance" he had specified could be six credit hours of biblical studies and six credit hours of Bible-related coursework. The proposed curriculum revision in the college's general education program seemed to meet that standard, although it might require further explanation of how the values component of the second year of the Man course and the alternative program could be reckoned as Bible related.

The Lilly team's report generated a flood of controversy. At the start of the 1980–1981 academic year, Dean Duff was introduced to a faculty up in arms about nearly every aspect of the report. General disbelief prevailed that four members of the faculty had been so presumptuous as to propose a thorough revision of the curriculum essentially on their own. The team's response—that a direct correlation existed between the proposed revision and earlier proposals that the faculty had endorsed in the mid-1970s—proved unconvincing. Some wondered how the revisions could be implemented: for example, would the natural science faculty teach the sophomore alternative to the Man course? Others favored less structure, not more, in the college's degree requirements. Some members of the Man staff openly disclaimed the central role granted to the Man course in the proposed curriculum, arguing that no one wanted to teach conscripts in a required course. Many faculty members believed that the course's proposed central role was simply an effort to comply with the stipulations of the Bellingrath-Morse Foundation.

By early October, not only had the Lilly team's proposal been weakened, but no viable alternative that would reinstate the college as a beneficiary of the foundation had replaced it. Thus, on November 5, 1980, in response to requests from Duff and Llewellyn, the curriculum committee (chaired by Harold Lyons from the chemistry department) formed a subcommittee (chaired by Kenneth Williams from the mathematics department) to study the Bellingrath-Morse matter and, in particular, to determine what role a religious studies program should have in the college's degree requirements. Five days later, the executive committee of the college's board of trustees authorized special arrangements to bring in John Wade, an expert on torts, to assist the curriculum committee in its work. In addition to being a professor of law at Vanderbilt University, Wade was a member of the Southwestern board and a longtime adviser to the faculty on personnel and curriculum matters.[21]

In early January 1981, the curriculum committee distributed to the faculty a new proposal for a "general structure for the College's degree requirements." The structure contained two components. The first, an Educational Skills component, required a course in English composition and a demonstrated proficiency in a foreign language. The second, a General Education Requirement established a "core curriculum" consisting of twelve credit hours in an interdisciplinary humanities course, nine hours in an interdisciplinary natural science course, nine hours in an interdisciplinary social science course, and six hours in an interdisciplinary fine arts course.[22] The new proposal also addressed the biblical studies issue, and the Man course again was cited as a standard:

[A] religious studies element is an appropriate component of the College's degree requirement program, provided it is presented in a context of interdisciplinary studies and includes a study of Eastern religions. . . . [T]he current "Man in the Light of History and Religion" course is established and with some changes could be the "Humanities Course" in the Core Curriculum. . . .[23]

The faculty met on January 14, 1981, its main agenda item being to consider the curriculum committee's proposal. It became clear that the proposal was not supported, in large measure because of doubts by the

natural science faculty about whether an interdisciplinary science course
was feasible. To many other faculty members the proposal seemed to suffer from hasty construction.

A substitute motion was made by Angelo Margaris from the mathematics department to adopt the curriculum proposal of the Lilly team.
During the discussion that followed, Winton Smith, the college's staff
legal counsel, was questioned at length about the details of the
Bellingrath-Morse trust, the possibility of requalifying as a beneficiary if
the Man course was required of all students, and the potential value of the
income from the foundation. Smith replied that it was reasonable to believe that the foundation's trustees would accept requiring the Man
course as an appropriate way to comply substantially with the deed of
trust. He also reported that the annual distribution to the college, assum-
ing the foundation sold the bottling company, was now estimated to be
approximately $750,000 per year.

Following this discussion, Donald Tucker from the foreign languages
department made a substitute motion: "That the course known as 'Man
in the Light of History and Religion' be adopted as a universal degree requirement for Southwestern students at the earliest possible date and that
the course be taught in a two-year sequence and be offered in Terms I
and II for the freshman and sophomore years."[24] After the faculty received
additional assurances from Smith that the Man course, taught over a two-
year period, would place the college in a strong position to requalify as a
beneficiary, Tucker's motion was passed by voice vote. Although the vote
was not unanimous, the ayes were loud enough that no division of the
vote was requested. In general, the faculty was relieved that the issue of
compliance with the Bellingrath-Morse Foundation's deed of trust
seemed to be settled.

In a letter to Downing on January 28, 1981, Daughdrill informed the
foundation of the faculty's action and the subsequent approval of that action by the college's board of trustees at its January meeting. He asked
Downing to confirm Southwestern's reinstatement as a beneficiary.

Downing replied on February 11, 1981, with a letter that was encouraging but not definitive; indeed, he indicated that the matter might
have to be decided by a court of law. The two other college beneficiaries were continuing to challenge the foundation's management, and
Downing believed that a judicial decision might be needed to resolve the
disputes. In the meantime, Southwestern was left in limbo. This state of
uncertainty affected the continuing discussion of the Man course at the

college. How properly to describe the course to the foundation and in the college catalogue was the new concern.

Implementing the Man Course as a Degree Requirement

The faculty's decision to require the Man course of all students, beginning in fall 1981 with the incoming freshman class, left considerable follow-up work to be done. Lecture room B in the Frazier-Jelke Science Center, the site of lectures since it opened in fall 1968, no longer sufficed; the 320-seat Hardie Auditorium was the only space on campus large enough (the gym excepted) to accommodate the anticipated class of approximately 280 students. As some students would later remark, "It is *Hardly* an *Auditorium*." The elevated platform and pulpit-style lectern made it difficult for lecturers to have reasonable eye-to-eye contact with students. The windows were not designed for darkening, which made audiovisual presentations virtually impossible. The sound system used a vacuum tube-era amplifier and was unreliable. No chalkboard was large enough to make outlines or notes visible to those who were seated in the back. The fixed seating, part of the original equipment of the room, was not elevated from front to back, was uncomfortable, and had no arm-tablets. President Emeritus Rhodes ameliorated the latter problem somewhat when, in consultation with the physical plant staff, he designed and oversaw the production of several hundred Masonite lapboards.

In addition to logistics, the structure and content of the Man course were changed to fit the two-year format. The daily schedule of class meetings was abandoned. Man continued its lecture-colloquium pattern, but only by meeting on Mondays for sixty-minute common lectures and on Wednesdays or Thursdays for ninety-minute discussions in colloquia.

The content of the 1981–1982 version of the Man course was not simply one-half of the previous syllabus. The new twelfth edition syllabus expanded the introductory unit and revised the biblical units, placing more emphasis on the creation stories in the Old Testament and the person of Jesus in the New Testament. The syllabus for the second year of the course, first used in 1982–1983, contained new materials on conservatism and liberalism in the nineteenth century and a reformulated structure for the twentieth century unit (communism, fascism, existentialism, and prospects for the American future and for the feminist initiative).

The staff of the Man course was nearly doubled to twenty-two faculty members to accommodate the influx of students. Returning veterans included Fred Neal (religion), Granville Davis (history), George Apperson (history), James Jobes (philosophy), Larry Lacy (philosophy), Robert Llewellyn (philosophy), Milton Brown (religion), Richard Batey (religion), Robert Patterson (religion), Horst Dinkelacker (foreign languages), Donald Tucker (foreign languages), and Richard Wood (English). Hatfield had joined the Man staff in 1980 after working with the Lilly team and, thus, was already a veteran of one year's standing. In addition, nine new members joined the staff: Robert Amy (biology), Diane Clark (music), John Bruhwiler (foreign languages), Llewellyn Queener (psychology), Elaine Whitaker (English), Bernice White (English), and three administrators: Robert Norfleet, the college chaplain and career planning and placement director; Ray Allen, the dean of admissions and financial aid; and Bo Scarborough, the dean of student affairs.

Neal anticipated the teaching needs of the staff, especially the nine new members, with a workshop held during the summer of 1981. Funds recently obtained by the college from the Andrew W. Mellon Foundation to support interdisciplinary teaching were used to provide a modest stipend to participants. The staff spent a week in June, reviewing the structure of the course; hearing presentations from experienced instructors about the main ideas presented in lectures; discussing certain problematic texts assigned for colloquium sessions, such as the documentary hypothesis concerning the Pentateuch; and determining general course expectations and standards. In a report to Duff, Neal summarized the results of the workshop, then added:

What came as a "bonus" was a feeling of unity as a teaching team. The old members and new members came to understand each other, to gain a sense of respect and trust in each other. I feel that we start a difficult two-year experiment with good morale, a sense of common purpose and a mutual concern and respect.[25]

As a result of the workshop, the staff agreed to gather weekly during the academic year to discuss materials in the course, and another summer workshop was projected for 1982 to prepare for the second year.

The expanded size of the Man staff militated against efficient business meetings, so Neal formed the Man Administrative Committee to help him address the week-to-week logistical challenges of the course. One of the committee's first items of business was to create the calendar for the sophomore year, which would be taught for the first time beginning in fall 1982.

While the Man staff prepared to teach the course, students were re-acting strongly to the new requirement that all must take it. Two weeks after the faculty voted to require the Man course, the lead article in the January 23, 1981, issue of the *Sou'wester*, headlined "Man Requirement Creates Opposition," summarized the reactions expressed at a Student Government Assembly (SGA) meeting chaired by Vice President David Eades: "[T]he requirement will make it more difficult to fulfill major re-quirements, scare away prospective students and infringe on students' freedom to shape their own academic program." On February 13, the *Sou'wester* reported that 90 percent of the 493 students who had re-sponded to a special poll wanted an alternative to the Man requirement, preferably a selection from a list of "acceptable" humanities courses.[26]

Faculty sentiment for an alternative to the Man course was also wide-spread. During the revisions of the college's curriculum and calendar in the late 1960s and early 1970s, the faculty had worked diligently to pro-vide multiple ways for students to fulfill degree requirements. In April 1981, an ad hoc committee formed by the curriculum committee pro-posed a revision of the humanities requirement that would establish, as an alternative to the Man course, discipline-based courses in the religion and philosophy departments, such as Introduction to the Old Testament and Social Issues in Ethical and Religious Perspective.[27] But it was too late in the academic year for such a proposal to be considered, to say nothing of the approval that any alternative to the Man course would have to receive as substantially complying with the deed of trust of the Bellingrath-Morse Foundation.

The Man Course Description

Both faculty and student feelings about the Man course were fueled by yet another concern. A statement about the course had been prepared by Neal in response to a request from legal counsel Winton Smith at the end of 1980, a time when the college's compliance with the deed of trust was still undecided. Neal's statement emphasized Man's biblical and reli-gious content so that this aspect of the course could be made explicit to the college's Alabama legal counsels, Douglas Arant and Wallace Sears. They in turn could then effectively present the Man course to the trustees of the foundation as substantially complying with the deed of trust.

A version of Neal's statement, edited by Duff and possibly by others, including the Alabama legal counsels, had accompanied Daughdrill's January 28, 1981, letter to Downing informing him that Man was now a required course. The statement was referred to in the letter as "a course description." This characterization was immediately challenged by Neal and the staff of the Man course. They argued that Neal's statement was not a complete course description, but rather a statement about "the religious dimensions" of the course. What is more, although his statement had intentionally emphasized that aspect of the Man course it nonetheless had set it alongside, and sometimes in contrast with, other formative influences on Western civilization. The edited version that accompanied the January 28 letter removed any mention of nonbiblical course materials.

As the controversy on campus grew, the legal issue was drawn in no uncertain terms by the college's Alabama legal counsels. If the college was to be reinstated as a beneficiary, then its catalogue for 1981–1982 not only must state that Man was a required course, but also must include the statement submitted by Daughdrill with his January 28 letter. The reasons for the counsels' position were twofold: first, the statement was part of the case before the Bellingrath-Morse trustees that the Man course was six credit hours of biblical studies and six credit hours of Bible-related study; and second, the statement had to be part of the college's contractual obligation with its students, as stated in the catalogue.

Neal and the Man staff insisted that Man was not a Bible course, narrowly defined, but that it was clearly a valid substitute for a Bible course because it taught students about the content of the Bible, methods of biblical study and interpretation, and the reciprocal influence of the Bible and its cultural setting. Further, in the late 1960s the Man course had been accepted by the foundation, at least implicitly, as meeting the curriculum conditions of the deed of trust. Indeed, from the very beginning of the college's ties with the Bellingrath-Morse Foundation in 1950, the first six hours of the Man course had always been reckoned as an acceptable substitute for required courses in the Old and New Testaments.[28]

After many attempts to revise the statement that had accompanied Daughdrill's January 28 letter, a compromise version was reluctantly approved by the staff of the Man course in March 1981. The compromise statement closely resembled the version that had accompanied the letter, but it did call attention to the study of Greco-Roman civilization in the first year of the course. The statement stressed that Greco-Roman civilization was studied "as important in its own right and as part of the background of early Christianity."[29]

Agreement on the compromise statement did not end the matter. According to the conditions under which it was approved by the Man staff, the statement was to be published as a description of the religious dimensions of the course and placed in a narrative portion of the catalogue, not among the course listings. Reference could then be made to this longer statement in the standard listing of the course.

The catalogue for 1981–1982 was distributed in April 1981. The long statement appeared as the official course listing for Man. It occupied almost three columns of text, substantially more than any other course listing in the catalogue.

Student and faculty members objected strongly to the new catalogue's presentation of the Man course. David Eades, now the SGA president, questioned the honesty of the description: "The description in the new catalogue does not accurately describe the course I took as a freshman. . . . It seems that we may be misrepresenting ourselves to the Bellingrath-Morse Foundation and to prospective students who read the catalog."[30] Larry Lacy, a longtime member of the Man staff, said, "Either we must insure that the course description faithfully reflects what has been done in the course, or we must bring the course as it is actually taught into conformity with the catalog description." If the catalogue stated that the Man course consistently made "reference back to the formative ideas of the Western tradition in the Bible and the classical heritage," Lacy continued, then those who taught in the course must understand their obligation to do just that.

Duff and Llewellyn insisted that no pressure had been exerted by the dean's office to construct the statement in any particular way. According to Duff, "We wanted to be as affirmative as possible in describing how [the Man course] is in compliance with the Bellingrath-Morse Trust and to be as accurate as possible." Llewellyn insisted that an honest mistake had been made in placing the compromise statement amid the standard course listings. He argued that the mistake must be corrected in the next printing of the catalogue.

The Man staff weighed in with its own corporate statement: "[The staff] is not changing the present Man course in general content, purpose, perspective or methodology. . . . The staff did not ask to have the Man course made into a course mandatory for graduation, but agreed to the proposal. . . . The Man staff believes that the Man course, as it is presently conducted, does satisfy, without equivocation, the terms of the Bellingrath Trust interpreted under the rubric of 'substantial compliance.' . . . The Man Staff is opposed to changing the Man Course to fit any ex-

ternally imposed directives—apart from the general supervision of all
curricular matters by the faculty."[31] Expressing the widespread preference
for an alternative means of complying with the Bellingrath-Morse stipulations, the Man staff urged creating optional ways to fulfill the humanities requirements for graduation.

The summer of 1981 brought good news to the college. In June
Southwestern learned that the Bellingrath-Morse trustees had sold the
foundation's stock in the Coca-Cola Bottling Company.[32] A month later,
Downing informed Daughdrill that "The Trustees have concluded . . .
that Southwestern at Memphis is requalified as beneficiary of the
Bellingrath-Morse Foundation and is therefore eligible to participate in
the next distribution to the college beneficiaries of Foundation net income."[33] Downing's letter was read to the executive committee of the
college's board of trustees at its meeting on July 28, 1981. Walter P. Armstrong, the acting secretary for the meeting, recorded the trustees' reactions:

It was generally agreed that returning the Bible to the center of the curriculum,
together with the requalification, form[s] one of the three most important events
in Southwestern's history, the others being the reopening of the college in 1873
when the church raised $6000 and directed the Board to keep the college going,
and the move to Memphis in 1925.[34]

For students and faculty, however, the good news was tempered by the
continuing controversy about the catalogue description. In addition, discussions between the foundation and its beneficiaries concerning issues
such as the proper amounts to be paid to the two church beneficiaries
were not yet ended. The threat that all of these matters would have to be
settled in court was real.

When the 1981–1982 academic year began, the catalogue controversy was once again front-page news on campus. Students objected to both
the content and placement of the long description.[35] They were led by a
new entity, the Man Advisory Council, which had been formed in 1980.
The council was the idea of Neal, who wanted to give more recognition
to students who had excelled in the Man course and who could be called
on to help the staff in a variety of ways.[36] Neal used council members to
assist with book sales, tutoring, and, from time to time, as substitute colloquium leaders.

On October 9, the *Sou'wester* reported that thirteen members of the

Man council had "pledged to begin work on a new description after unanimously agreeing . . . that the current catalogue description is inaccurate." They had been encouraged to take on this task after student leaders at an opening retreat at Camp Pinecrest "concluded that united opposition to the current description by the course's top students might cause the description to be reconsidered."[37] In the same issue, the *Sou'wester* published an open letter from student leaders to the college's board of trustees that identified the Man course description as an issue of "utmost concern" to students. The Man Administrative Committee—the faculty advisory group to Neal—formally asked the Man Advisory Council to work on a course description, and student members Boyd Chitwood and David Eades were made the conduit for combined student and faculty consideration of a new proposal.[38]

The college's Alabama legal counsels remained adamant that the long catalogue statement about the Man course must not be changed in content or location.[39] Considering that Southwestern had requalified as a beneficiary based on the required Man course and the catalogue's statement about the course, any modification might jeopardize the college's status. Litigation involving the foundation and its beneficiaries was still possible. Daughdrill believed that the continuing controversy on campus meant that the faculty questioned whether the Man course was six credit hours of biblical study and six credit hours of Bible-related study. He also feared that the controversy would be interpreted as a refusal by the college to have any biblical requirement at all, and thus might remove the legal basis on which the college had requalified as a beneficiary.

The college's board of trustees surprised students and faculty alike. At its October 1981 meeting the board agreed with the student representatives that the long description of the Man course should appear in a narrative section of the catalogue and that a new description should be written as the standard course listing. It addressed the concerns about the college's legal position by adopting a resolution that clearly affirmed, in language that echoed the Bellingrath-Morse Foundation's deed of trust, Southwestern's commitment to biblical studies as a degree requirement: "It is the intention of the Board that the college substantially comply with requiring two years of a sound and comprehensive study of the Bible for the granting of a degree." The board then directed that its resolution be incorporated into the college's statement of purpose at the beginning of the catalogue, that it be followed both by a declaration that the

Man course was required of all students and by the long statement about
the religious dimensions of the Man course, and finally that the catalogue
state that the Man course was one year of Bible and one year of Bible-
related study.[40]

Students greeted the board's decision enthusiastically. Christe Ray, a
student representative to the board, said that although she had not expected the trustees to pay much attention to the students' concerns, "The
almost hour-long discussion over the description proved me wrong.
Trustees John Smith and Eleanor Shannon were thrilled with the 'con-
scientious' students they had talked with, and they felt the students' concern to be genuine and in Southwestern's best interest."[41]

The controversy about the description of the Man course speaks
forcefully about the course and its intended effect on students. From the
beginning, the disputed description itself had concluded with a statement
about the staff's intent in teaching in the course: "[It is] the kind of teaching which we believe makes ideas come alive and become part of human
character and where values are not merely something to be learned but
something to be experienced and cherished." In a *Sou'wester* editorial,
Mark Hurley penned a "more personal statement about the Man course
description controversy" that gave eloquent testimony to the truth of this
claim. Noting that students and faculty did not step aside in the face of
discouraging legal opinions and unreceptive audiences, Hurley concluded, "Personally, I would like to thank them for teaching me a lesson about
idealism, integrity and courage."[42]

A National College

With the agenda cleared of controversy, events at the college moved
rapidly during the first six months of 1982. New covenants with the synods of the Mid-South and the Red River continued the college's historical ties with the Presbyterian church. More important, the reunion of the
denomination's northern and southern branches aligned Southwestern
with a national church. At the May 1982 meeting of the faculty, Daughdrill proclaimed that the goal of the college was to be "the best college
in the South and the best church-related college in the country." He also
reported that on April 30, the Alabama court had sanctioned agreements
between the trustees of the Bellingrath-Morse Foundation and the foundation's beneficiaries. Southwestern was declared in substantial compli-

ance with the deed of trust. A few weeks later, on May 26, 1982, Daugh-drill announced that the college had received its first check as a requali-fied beneficiary, in the amount of $1,106,747.

During the summer of 1982, the executive committee of Southwest-ern's board of trustees decided that the college would honor the Bellingraths by using its share of the return from the foundation as an en-dowment from which to award each year, on a merit basis, four Bellingrath scholarships for tuition and room and board, and eight Morse scholarships for tuition. The purpose was to attract a larger number of applications from students of exceptional academic promise and, in the long run, to achieve for the college increased national recognition for academic excellence.

In October 1982 the faculty voted to modify the college's degree re-quirements to include an alternative to the Man course, a program ini-tially labeled "Track B" of the humanities requirement and eventually titled Life: Then and Now. The alternative program was accepted by the administration and ultimately certified by the Bellingrath-Morse Foun-dation as being in substantial compliance with the deed of trust.[43] The "Life" alternative to Man required two biblical studies courses during the student's first year and, in subsequent years, two additional Bible-related courses chosen from an approved list of philosophy and religion courses.

The Life program was in place in time for the 1983–1984 academic year. The Man course, therefore, existed for only two academic years as a universal requirement for graduation. But even with Life in place, Man continued to enroll more than half of the students in each entering class. In fact, enrollment had to be capped at 245, which was the capacity of lecture room B in Frazier-Jelke Science Center, the largest classroom on compus. Typically sixteen colloquium sections were scheduled each year so that the average enrollment in each section could be held to fifteen students.

Name Handicaps

The biblical image of new wine requiring new wineskins fits the col-lege's experience in the aftermath of the curriculum controversies. Daughdrill believed that the college must capitalize on its new financial strength in order to achieve the national prominence it sought in higher education. From 1975 to 1985 the college's enrollment fluctuated around the one thousand mark, ranging from a high of 1,103 in 1975–1976 to a low of 985 in 1983–1984. Yet with the number of American eighteen-year-olds expected to drop 26 percent during the next ten years, it was generally agreed that the continuing financial health of the college depended on reaching a stable enrollment of 1,450. Competition for good students would be keen, and the merit-based Bellingrath-Morse scholarships would play an essential role in attracting superior applicants.

At the same time, Southwestern needed to ensure that its faculty was strong and had the resources necessary for active professional development. Faculty recruitment became more ambitious, and a concerted effort was made to increase the number of women and African Americans on the faculty. Detailed standards for evaluating faculty performance were established. Significant endowment funds were secured to support scholarly and creative work by faculty members that would result in publications or performances.

At Daughdrill's call, the board of trustees met in a retreat in February 1984 at Point Clear, Alabama. During that meeting the board established a new goal for the college: "Southwestern is committed to being a truly national liberal arts college in academic quality and in national recognition."

As part of the college's effort to achieve excellence and renown, in 1984 it changed its name to Rhodes College. In doing so it removed what some considered to be its greatest handicap. "Southwestern at Memphis" did not contain the word *college* and was too easily confused with a plethora of other institutions with *southwestern* in their names; indeed, *southwestern* was not an appropriate geographical designation for the college's Mid-South location. Rhodes College was thought to have the right sound; it also honored the lifetime service of President Emeritus Rhodes.[44]

Another issue of nomenclature, on a smaller scale but evoking strong sentiments from many faculty members and students, had first surfaced in December 1981. The disputed name was *Man,* and the challenge to it drew attention once again to the description of the course in the catalogue.

At its December 4, 1981, meeting, the Man staff recommended that a footnote be added to the catalogue description at the end of the first sentence. The first sentence stated: "'Man in the Light of History and Religion' is an interdisciplinary study of the ideas, beliefs, and cultural developments that have formed Western man." The recommended footnote was: "For brevity and clarity, the title and description of the course use the noun 'Man' to denote both men and women."[45] Although the footnote never did appear in the catalogue, the motivation for recom-

mending it did not vanish. Hatfield, the secretary of the Man Administrative Council, recorded that at a meeting in January 1984 "Prof. Jobes
raised a concern which the entire staff will need to address and deal with
in the near future. That concern has to do with the serious gender objections to the title of the course which are held by many of our colleagues and students."[46] Contributing to this concern was the college's
success in recruiting women to the faculty. Especially for those women
who taught in the course, the use of *Man* in the title appeared to give un-
acceptable prominence to men.[47]

   In fall 1984 the revised second-year syllabus for the Man course tried
to respond to the issue of gender bias. As noted earlier, the cover displayed
"M A N" in large block letters, each letter printed sideways in a vertical
column and comprised of "MAN~WOMAN~MAN~WOMAN~" printed
left to right, a design made possible by early computer-generated sign
software. In addition, for the first time, the title page contained a subtitle
for the course:

> A Study of Ways in Which Men and Women of the Western World
> Have Understood Themselves as Human Beings in the
> Light of Their Significant Experiences and
> Their Highest Hopes and Values

   According to Neal, who wrote the subtitle, it expressed the *logos*—the
formative principle—of the Man course.[48] The preface to the syllabus explained that the change of images on the cover merely affirmed what the
Man course had always maintained: "We use the word *Man* in its true
generic sense as encompassing in one species both men and women."[49]

   Neal resisted the entreaties of those who felt strongly that the next
step was to replace *Man* in the title of the course, an issue he eventually
lost (see chapter 4). But even in that controversy Neal held up for the
Man course a standard that was the measure of all who taught in it.

A New Director for the Man Course

   Course development and faculty recruitment dominated Neal's work
as the director of the Man course in the period 1975–1985. The end of
that decade reflected significant advances in both areas as a result of his
leadership.

   No faculty member at the college was hired for the specific purpose of teaching in the Man course. Indeed, not until Man was included in the freshman colloquium program was teaching in the course counted as part of a faculty member's standard teaching load. Even then, at a time when the course met five days a week for both semesters and accounted for twelve credit hours in a first-year student's schedule, Man was never counted as more than two three-hour courses per academic year in a faculty member's teaching load; for most, if it was counted at all, it was as only one course.[50]

This problem became acute in 1981 when the Man course began to be taught over a two-year period. Before then the fact that Man represented four courses was concealed by the lecture-colloquium pairings; a faculty member seemed to be on duty only every other day. When the course was distributed over four semesters, however, the share of colloquium sessions began to rise, and it became clear that staff members needed to prepare as fully as if four separate courses were being taught. In a memorandum to Duff, Neal put the matter plainly: "The experience of teaching Man in addition to departmental responsibilities has made several of our new staff loath to undertake the teaching of more than one-half of the Man course next year"—that is, either the first year or the second year of the course, totaling three credit hours per term rather than six.[51] Not reflected in this comment, but certainly true of some faculty feeling, was that the preparation needed to teach Man not only took one outside one's field of expertise, but also diverted time away from research in one's discipline. As the college began to place more emphasis on research and other scholarly activity as part of the effort to attain national distinction for its faculty, the tendency was to safeguard one's time for such work.

Faculty recruitment for the Man course exceeded all reasonable expectations because Neal "worked all the angles." Personal friendship was one. Robert Amy, a member of the biology department and a longtime bridge player with Neal and his wife June, related his experience:

In the twenty-three years I had been teaching at the college, many students had told me how valuable the course had been to them, so I was well aware of its merits. I had always been interested in history and religion but had not been able to pursue them. . . . [B]ecoming involved in the Man course seemed like a good opportunity to learn more about these subjects. Finally, how could I refuse a request to join the Man faculty from my good friend Fred Neal, the leader of the group?[52]

Opportunism also worked. Whitaker, a member of English department, described her first encounter with Neal:

Fred was apparently looking for more faculty due to the Bellingrath-mandated requirement [that all freshmen take the Man course]; he was also looking to put women on the team and had already lined up Diane Clark. I was in the mail room when I asked him if I could audit the course because I thought that, as an instructor in English 151, I should know what was going on in Man so that I could make some cross references. At that point, he said that if I was going to audit anyway he thought I might consider teaching Man.[53]

Both Amy and Whitaker were members of the group of faculty that participated in the first Man staff workshop in the summer of 1981. For Neal, faculty recruitment was never pursued without provision for faculty development.

Neal stated the need for workshops in the Man course boldly: "Pro-

English professor Elaine Whitaker (right) with student Leigh Belyeu.

fessors generically do not fit into the style of the course." For new recruits
to the staff, the summer workshops were necessary to become acquainted with the full range of materials to be studied, to prepare for teaching
especially difficult texts, to make connections between the various units
of the course, and to develop facility at leading discussions. Neal characterized the greatest danger for a faculty member in a colloquium as acting as "a fountain of knowledge. The successful Man discussion leader
must learn to keep his or her mouth shut." Because a similar problem
might plague even a veteran teacher, Neal was not inclined to allow
members of the staff "to lecture in areas of their specialties. Lectures that
are suitable in a special discipline are much too detailed, and the material is lost on the Man student."[54]

As noted earlier, Neal was able to fund the early workshops with
grants that the college had received from the Mellon foundation and,
when these funds were exhausted, from the dean's discretionary fund. The
unanimous praise with which participants greeted these workshops inspired Neal to try to make them annual events. Among other things, each
workshop became a forum in which the content of the course could be
reviewed and altered. New recruits to the Man staff brought convincing
arguments for adding new texts and rearranging or replacing existing
ones. Whitaker recalled that "what I remember most as my 'contribution'
was getting Fred and company to accept an extract from Simone de
Beauvoir's *The Second Sex* for the revision of the sophomore *Readings*.
The truly best part of this was that Fred altered the cut in the following
way: I had stopped prior to a sentence that called for men and women to
work together; Fred insisted that the reading continue to include this."[55]

As the workshops continued Neal delegated more and more responsibility for syllabus revision to the staff. He insisted that each syllabus be
projected for only a three-year run, making revision a customary and ongoing part of the course. For students this meant that the course was constantly being reviewed and updated. The Man Advisory Council provided
the staff with a significant student voice in the process.

Neal persistently lobbied the administration for an endowment fund
to support the workshops. Yet it was not any direct request, but his own
relationship with David and Mary Elizabeth Walker that in 1985 inspired
the endowment for the George Douglass Faculty Seminars for Interdisciplinary Teaching, an endowment that continues to sustain the annual
workshops. Mary Elizabeth Walker was a graduate of Southwestern and,
along with her husband David, who taught mathematics at Memphis

State University, was a longtime member of the T. K. Young class at Idlewild Presbyterian Church, which Neal taught on Sunday mornings. In 1976, when the Man course was first adapted for the college's adult continuing education program, the Walkers became charter members.[56]

The summer workshops did more than enable the staff to meet the year-in, year-out needs of the Man course; they also served as a gateway into the course for new instructors. Teaching Man was the measure of a faculty member at Neal's "perfect college." In an interview with the *Sou'wester* he explained: "If I had a chance to make my perfect college, I would want every professor who joins our faculty to teach the Man course in one round, at least. . . . Education is a moral endeavor whereby we're all joined together in this common pursuit of knowledge, and if you can do it around certain tasks, it gives you a real sense of community."[57]

As might be expected, major changes in the content of the Man course were made as a result of spreading the course over a two-year period. The second year of the course, first taught in 1982–1983, met on Tuesdays and Thursdays for ninety-minute sessions. The pattern of pairing a lecture with each colloquium was continued but at a high price: hour-and-a-half lectures were exhausting for lecturer and students alike.

Neal insisted that the students not be lectured to for the entire period. More audiovisual materials were incorporated into the course, including movies like *Ordet*, a reflection on the Gospel of John that was first used in the course in the early 1970s and that almost became a Man course tradition. Neal purchased a large slide collection and obtained capital improvement funds to equip the Frazier-Jelke lecture room B with a remote-controlled slide projector. In addition, "mini-lectures" were presented by teams of staff members rather than one lecturer. In one session, for example, Llewellyn talked about Friedrich Nietzsche, then Queener introduced Sigmund Freud.

Special two or three-session seminars continued to break up the lecture-colloquium routine in all four terms of the course. These seminars provided each student with an opportunity to study topics that could not be included in the basic syllabus and were taken from Man instructors other than the student's colloquium leader. During the period of seminars, which lasted until 1983–1984, an amazing variety of topics was presented: Creationism and Evolution (Robert Amy), Pottery and the Prophetic People (Carl Walters), History and Revelation (Douglas Hatfield), Erasmus on Marriage (John Bruhwiler), The Concept of Holy War (Michael McLain), Courtly Love (Richard Wood), Alice Walker's *Meridi-*

an (Elaine Whitaker), and The "Second" Sex: or, There Really Are Women in the Bible (Bernice White).

In 1984, the staff decided to abandon the lecture-colloquium pattern in favor of more colloquia in the first year of the course, and to adopt a Monday-Wednesday-Friday schedule of sixty-minute classes.[58] For Neal, the change was in keeping with his own assessment of where learning takes place:

We've kept as a basic rule that our colloquia are the places where the real learning is done. So, without fail, we always must have more colloquia than other sessions in the course. Dr. Lawrence Kinney and Dr. Granville Davis [were] masters of the discussion method of teaching. I've made a lifetime of trying to learn how to do it. We really aim for a setting in which people will learn in the process of talking out their ideas of great thinkers and seeing how these ideas agree or disagree with each other. If we could really do our job well, we would be developing a full generation of students who can analyze, interpret, and evaluate. . . .[59]

Discussions do not go very well when students do not have their own copies of the basic sources. Throughout the decade 1975–1985, syllabus revision went hand-in-hand with the monumental task of producing the *Readings* books. These books did two things for the course: they eliminated the staff's dependence on commercially-published anthologies, which never contained the right mix of texts, and they reduced the need to have extensive library reserve readings, which could not be marked up or brought to class by students. Staff members provided translations and commentary for important texts in *Readings.* Tucker's translation of selections from Machiavelli's *The Prince* and Wood's commentary on Coleridge's "Rime of the Ancient Mariner" appeared in the first two-volume edition. Later editions contained translations by Brown (a text on Epicurus), Wood (a text from Cicero), Tucker (cantos from Dante's *Divine Comedy*, selections from Rabelais's *Gargantua*, and an extract from Calvin's "Confession of Faith"), and James Vest (Sartre's "Existentialism as a Humanism").[60]

The controversy about what some considered the androcentric name of the course shadowed the final years of Neal's directorship as he approached retirement in 1985. Never one to promote male chauvinism, always one to emphasize the inclusive scope of the word *Man* in the course; never one to restrict the makeup of the staff, always one to recruit any faculty member with the slightest openness to interdisciplinary teaching; never one to limit the materials of the course to selected per-spectives, always one to encourage the use of new materials, including feminist literature, Neal nonetheless resisted efforts to change the name of the course. *Man,* he believed, properly conveyed that the subject of the course was a special order of being—mankind. "We are talking about a particular species of which men and women exemplify certain qualities which they hold together." "Humanities"—the standard listing for the course—and even "The Search for Values"—the core of the eventual name of the course—were too broad and undifferentiated for Neal; in fact, they seemed "value-neutral," contrary to the course's essential na-ture.[61] Besides, the controversy spawned by the "Man" title could be an asset: "Why remove the controversy by changing the title? Discuss the title and the problem with students and faculty. It is the discussion of the issue that is important."[62]

Because advance planning was needed to accommodate Neal's retire-ment in 1985, the question of a new director for the Man course was raised officially in October 1983. It was answered in February 1985 with the appointment of Douglas Hatfield, who in 1989 became Granville Davis's successor as the J. J. McComb Professor of History. Hatfield had earned his B.A. at Baylor University and his Ph.D. in history at the Uni-versity of Kentucky, then taught briefly at Baylor before coming to Southwestern in 1967. In the process of defining the nature of the as-signment, Neal obtained from Duff commitments to recognize properly the work of both the director and the staff.[63] Beginning in 1985–1986, the director was to be recognized as a department chair and compensat-ed accordingly. (Neal's title as director of the Man course had never been official; nor had a contractual definition of the job ever existed.) As for the Man staff, members would have their involvement in the course counted fully in the computation of their teaching loads, and new ap-pointments to the faculty would be made with possible participation in the Man course in mind. For Neal, this latter condition was another way of expressing his belief that teaching in the Man course was the measure of a faculty member at the college:

A willingness and ability to teach periodically in the Man course could be one of the qualities sought in new appointees not only in the area of the humanities, but in the natural and social sciences. To broaden the base of the teaching staff not only enhances the course with new points of view, but also serves as a bond of unity among the faculty and between departments. Additions to our teaching staff from Biology and Psychology, for example, have been both happy and productive. Taking the Man Course has been a bond of unity in the student body. Teaching in the Man Course has been and can be a bond of unity in the faculty also.[64]

The decade 1975–1985 ended for Man with the final lecture in the sophomore year of the course, announced with the title The Heritage We Stand On. Neal was the lecturer, and his peroration concerned the vocation of the student:

The vocation of students . . . is channeled and expressed by those peculiar understandings and skills which their experience of study has given them and which they can contribute to the common life of mankind. They are the gifts of *mind*, and *heart* and *spirit* which have been sharpened through years of trial in the community of learning. . . . There is no area of human life and knowledge which should be spared from the questioning and disciplined mind: politics, business, society, religion. . . . By what values do you appraise yourself? As a man seeketh in his heart, so is he. . . . In the midst of the pluralism in which we live, where competing principles of truth and value confront each other daily, where all judgments seem to be relative and all values transitory and fleeting, there is hunger in mankind for some *unity* to experience . . . some ultimate meaning.[65]

Conclusion

"Man is the measure" characterizes the role and the place of the Man course at Southwestern from 1975 to 1985. Man embodied an ideal to be sought in designing a curriculum for the college. For two academic years it was a standard that all students had to meet in order to graduate. In becoming a standard the course itself had to measure up to a curriculum requirement not of its own design, and it was found not to be lacking. Members of the faculty who taught in the Man course were challenged in their teaching by a standard of humbling proportions: namely, Fred Neal, their director, who not only encouraged them to reach for the ideal but also believed that they could measure up to it. As for students, few speak more eloquently of Man as the measure of the Southwestern experience than John Gladney, a student of Neal's in Man and a 1974 graduate. "In the Man course I knew that I had arrived," says Gladney. "I said, 'For me, *this* is college.'"[66]

Of Great Books and Conflicts

D A N I E L   E .   C U L L E N

I volunteered to teach in Search because I believe in what is called, often disparagingly, "Great Books" education. My conviction does not arise from the voguish concern for "cultural literacy" or from a political agenda to restore the country's moral fiber; a case could be made that these are needful things, but they are not the end of liberal education. The latter means education for a certain kind of life: a life of freedom, which requires moral seriousness and the capacity for judgment. The great books are useful in developing that capacity and in nurturing the taste for freedom. The proper method of a great books course is, I would argue, not adulatory but *zetetic*, probing, skeptical. Recent critics of courses like Search associate them with an attempt to instill a narrow moralism in students, but this belief is doubly mistaken because it disregards the genuine diversity within the Western tradition and ignores the fact that the great books are typically disturbing and dangerous, more likely to upset than to ratify the conventional opinions that support morality.

The Search curriculum is, therefore, inherently radical. But, as the saying goes, is it relevant? In my experience, students are naturally inclined to ask (to paraphrase Tertullian): What do Athens and Jerusalem have to do with me? It's a fair question, and a demand I take seriously, believing as I do that most students arrive at college without an educational plan, but longing for fulfillment and self-knowledge. The Search course responds to that longing with the implicit suggestion that students can begin to find themselves with the aid of books that challenge them to make sense of human experience, often by exploring a dimension of humanity that is unknown to, or forgotten by, our culture. Nothing will be gained by studying the great books unless we can learn something from them—merely to admire them for their canonicity is both empty and ridiculous. I approach Search with the idea that one can learn *from* Homer or Plato, not merely *about* him. To ponder why Odysseus rejects Calypso's offer, choosing instead the bounds of mortality and the hazards of homecoming, is to confront the question of what it means to be human. Similarly, coming to grips with the insistence on radical humility in the Rule of St. Benedict can bring home, perhaps for the first time, the ramifications of acknowledging one's status as a created being.

Such, at least, has been my experience. The tension between Jerusalem and Athens had for a long time been a touchstone for my reading and thinking. But being a partisan of philosophy, I had failed to consider seriously the religious component of the Western tradition as a source of truth. My reading of the Bible had been occasional, and I had certainly never studied it. During my preparation for teaching the Hebrew prophets, which required entering into their perspective sympathetically, I was struck by the profound rejoinder to the Socratic insistence on the unworthiness of the "unexamined life" in Micah 6:8: "He has told you, O mortal, what is good; and what does the Lord require of you but to do justice, and to love kindness, and to walk humbly with your God?" In subsequent readings of Pascal, Kierkegaard, and Dostoyevsky I found new sympathy for these strange knights of faith. I have never experienced anything like Pascal's night of fire, but thinking about it, and discussing it with my students, has given me an appreciation of the case against rationalism.

It is a daunting task to guide students through the two years of Search. I find solace in the fact that the great books are themselves teachers, and I try to guard against letting my own voice render their authors inaudible. I once heard an experienced teacher say that "students aren't very interested in what *we* have to say about these books, but they are very interested in talking about the books themselves." Fortunately, the format of Search has always acknowledged that interest. It behooves us as teachers to remember that before thinkers like Aristotle, Rousseau, and Nietzsche were canonized, they were troublers of settled opinion, radicals who reached out through their writings to touch the souls of others—to teach, to persuade, perhaps to seduce. As Pascal put it, one opens a book expecting to encounter an author—and meets a man.

What students make of these encounters is, properly, their own business. Good teachers, in the apt characterization of Allan Bloom, are merely matchmakers who bring together book and reader. Without underestimating the disciplined effort required to enter into the world of Sophocles or Shakespeare, Search remains guided by the awareness that literature is about life, and that the task of reason is to judge action, even action that lies beyond our immediate experience. Liberal education should, of course, promote an exacting scholarship and the subtleties of the great books require it; but it is the subtleties of life that matter most, and Search aims at bringing them into view. The course has not allowed literary theory to usurp the place of literature. It preserves the fundamental questions concerning how to live in all their clarity—and in all their ambiguity.

My perspective is, of course, out of fashion. To speak of books and authors rather than "texts" and "readings" is, in today's intellectual atmosphere, to announce one's backwardness. The Search course may appear at first glance to present a fat target in the war over the canon. Some will ask: Where is the attention to race, gender, and class? One response is to point to what the Western canon actually contains. *Othello*, *The Merchant of Venice*, and *Antigone*, with their profound examinations of blood and belonging, hunt bigger game than most contemporary discussions of multiculturalism. Similarly, an analysis of the permanence of class conflict and the structure of revolutionary passions is available in Aristotle's *Politics*. Detractors of the great books are perhaps too confident in their opinions about the meaning of justice, equality, and freedom. At a minimum, to attack certain books as surrogates of an oppressive social order begs the question of what the just social order is. The Search curriculum preserves, indeed intensifies, many of the permanent questions of human life; in that sense, it is nothing but a study of conflicts.

Gerald Graff, a prominent critic of traditional liberal education, suggests that the solution to the quarrel over great books education is to "teach the conflicts." But what he has in mind is the intramural academic disagreements about what should go into the canon. As Graff puts it: *King Lear* or *King Kong*? Rimbaud or *Rambo*? Plato or Puzo? But surely more important issues await to be taught—and lived out—in and through the great books themselves, philosophy versus faith being the most prominent example. The conflicts, which often span the centuries, between an Aristotle and an Augustine, an Erasmus and a Luther, a Galileo and a John Donne, or a Voltaire and a Rousseau, amount to crucibles for any soul that seeks understanding. Near the beginning of the twentieth century, Max Weber warned that the ethos of modernity threatens to produce "specialists without spirit, sensualists without heart." Some maintain that the great books, and the Western tradition they embody, are part of the disease. I believe they can be part of the cure.

The Feminist Search for Values

GAIL CORRINGTON STREETE

It has become an academic truism that there is no such thing as disengaged scholarship, although this has perhaps been most openly recognized and practiced, and for the longest time, by feminist scholars. Even one trained as I was in the traditionally "objective" disciplines of religious studies and the classics can not help but engage them as a feminist and a woman, as well as a scholar. (Nor would I want to do otherwise.) The approach to undergraduate teaching to which I have committed myself invites a similar personal engagement on the part of the student. It would be dishonest to pretend that the professor, however receptive and academically liberal she may be, stands without passion or commitment above the material she teaches, as she may often stand literally above her students at the lecture podium. (What one must keep in mind is not to abuse that podium as an ideological "bully pulpit.") Anything that I have to say, therefore, about my engagement with the Search course will employ the personal to interpret the academic.

As a newly hired professor at Rhodes in the summer of 1990, I was invited to attend the May workshop for those who would be teaching in the 1990–1991 version of the first-year Search course. I was excited, not only because the course incorporated the areas of my primary expertise, but also because the title (and, I presumed, the focus) of the course had recently been changed from "Man in the Light of History and Religion" to "The Search for Values in the Light of Western History and Religion."

I was also somewhat apprehensive. Experience had taught me that such changes do not come about rapidly or without lingering rancor and that they are often merely cosmetic. I also knew that courses such as this one had become storm centers of academic controversy, having had a good deal of personal experience with both the defenders and detractors of the dual "canons" of the Bible and classical antiquity.

Thus I sat down for the first session of the workshop with not a little anxiety, a feeling that immediately increased when I found that I was the only woman there. Being an "only" has not been an infrequent occurrence for me, but I continue to feel that a highly visible "gender marker" raises definite expectations, both in me and in others. Taking a (figurative) deep breath, I resolved that as a new faculty member at Rhodes I would feel my way around before rocking the boat on matters of course design. As for my own colloquium, I was fairly confident, from courses I had previously taught, of my ability to deal with the "canonical" by using a strategy of subversion—that is, of "turning under" the text so that other, hidden perspectives could emerge, thus challenging students to examine and to question the assumptions embedded in the text.

All my resolve fled when I glanced down at the cover of the readings book that the staff had compiled for the course: a series of concentric, beautifully calligraphed quotations, all drawn from the western tradition's "greatest hits," and all highlighting the word *man*. This was the most literal illustration of androcentrism that I had ever encountered in a text. Unable to believe that no one had questioned this design, I continued on to the first two readings: "What Is Man?" and "The Historian and His Facts."

I took another deep breath. I reminded myself that I was in the midst of scholars who had helped to develop this course, had worked constantly to refine it, had taught in it for many years, and who I hoped would be my colleagues for the foreseeable future. I did not want to alienate them and perhaps be conveniently labeled (and thus dismissed as) a "politically correct" feminist. But more powerful than my hesitation was my conviction that I would be doing my students, my colleagues, and ultimately myself an injustice if I failed at least to raise the question of inclusive language and inclusivity of perspective. "I can't teach this," I said. But as it turned out I did teach it, or a version of it, and I have continued to teach it and struggle to transform it subtly, gradually, and not without frustration for the past six years.

How do I teach what I had declared unteachable? A feminist can approach an androcentric canon in several ways. One can reject such texts as irretrievably patriarchal, discover what lies hidden in the margins or underneath the texts, expand the concept of "canon" (as the concept of "history" has been expanded) to include the excluded, or treat the canon as a map of enemy terrain that needs to be studied for purposes of cultural survival and transformation. I have not used the first approach because I firmly believe that we cannot afford to be ahistorical or antihistorical, however much history has abused us. (We may rightly deplore the viewpoint of the National Socialists in Germany, for example, but we must also understand it to get a fuller picture of human potential and propensities.) But I have used the other three approaches because I believe that it is as absurd for students and teachers, male as well as female, to believe that history, literature, philosophy, and religion are neutral with respect to the gender, race, class, and social location of their authors and audiences as it would be to assume that texts are value-neutral.

Hence I believe it is essential that, when reading the Hebrew prophets, students understand that oppressing the poor comes in for much greater condemnation than spiritual infidelity. When reading Plato's *Symposium* they should understand that homoerotic attachment is its norm, just as they should realize when reading the *Republic* that, despite the gender equality of the Guardians, Plato prescribes an entire servant class whose existence is supported by a "noble lie." When reading Aristotle's *Politics,* students should not simply remember mottoes like "Humans are by nature political animals" (often mistranslated, "Man is by nature a political animal") while ignoring his belief that women, non-Greeks, and slaves were inferior by nature. Aristotle's claim, expressed in *On the Generation of Animals*, that females are defective males has influenced Western values far more than his physics, politics, or ethics.

If most students read of the noble deaths of Socrates and Seneca without reading one of the most influential early Christian works, *The Martyrdom of Perpetua and Felicitas*, written in large part by one of its heroines, they are being shortchanged, just as they are shortchanged by reading the epic poetry of *Gilgamesh*, the *Iliad*, the *Odyssey*, and the *Aeneid* without reading the great lyric poet Sappho, who expresses the intensely personal realm of passionate attachment. Similarly, students should not be seduced into believing that "Western" equals "European." One need not be an Afrocentrist to know that Augustine was a North African.

In conclusion, I endorse with modification (as is my *modus operandi*) a saying attributed to the great antagonist of Athenian democracy, Socrates: "The unexamined life is not worth living." He is right, and the unquestioned text is equally without value—including the *Apology of Socrates*.

4

Redefining the Search 1985–1995

J A M E S   M .   V E S T
and
D A N I E L   E .   C U L L E N

In the period from 1985 to 1995, developments in the college's operations and policies, and in the larger society and culture as well, brought about dramatic alterations in the Man course. These changes affected matters as varied as the name of the course, the manner in which faculty members were recruited and trained to teach in it, the selection of materials to be studied, the presentation and testing of those materials, the nature of lectures, and the computerization of lecture materials, syllabi, readings, writing assignments, and tests. All of the changes were made under the leadership of the program's new director, Douglas Hatfield.

Hatfield and his colleagues were aided in their efforts by dramatic advances in the academic quality of the college. As noted in chapter 3, in February 1984 the board of trustees had committed itself to making Rhodes one of the finest liberal arts colleges in the nation. That commitment was supported by initiatives in areas such as scholarships for students, faculty recruitment, new facilities, and fundraising. Afterward, the student body was increased in size and selectivity: enrollments went from around 1,000 in 1985 to around 1,450 in 1995 and, in the same period, the entering class's average score on the Scholastic Assessment Test (before the SAT was "re-centered") rose from 1,155 to 1,218. The burgeoning college-rating industry took note of Rhodes's success. In 1990, *U.S. News and World Report* identified Rhodes as first on the list of "up-and-coming" national liberal arts colleges in the judgment of college presidents and deans. By 1995, the college had risen to the magazine's top category of national liberal arts colleges.[1]

New Leadership, New Structure, New Name

In 1985, when Fred Neal retired from full-time teaching and gave up the directorship of the Man course, Hatfield was appointed as Neal's successor. As a former head of the history department, Hatfield had the administrative qualifications to supervise a large and complex program. More importantly, as a longtime teacher in Man, Hatfield was imbued with the spirit of the enterprise and possessed a fine-grained sense of the course's needs. Having served on the Man Administrative Council for several years, he had worked closely with Neal on budgeting, scheduling, and other administrative business. This apprenticeship had made Hatfield thoroughly familiar with the operations of the course by the time he assumed its directorship. According to Neal, the transition went without a hitch: "I simply stepped down and Doug started. . . . He was so in tune with how things worked that there was no need for any formal period of transition or training."[2] "When Fred Neal retired," Hatfield recalls, "al-

Douglas W. Hatfield, director of the Search course since 1985.

though he was still around, he stepped back from the course and gave me a free hand. He did that so people wouldn't be tempted to look back to him. That was a big help to me, not having to compete for people's attention or loyalties."[3] Hatfield officially took the reins in the summer of 1985 and immediately charged into the task of guiding the course, its staff, and its students into a new era.

Hatfield had been selected in part because of his skill at fostering cooperation and teamwork. His personal style was marked by a distinctive blend of thoroughness and good humor, an amalgam of the meticulous and the whimsical. As one colleague who worked closely with Hatfield put it:

In all areas . . . from the most routine memoranda to the substantial assessment of programs, [his work] has been carefully articulated, clear, and accurate. Those of us who have served with Hatfield value very much this sense of direction, and . . . serve the students of the College better because our time and energies are always focused.[4]

Hatfield's quiet sincerity and willingness to get along with just about anyone were assets in managing increasingly diverse viewpoints and demands within the course staff. Cognizant of the strong feelings of proprietorship that teachers have in their classes, he was patient as numerous and conflicting ideas regarding the structure and content of the course were proposed in the annual process of revision: Should students be required to read secondary works, or not? Which play by Aeschylus should be assigned? Should Aristotle be dropped altogether in favor of more Plato? Understanding that there was no single answer to these sorts of questions, Hatfield presided over staff discussions with a keen eye for an emerging consensus, gently but doggedly keeping the faculty on task.

On a larger scale, Hatfield committed himself to consolidating the soon-renamed Search course, which, because of its size and complexity, naturally tended toward disintegration. He sought to bring stability to the course, viewing it as the cornerstone of the college's curriculum. The general problem facing courses like Search had been identified as early as 1971 by the philosopher John Searle, who remarked on the predicament of higher education: "We have lost confidence in our traditional conception of a liberal education, but we have not yet found anything to replace it with."[5] In the traditional conception, which had been the practice at most liberal arts colleges, students devoted two years to acquiring a general background in Western civilization, followed by two years of more concentrated study in a discipline. Searle pointed out that,

Over the years the excitement has drained out of these general courses. The better faculty do not like to teach them, as their own intellectual interests have grown more specialized and professionalized. The lecturing has devolved onto the most junior faculty, who regard the whole affair as an obligatory chore. Large lecture halls of bored students face nervous assistant professors reading their notes on man's greatest cultural achievements.[6]

The Search course was not immune to such ills, and it is fair to say that avoiding them was the principal challenge of Hatfield's leadership.

Keeping the course vital and coherent and attracting talented and enthusiastic faculty to teach it became his dominant concerns. He identified the
crucial requirements of effective teaching in Search as a commitment to
the intrinsic goodness of an interdisciplinary approach and "values-oriented emphases," along with a spirit of collegiality, a "willingness to work
as part of a group." Bucking the trend described by Searle, Hatfield resolved to recruit staff from the senior faculty of the college, looking for
"those who are secure enough in their own professional accomplishment
not to feel side-tracked by such an endeavor as Search, and those who
have been here long enough to have developed a sense of community
within the faculty." He also persistently lobbied the administration to hire
new faculty who would relish the opportunity for interdisciplinary teaching and whose primary responsibility would include teaching in Search.[7]

Apart from these structural problems of academic culture and personnel management, the Search course faced what might be called an ideological challenge. In the 1980s and 1990s, the politics of liberal education
attracted as much (if not more) attention as liberal education itself.
Throughout the country, but particularly in the elite colleges and universities, the curriculum of courses like Search became a battleground in
the "culture war" between one party that regarded the study of Western
civilization as a continuation of political and cultural oppression and another that tended to associate defense of the canon with the defense of
civilization itself.[8] The ferocity of the struggle bespoke an intellectual and
moral crisis in academia, which was played out in the pages of quarterly
journals, at professional meetings, and in departmental battles over hiring
and curriculum.

Whiffs of this conflict occasionally intruded on the Search course, but
deliberations among staff members proceeded in a spirit of moderation
and collegiality. Part of the explanation for Search's success is that the
course's staff generally was both committed to cultural inclusion (and
therefore sympathetic to criticisms of a rigid canon) and persuaded of the
enduring value of the classics of literature, religion, philosophy and history. More importantly, those critical of traditional "Western civ" approaches were invited to bring their concerns into the course by joining
the staff, serving as a summer workshop leader, or in some other advisory capacity; no one was left to rail outside the gate. As Hatfield noted in
1990:

Diversity is provided by the fact that the course is interdisciplinary and draws on the perspectives of several different approaches to learning. The professors are also diverse, being drawn from seven different departments in the College and representing a range of different ages and experiences in the faculty, and a broad range of religious (denominational) and ethical perspectives.[9]

Since its inception, the content of the Search course has been shaped and reshaped almost continuously, reflecting in its own way the syncretistic character of the Western tradition. For that reason, Search had long been engaged in discussion of some of the issues that the new *Kulturkampf* brought to national attention. Hatfield's style of leadership, which encouraged open discussion and relied on consensus decision making, reflected the cooperative ethic that had always informed the course but was particularly suited to a time when the very purpose of the humanities had become a contentious issue. Those cooperative habits were put to a test in the spring of 1986 when, after more than forty years of existence as Man in the Light of History and Religion, the course was rechristened The Search for Values in Light of Western History and Religion.

The catalyst for the name change was Dean Gerald Duff, who was responding to a number of trends then cresting in the humanities and social sciences. Theorists from various disciplines had made the long-revered books of the Western canon the site of a new cultural conflict, attacking the notion that there was an essential "core" of civilization or of civilization's texts. Semioticians heightened awareness of names as "signifiers," structuralists called attention to the ordering of knowledge and power as a function of cultural production, and feminists denounced the androcentric bias of the Western tradition. At Rhodes, newer staff members in particular complained that they were embarrassed to be associated with a course named Man that included few women authors, involved few women faculty, and was, moreover, limited to the Western tradition.[10]

At this juncture, political and literary concerns that were ascendant in academe were brought to bear on Man in the Light of History and Religion. The title (and, it was felt, much of the content) of the course obscured or devalued women's experience—what about *Her*story? Postmodern critics had drawn attention to Western civilization's "erasure" of women's history, arguing that the usage of *man* as a synonym for *human being* was not and never had been neutral. In the new critical perspective, the category of human being was regarded as an essentially contested concept, and the practical task of criticism was to deconstruct norms that reflected established patterns of social life, particularly the historical dominance of patriarchy.[11]

The accuracy of this analysis was taken for granted by some Rhodes faculty and treated with skepticism or neutral interest by others. In any case, concerns about the name change were broadly aired on the campus. One of Hatfield's first administrative acts was to appoint a committee to study the issue. That committee, which consisted of faculty members and administrators, wrestled with the centrality of the Western tradition in the course as well as its name. Religious studies professor Valarie Ziegler, a strong critic of the course, was the committee's head. She recalled those sessions as impassioned: "We agonized for weeks. We struggled to figure out what it was that the course attempted to do and how we should (or should not) attempt to reconceive it."[12] Student opinions were solicited via a huge piece of newsprint attached to a wall in the dining hall and bearing the label: "What should we call the Man course?"[13]

The committee concluded that in view of the externally mandated features of the course (mainly, the substantial component that had to be devoted to the Judeo-Christian tradition), it would have to be confined to the Western experience—a limitation that should be signaled in the new title. At the same time, the course should bring a new perspective to that experience. After much discussion, the committee issued a report recommending the title The Quest for Meaning in the Light of Western History and Religion. Ziegler explained: "The committee thought that 'meaning' was better than 'values' because we didn't conceive the course as an attempt to teach values. Rather, we saw the course as an historical investigation into the ways that a variety of notable Western persons . . . had constructed world views that gave meaning to their lives."

At subsequent plenary sessions of the course staff, some took issue with the proposed title—Quest for Meaning sounded vacuous to some, quixotic to others, and still others found it a potentially confusing replication of the title of an existing course in the religion department. Several other names were proposed by staff members, and the issue roiled through what Hatfield recalls as "long and stormy sessions" leading to the adoption of the present name: the Search for Values in the Light of Western History and Religion. Committee member Robert Llewellyn recalled that the group "'fell' into the title after much discussion."[14]

The name change reflected the feminist critique of the Western tradition and acknowledged the multiculturalist sensitivity to "Eurocentric bias." What went virtually unremarked at the time was the new title's implicit acknowledgment of Nietzsche, who coined the current meaning of the term "values" to displace the old notions of "good" and "evil" and for whom reason and revelation had been superseded as sources of authority by the creative genius of philosophic legislators.[15] *Values* appealed to the Search staff as a benign synonym for *morality*, avoiding the latter's implicit claims to finality. To many, the new name suggested a renewed vigor and a new perspective on the past and the future.

One practical implication of the change in nomenclature was increased attention to values issues in the selection of course materials and class discussions. Themes such as justice, freedom, equality, and the relation of humans to the divine had always pervaded the course, but the term *search* seemed explicitly to convey the idea of human beings grappling with fundamental questions and forging responses that might constitute the intellectual horizon of one epoch but be superseded in another. It was also felt that "search for values" spoke to the anticipated experience of students who would be exposed to a variety of conflicting moral perspectives.

The foundational idea of the course—small-group discussion of classic readings from the Bible and other formative texts of Western civilization—remained unchanged while approaches to that idea and strategies for implementing it evolved. The latter would now include, at least for some of the staff, employing the "hermeneutic of suspicion," especially toward those texts, such as Genesis 1–3, whose misuse had historically played a part in constructing a subordinate role for women. The interpretive strategy of "getting behind the text" to the social and political interests that shaped it opened up the possibility of reading familiar works in unfamiliar ways. Perhaps that was the key to the endurance of the course in its fifth decade: a policy that allowed new approaches, yet preserved the kind of works that seem withal to have an intrinsic yet inexhaustible meaning to impart to readers who have eyes to see. A brochure prepared for the college's humanities division in the early 1990s managed to capture this quality of continuity amid diversity:

The Search course, a staple of the college's curriculum since 1945 . . . is taught by professors who are drawn from many different academic disciplines and experiences in life and who share with students the intellectual stimulation that comes from exploring materials drawn from history, religious studies, biblical literature, the arts, philosophy, and imaginative literature. . . . The Search course has introduced thousands of Rhodes students to the excitement of the "life of the mind" and to the possibilities of beginning a lifelong engagement with the persistent issues of human experience.

That feature of existential engagement has come to characterize the program in the minds of many participants, especially, perhaps, those adult students who came to the course with significant life experience. In 1988 the Search course became an integral part of the new Adult Degree Program, established by Sally Thomason, the director of the college's Meeman Center for Special Studies, to enable individuals to finish their undergraduate degrees on a part-time basis. All of the adult learners began the program by taking the Search course and were grouped together in a colloquium with younger undergraduates. Historian and Episcopal priest Robert M. Watson, who served as the first instructor and faculty mentor for this group, remarked on its congeniality and penchant for lively argument.[16] Gail Corrington Streete of the again-renamed religious studies department, who had taught in the course since coming to Rhodes in 1990, succeeded Watson as the group's colloquium leader and was affected deeply by the experience:

There were people attending adult Search for whom entire new vistas, on history, religion, and themselves, were opening up. Some people, especially women, who had nothing to say at the beginning of the term, were eagerly participating in discussions and raising questions in the lectures as we went on. For many, biblical literature, which they had never studied in depth or in an academic setting, became exciting. I formed some lasting ties and met some people fascinating in their own right: writers, musicians, morticians, flight attendants, entrepreneurs. Several shared with me literature or music they had discovered or rediscovered. ...Teachers frequently claim that their students teach them as much as they teach their students, but in this case it was the truth.[17]

Because of administrative problems unrelated to the Search course, the Adult Degree Program was ended in 1993. But those who participated in the program remember it with special pleasure. Linda Nelson, who began the course in 1991, recalled a feeling of personal accomplishment after reading and evaluating a large amount of material, then writing about it. "Search set the tone, gave me a feel for history, philosophy, religion, politics," she reported, "and it guided me in making later course choices. It helped to shape my understanding of current issues." Peggy

Harlow and Chesley H. Dickinson, who both started in the program in 1992, remembered the challenge of adapting to a classroom situation in which traditional students and adult learners were mixed and how, in time, the two groups grew to a deep appreciation of each other. Harlow recalled warming to the Search professors' probing questions and her own delight in passing on to her family discoveries made in class discussions and in reading assignments. "It was that experience with Search that convinced me to go back to school full-time to complete my degree" Harlow said. "It made me rethink everything, made me question," added Dickinson. "Search was the perfect first class in college. It set the stage for learning, opened me to new ideas, and prepared me for the rest of my college studies. I wish it could go on for all four years."[18]

In 1986, the same year that the course's name was changed, the Rhodes faculty voted to alter the academic calendar from the three-term format—two twelve-week terms followed by a six-week term, with Search taught only during the long terms—to two fourteen-week semesters. This structural change was accompanied by a shift in faculty teaching loads from seven or more courses per year to six. Not everyone on the Search staff ended up teaching only six courses during the first year or so of the new policy, however. According to Hatfield, the dedication of some faculty members to the course led them to continue teaching Search even though it amounted to an overload in their schedules.

Newly appointed dean Harmon Dunathan (a humanities-oriented chemist who arrived in 1987 from Hampshire College, where he also had served as dean) and Associate Dean Robert Llewellyn (a philosopher and veteran Search staff member who continued to teach in the course while performing his administrative duties) responded to Hatfield's repeated admonition that "if we are going to do [the course] right, we must look toward the appointment of some positions in Search."[19] In the late 1980s, for the first time, a concerted effort was made to recruit new faculty members with the Search course in mind. Dunathan viewed this as a special challenge, tied to the distinctive heritage and purpose of the college: "I don't know of any other nationally recognized liberal arts college that attempts anything so ambitious as the four required semesters of Search, or that successfully incorporates a religious theme in such a sequence," he said. "Coming to Rhodes in 1987, I saw the existence of this requirement as a great opportunity to strengthen and preserve the very center of Rhodes' liberal arts tradition."[20]

Dunathan was particularly concerned about the quality of teaching in Search, considering its weight in the undergraduate curriculum:

I felt that there was an ethical issue at stake here. We bring students to Rhodes, telling them, "The institution really believes in the Search requirement, to the point that you must spend more than 10 percent of your academic work in that course." Having made that statement of belief, we had an obligation to see that the course was taught exceptionally well and that all possible improvements were made in its organization and content. . . . The best evidence that an institution is committed to its vision of the liberal arts is in the resources given to [its] requirements and in an institutional ethos that supports them. This was behind everything I felt about Search.

The sense of ethical obligation led Dunathan, assisted by Llewellyn, to push vigorously to have more full-time faculty members in Search (the course, Dunathan believed, had leaned too heavily on part-timers in the recent past), and to find more people who would be committed to Search as an integral and important part of their teaching assignment. Llewellyn recalls this process as an exciting one in which new tenure-track openings were "consciously defined as including teaching in the interdisciplinary program, so that the interviews for hiring new professors were in part focused on candidates' affinity with that kind of teaching and desire to do that kind of teaching." [21] During the hiring process, members of the academic dean's staff regularly evaluated candidates' public lectures with a Search-related criterion firmly in mind: the ability to communicate well with a multidisciplinary audience.

Harmon Dunathan, dean of academic affairs, 1987–93.

The efforts of Dunathan, Hatfield, and Llewellyn to improve the Search staff bore fruit abundantly. A number of faculty appointments eventually were made with the interests of the Search course taken into consideration. Daniel Cullen, hired to strengthen political philosophy within the political science department, joined the Search faculty in 1989, his second year at Rhodes. Sandra McEntire, a specialist in medieval English literature, joined the second-year staff. Michael Nelson, a scholar of the American presidency, left a tenured position at Vanderbilt University with the idea of beginning a new intellectual odyssey in Search. These and other appointments (including the recent addition of two classicists, the first ever to teach in the course) went a long way toward fulfilling Hatfield's goal of establishing a stable and committed Search staff. Several of the newcomers were female faculty members, bringing an added degree of balance to the teaching staff of Search and of the college as a whole.

Taking a historical perspective, Dunathan articulated a persuasive conception of the intrinsic value of the Search course in the broader scheme of things, as well as of what it could mean for students and for collegiate learning:

Ever since the Second World War academics have lamented the gradual loss of coherence in the liberal arts curriculum. Interdisciplinary studies became fashionable in part to recover lost connections across the curriculum. When these courses work well they communicate a belief that the subjects treated are of great value. Students may resist appropriating this knowledge for themselves, but at least they will know that they have been in contact with ideas that are transcendent. Faculty members teaching in these courses should not be afraid to make claims for the material [and] not be afraid to say that these are great things.

Dunathan was fully aware of the pressures of contemporary academic life, especially the lack of professional incentives to participate in a course like Search. But he steadfastly maintained that it was possible to take a professoriate that is narrowly trained and convince it of the fulfillment and joy to be found in interdisciplinary teaching.

The new name, the more deliberate hiring strategy, and the two-term calendar produced a new form and new focus for Search. The calendar change, which went into effect in the fall of 1987, forced faculty to reformulate the syllabi of nearly every course in the curriculum, and Search was no exception. Although the basic emphases of the course remained unchanged, some fresh materials were added to the syllabus of the first year, and the idea of discipline-based "tracks" was implemented in the second year of the course.

Developments in First-Year Search:
New Materials, New Strategies

With the expanded fourteen-week semesters, the first-year Search syllabus underwent significant alterations, particularly the units dealing with the Hebrew scriptures and the New Testament. Updated materials fleshed out the "What does it mean to be human?" introduction to the course. Substantial sections of the books of Genesis, I and II Samuel, and I Kings were added to the colloquium readings, as were the Caananite stories of Baal, which shed light on the cultural and religious environment of ancient Israel. Selections from the *Iliad* joined those from the *Odyssey*. The New Testament unit now included readings from the intertestamental Apocrypha (II Esdras) and additional selections from the gospels and the Acts of the Apostles. The revisions generally aimed at providing more depth and thematic unity to the course, sometimes by pointing up cross-cultural parallels, such as those between the Hebrew and Babylonian creation stories.

Various other changes occurred in subsequent years. In 1988, for example, selections from II Kings, Leviticus, and Proverbs were added to the Hebrew unit. The Greek unit was revised in 1991 to include more Thucydides and to shift all of the nonphilosophical materials to the fall semester so that Plato could be considered in the spring in conjunction with increased coverage of Aristotle.[22] The purpose of these modifications was to highlight the *polis* as the focus of the Greek understanding of civilization. That same year produced two other major adjustments. First, the Search staff decided to use Augustine's *Confessions* at the beginning of the first year as well as at the end, thereby framing the course with the chronicle of a young person's intellectual and moral struggle, a struggle with which students embarked on their own search for meaning might identify. Second, in addition to the staff-produced *Readings* books, students were asked to purchase all the primary texts for the course rather than use library copies. The staff wanted to emphasize that these works were to be marked up, brought to class, and, not least, added to each student's own permanent library.

In 1994, the Book of Ruth and supplemental readings from ancient Egypt, including creation and flood stories and incantations from the

Book of the Dead, were added to underscore the diverse cultural context of the Hebrew scriptures. The New Testament unit was expanded to include the Epistle to the Hebrews, as well as ancillary readings from non-canonical gospels, early Christian apologists, and the lives and deaths of the martyrs (*The Martyrdom of Saints Perpetua and Felicitas*). These changes addressed crucial developments in Christianity that occurred during the two centuries between the gospels and Augustine and also served to anchor the biblical texts more firmly in the context of the Greco-Roman world.

With the arrival of classicists Kenneth Morrell and Livia Tenzer on the staff in 1994, a unified Greco-Roman unit took shape. This unit included larger chunks of favorite texts—the *Aeneid* and the *Odyssey* would now be read nearly in their entirety, as would the complete cycle of Sophocles' Theban plays. New works by Cicero, Sallust, Seneca, Tacitus, Philo of Alexandria, and Plato (the *Phaedo*) also were added. Other authors, such as Horace and Plutarch, were dropped to make room for the additions.

As for the organization of the course, a new division of labor was instituted in 1988, when the first year was separated into two teaching teams of seven professors each. Half of the first-year students in the course continued to meet at "D" hour (11:30 to 12:30) with one team, and the rest met at "F" hour (1:50 to 2:50) with the other team. This change allowed for a halving of the lecture sections, which met approximately once per week, to 120–140 students, and created a greater sense of collegiality and participation among staff members. It also allowed students greater flexibility in scheduling their courses and reduced the magnitude of the stampede on the refectory at 12:30.[23] Under the new scheme the D- and F-hour staffs initially had considerable control of their respective sections. Although the content of the two courses remained virtually identical, some variation occurred in the order of topics and the character of exams and writing assignments—testimony that no two groups of faculty, left to their own devices, will plan a course in exactly the same way.

Hatfield suggested that the two teams meet together in the summer of 1991 to agree on an identical structure, calendar, and set of readings. Standardization would remove most occasions for student griping about one section being more difficult or rule-bound than the other; it also would make it easier to distribute lecture responsibilities across the sections—whenever possible, the same person would give the same lecture at both hours. Changes in readings necessitated a new syllabus. The staff threw itself into a thorough revision of study questions for each colloquium to give students more guidance in the actual examination of texts and resumed the perennial task of trying to increase the coherence of the course's thematic focus and goals.

The staff also experimented with innovative instructional approaches. "Special sessions" were worked into the first-year program to enhance the standard daily schedule. These occurred at long intervals and were designed as breathers, intended to alleviate the intensity of the course's driving pace. That lockstep rhythm, described by some students (and faculty) as "unremitting" and by others as "rapid-fire" or "break-neck," was characterized by one frazzled wag as the "If this is Monday, it must be *Gilgamesh*" syndrome. On special-session days no new assignments were introduced. Instead the class meeting was devoted to a pedagogical end, such as assimilation and review of particularly difficult course materials, instruction in preparation for writing assignments, or the common viewing of pertinent films. Sometimes the sessions consisted of panel discussions led by all colloquium leaders, answering students' questions concerning a unit or an entire term; sometimes they featured a guest speaker, such as Memphis rabbi Micah Greenstein discussing modern Judaism at the end of the unit on the ancient Hebrews. Beyond regular class hours, a videotape of Sophocles' *Antigone* featuring Rhodes students was viewed one year. Other years *The Gospel at Colonus*, a filmed musical adaptation of *Oedipus at Colonus*, was shown in conjunction with the reading of the play. Luncheon sessions open to staff and students were sometimes offered when visiting lecturers delivered talks. The inception of Search Suppers in 1994 was a natural extension of the idea of out-of-class common experiences, offering students a weekly chance to discuss with a professor those issues that might not get treated (or satisfactorily completed) in regular colloquium sessions.

Some of these experiments and initiatives were more successful than others, but taken together they testified to the staff's continuing commitment to explore innovative ways to engage students and stimulate their interest. New lecturing techniques evolved, reflecting changes in personnel, technical aids, and course emphases. Slide presentations, music and drama, and computer-assisted lectures became increasingly common. In the mid-1980s Diane Clark of the music department organized two lectures, one involving dramatic readings and dance performed by students, and the other a cantor from a local synagogue. "Both these sessions were a good way to involve some of our students and faculty in the arts," Clark recalls.[24] In 1991, Search lectures moved from Frazier-Jelke B to Blount Auditorium in the newly constructed Buckman Hall. Blount substituted state-of-the-art audiovisual facilities for those in the older, larger room.

As the staff experimented freely with modes of instruction it was mindful of the adage about "the best laid plans." Consequently, additional methods for evaluating the course were implemented in 1992. The first was a questionnaire distributed to all students near the end of the second semester to solicit their opinions about lectures, readings, exams, and writing assignments. In 1994 the questionnaire was expanded to ask, "What issue was of greatest importance to you in the development of your own thinking?" and to pursue the implications raised by the students' answers to that question. A second type of assessment involved inviting the Search Advisory Council, which included the best students from all sections, to meet with the staff and discuss in small groups their reactions to the course and their suggestions for improving it. These student responses led the staff to reevaluate the role of lectures. Students had complained that the lectures were disconnected from what they read and discussed in colloquium meetings. Although the staff did not share this view, it responded to the students' perception and, in the 1994 revision of the course, reduced the proportion of lectures from around one-third to one-fourth of the class meetings.

In response to other of the students' recommendations, the staff modified some of the reading and essay assignments and experimented with testing and evaluating techniques.[25] Flexibility was introduced into examination procedures in the hope of reflecting more accurately the individualities of teaching and learning styles. For years Search tests had been forged by the staff as a whole and administered to all colloquia during the regular class hour. Innovative testing procedures implemented in 1994 included take-home tests, tests for which some of the essay topics were distributed to students prior to the test date, open-book tests, and final exams with a major comprehensive essay constructed in conjunction with one of the term's paper assignments. In 1995 the staff decided to allow colloquium leaders to design their own essay questions, while retaining a common objective portion of the test for all the sections in each hour of the course.

This sense of innovative engagement extended to writing assignments, which were reconceived in light of workshops conducted on campus in the early 1990s by Toby Fulwiler, the director of writing at the

University of Vermont. Numerous new approaches were tried by colloquium leaders: brief essays at the beginning or end of class; frequent
quizzes; out-of-class essays, coordinated across both semesters to allow for
monitored progress and development; and increased use of the college's
Writing Center. The second semester writing project included a paper
that encouraged students to compare in an inventive way characters from
more than one unit of the course—Jesus and Oedipus, Moses and Aeneas,
or some other pair.

The care given to the design of exams and writing assignments was a
reflection of the painstaking attention that the Search staff gave to the coherence of the course, as well as an awareness of the peculiar needs of
first-year students who are developing their reading and writing skills. Although the staff was not interested in change for its own sake and was
particularly careful not to reinvent the wheel, it was united by a desire to
improve all aspects of the course, and approached the annual and the
(more comprehensive) triennial course revisions with the conviction that
things could be done better.

These habits of self-scrutiny placed the Search program in advance of
the trend toward institutional planning, goal setting, and evaluation that
swept through American higher education in the late 1980s and continued into the 1990s. *Proficiency, outcomes, accountability,* and *productivity* became the new buzzwords. This thrust was felt at Rhodes as a result of a
visit by a reaccreditation team of the Southern Association of Colleges
and Schools (SACS) in 1989. To satisfy SACS, every department and program in the college was required to state its goals and its plan for achiev-
ing them.[26] Search was no exception, and the following statement of
purpose was composed by the staff:

To encourage and guide students in exploring the persistent and significant issues pertaining to meaning and values in human experience; and to provide students with opportunities, through discussion in small groups of students and
faculty members, to relate that exploration to their own intellectual and moral
development.[27]

As an additional part of the SACS process, specific goals were to be
developed for accomplishing the stated purpose. These goals were to be
"assessable," stated in terms of "learning objectives for individual students," and "linked clearly to the department's mission statement." [28] The
staff expressed the goals of the Search course as follows:

1. To provide students with a firm foundation in the study of the Bible. This foundation includes a knowledge of the themes addressed and the approaches taken in addressing those themes in the different sections of the Bible as well as an appreciation of, and ability to employ, some of the modern methods of biblical study.
2. To provide students with direct introductions, through the assigned reading of primary sources, to the ideas and movements that have shaped and given character to the western world.
3. To provide students with an opportunity, through small group discussions, to discuss the ideas from the readings and to explore how those ideas relate to their own thinking and systems of values.
4. To provide students with a foundation for a continuing, life-long engagement in developing the "life of the mind" and to encourage them actually to commit themselves to such an engagement.
5. To provide students with an educational setting in which they can experience an approach to learning that cuts across the usual disciplinary lines of the curriculum.

In order to respond to the fundamental questions raised by the SACS committee—"Are you accomplishing what you propose to accomplish for your students?" and "How do you know?"—concrete descriptions of the ways in which these goals were implemented were devised. The purpose of each lecture was clearly formulated, its goals defined. For example, the lecture on post-exilic Judaism sought to explore the changes and continuities in Israelite religion as it emerged from the experience of exile, as well as to set the stage for reading and discussing the books of Ruth, Proverbs, Ecclesiastes, and Job. Similar evaluative criteria eventually were applied to every colloquium assignment: Were students reading appropriate selections and applying the principles of biblical criticism in their discussions of biblical texts? As part of the general move toward clearer expression of goals and the terms used to define them, the venerable Oxonian name *collection,* which had characterized Search tests for more than four decades, was jettisoned in favor of *test.* Similarly, the term *syllabus* was retired in favor of the more accurate, if more prosaic *study guide.* Colloquia, however, were still called colloquia rather than "discussion sections" because the latter implied a predominantly lecture course, which Search was not.

Not every development was positive. In the mid-1990s, national trends concerning "cost control" and "downsizing" reached the college

and affected operations in the course. Some faculty positions were eliminated or removed from the tenure track in departments that historically
had supplied numerous faculty for Search, introducing an element of in-
stability into a course in which staff continuity had been essential to effective planning, training, and coordination. In addition, colloquium sizes
were allowed to rise. For years, students had stressed the importance of
small Search colloquia and recommended that they be kept to a maxi-
mum of eighteen or fewer.[29] In the fall of 1994 administrative pressures
were brought to bear and, at the insistence of Dean Mark McMahon
(who had replaced Dunathan as dean in 1993), first-year Search colloquia
were enlarged to twenty-one. Hatfield summarized the opinion of many
who taught in the course when he stated:

The Staff remains adamantly convinced that this change will further erode the
integrity of the kind of teaching, and learning, that goes on in Search. While one
may argue that going from 18 to 20 [or more] is not such a big deal, the fact is
that the 18 limit had already surpassed the original ideal of sections of 12 to 15
students. Search classes depend on student participation, in discussion with one
another and in extensive interaction with the professor. Such a class cannot be
successful where there are . . . too many students, where discussion can never get
beyond the surface because there is not enough time for every student to develop fully his/her view or idea.[30]

Rethinking and Restructuring Second-Year Search

After the Search course was restructured in 1981 to be taught in four
semesters instead of two, the Hebrew, Greek, Roman, and early Christian
units were covered during the first year of the course, while the second
year began with the Middle Ages and continued to the present. Although
the content of the first-year program remained very much what it had
been in the past, the second year took on a new form that encouraged a
number of new approaches.

Innovation in the second year came in response to several pressures
and problems. Continuing the weekly structure (common lecture, then
colloquium) and methodology (common syllabus and core readings) of
the first-year course into the second year proved to be not only imprac-
tical, often yielding ninety-minute lectures and only one discussion meeting per week, but also somewhat monotonous. As sophomores, ready to
commit to a major and to be more involved in their classes than a diet

heavy in lectures permits, many students came to resent the required survey style of course design that they had encountered during their first year.

The staff had its own reasons for change. The second-year curriculum was a quick march through philosophical, literary, historical, and religious topics spanning fifteen centuries. A common syllabus prevented instructors from different disciplines from moving at different speeds or along different routes, all of which might be worthwhile. For example, whereas the natural tendency of the religious studies faculty was to work slowly through the theology of Augustine and Aquinas, the literature faculty would have gladly bypassed them both and considered religious questions through the prism of Dante.

In 1988, the staff of the second year embraced its own "law of uneven development" and decided to establish four discipline-based "tracks," each of which would pursue concerns particular to religion, philosophy, literature, or history. A large number of core readings common to all tracks were preserved to maintain unity in the course. But instructors in each track also were invited to supplement the core with readings of special significance to their own area. This scheme was implemented in 1989 with three sections of history, three sections of literature, and one section each of philosophy and religion.[31] In some cases these courses could be used to satisfy requirements in the major as well as degree requirements. The philosophy department, for example, used the philosophy track as an introductory philosophy course and required that its majors take both semesters. Because of the selections that students read from Machiavelli, Hobbes, Locke, Rousseau, Marx, and Nietzsche, a political science major could use the same track to satisfy the department's one-course requirement in political theory.

Hatfield enthusiastically supported reforming the second year of the course, then oversaw the implementation and fine tuning of this major structural change. After he and the staff defined the core readings for the sophomore year, he oversaw the staff work that resulted in a distinctive syllabus for each of the tracks. A major benefit of the clear disciplinary focus of the track system was that faculty members for second-year Search became easier to recruit than in the past. Another result was full enrollments in all tracks, reversing a trend of declining enrollments between the first and second years of the course.[32] As Hatfield reported:

The new approach was an overwhelming success. The enrollments for 1989 were approximately twenty percent above what they had been in the previous year. Even more striking is the fact that pre-registration for the fall of 1990 saw the filling of all eight sections to capacity (and beyond in one case) representing an increase of another thirty-three percent over the enrollments for this year. Evidence of approval for the change was reinforced by a survey of the students in the course. . . . The survey indicated a general, and even enthusiastic, endorsement of the track system. [33]

In the revised format, each second-year track began with the collapse of the Roman empire in the west and the emergence of the Middle Ages, continuing to the late twentieth century. The common core of readings included selections from Augustine, Aquinas, Dante, Petrarch, Luther, Calvin, Bacon, Descartes, Hobbes, Locke, Kant, Marx, Freud, and Sartre. The history track focused on issues such as the origins of feudalism, the relationship between ecclesiastical and political conflict, the rise of the modern state, revolution, nationalism, and the formation of the ideologies of communism and fascism. The literature track explored the genres of romance, drama, and the novel, and included such works as Cervantes's *Don Quixote*, Voltaire's *Candide*, Tolstoy's *Death of Ivan Ilyich*, and Sartre's *No Exit*. The philosophy track highlighted topics such as natural law, the origin of subjectivity, empiricist and rationalist epistemologies, theistic and atheistic existentialisms, pragmatism, and postmodernism. The religion track examined the development of Christian doctrine from Augustine and Aquinas to contemporary theologies of liberation.

All tracks of the second-year course remained organized by periods: Middle Ages, Renaissance and Reformation, Enlightenment, and nineteenth and twentieth centuries. For each period a list of core readings was provided to each instructor from which a certain number of selections were to be included. Some of these readings, such as Dante's *Inferno*, were mandatory for all tracks; others, at the discretion of the instructor, could be replaced by a different selection by the same author (Nietzsche's *Genealogy of Morals* rather than *The Will to Power*), or ignored altogether in favor of a substitute from the same period. Although the track approach was more closely aligned with the professional training of the staff than is the common syllabus used in the first year of the course, all second-year staff members continued to teach outside their disciplines to some extent.

One consequence of abandoning common lectures in the second year was that students could now spend more time reading and discussing primary texts. The separate tracks were, for the most part, reading the same authors but reading larger or smaller selections from a given work or, occasionally, reading different works by the same author. For example, the literature track would read more cantos from the *Inferno* than would the philosophy track, and history would read a short selection from Descartes's *Discourse on Method* while philosophy would read Descartes's *Meditations* in its entirety. Assignments distinctive to each track also were made. The religion and literature classes sampled the writings of female medieval mystics (Hildegard of Bingen, Julian of Norwich, Catherine of Siena); in contrast, the philosophy track, while not neglecting mysticism, focused on Christine de Pizan's defense of women's rationality.

The decentralization of the second-year course made it easier for each track to adopt themes, for instructors to select texts that develop those themes, and for students to cope with the enormous chronological sweep of the syllabus. One advantage of giving considerable control of the course to each instructor was the increased ability to respond in an ad hoc way to the difficulties inherent in teaching a survey course: lecturing when students need some context or overview; slowing the pace when particularly difficult subjects are being covered (Kant's epistemology being a notorious case in point); and permitting a class to continue a discussion of, say, Machiavelli's challenge to traditional ethics when a common course calendar would dictate moving on. Another benefit of the track system, universally acclaimed by the second-year staff, was the complete decentralization of testing. College professors tend to be individualists, and few things are more idiosyncratic than philosophies of testing. Some prefer conventional in-class examinations, others take-home exams; some assign a series of papers, some require journals. The freedom to determine at least some reading assignments and the complete control of testing went a long way to overcoming the standard objections of faculty members regarding team-taught courses.

The new structure of the second-year program made revising the course a gentle process. Every change did not need to be negotiated with one's peers, and individual instructors could experiment liberally with new readings and topics. At the same time, one could appropriate the results from another's laboratory. Colleagues asked each other: Was reading More's *Utopia* in the history track a success? Did the addition of Rousseau's *Discourse on the Origin of Inequality* to the philosophy syllabus shed light on the author's notoriously difficult *Social Contract*? Was Sartre's *No Exit* a better entrée to his thought than "Existentialism Is a Humanism"?

Almost to a one, faculty and students agreed that the change to the track system in the second year was a wise move. Was there loss as well as gain? Probably. The abandonment of common lectures increased the pressure on each instructor to be a jack of all trades. Moving from one era to another became more challenging than it had been when such transitions were the mainstays of the common lectures. But instructors who occasionally found themselves out of their element freely sought the advice of colleagues who were more comfortable with Calvinist theology, Cartesian rationalism, Romantic poetry, or Freudian psychology— whatever the case might be. It was not uncommon for a staff member to arrive in the morning to find an urgent e-mail message asking for tips on how to explain Locke's distinction between primary and secondary qualities, Rousseau's general will, or Coleridge's "Rime of the Ancient Mariner."

On occasion, when special opportunities arose, the second-year staff organized common sessions held outside of regular class periods. Dante scholar Giuseppe Mazotta lectured to the entire second-year course, as did the literary scholar Peter Stansky, who offered a 1994 retrospective on the "tenth anniversary" of Orwell's *1984*. The staff agreed that students could occasionally benefit from common lectures such as these, even when the tracks were at different historical periods in their syllabi, but such occasions would be infrequent, normally not more than once a semester.

The Douglass Seminars:
Staff Renewal and Course Revitalization

One of the first things Hatfield did when he was appointed director-designate of the Search course was to launch a workshop for the first and second-year staff in the summer of 1985, continuing the practice begun by Fred Neal. Hatfield prepared a five-day, ten-session schedule that addressed three important goals: review of significant themes common to the several segments of the course, intensive study of some of the more difficult sections to teach, and demonstrations of audio-visual materials and of techniques for leading colloquia. The twenty staff members who participated in the August workshop were joined by twenty-two students for sample colloquium sessions on justice and on existentialism, led by Neal and Larry Lacy, respectively. Faculty participants found the workshop "well-conceived and efficiently executed," and "a good introduction to the course, its purpose and goals." A seasoned veteran of the course noted that "the workshop was a good way to get reacquainted with the material and toss it around with each other." A newcomer to the staff commented: "I can't imagine a new staff member entering [this] program without first receiving the orientation the workshop provided. . . . Seeing how students actually confronted some difficult material helped me to realize what I need to do to insure that my students get the most out of the colloquium experience." Several seminar participants commented on the strong sense of bonding that emerged as the diverse staff came together to work toward a common academic purpose. "Best of all," said one, was "the fellowship aspect, [a] 'sense of the meeting' continually evoked. How important it is for us to love and respect each other." [34]

Several faculty members suggested that the workshop be made an annual event and that outside speakers be brought in to help guide the staff's discussions of difficult materials. As noted in chapter 3, that purpose was accomplished through the auspices of the newly endowed Douglass seminars. The document prepared by the college's development office in recognition of the gift began with the statement, "Interdisciplinary teaching is at the heart of the curriculum of Rhodes College," and concluded:

There is an important by-product of the Douglass Seminars that cannot be over-estimated. Because there is a working together on matters of importance in the education of our students, there is a sense of collegiality among members of the staff not found within the normal structure of college facilities. The seminars will promote a sense of connection across departmental and discipline boundaries; they will provide an opportunity for a sharing of ideas among experts in traditional liberal arts and sciences areas. [35]

Year after year, the Douglass seminars served to orient and acclimate new faculty, to cultivate an esprit de corps among the entire staff, and to facilitate fine-grained analysis and revision of the Search curriculum. Through the seminars, new perspectives, new readings, and new ideas were introduced into the course under the guidance of scholars from outside the college and across the humanities. They also helped new and continuing staff members to know one another better and to become more effective team members by working together closely.

Hatfield regarded the seminars as valuable training opportunities: "None of us who teach in the program has been trained in interdisciplinary scholarship. We have to learn as we go along: from our own mistakes, from one another, and from our students. . . . We have learned from experience how helpful staff seminars can be in assisting us in our development." [36] German professor John Bruhwiler, who taught in the course for a decade until his retirement in 1991, remarked on the challenging group dynamics of the Douglass seminars: "It was a matter of adjusting to others' ways of doing things, seeing insights others had, getting out of disciplinary isolation." [37] Bruhwiler also recalled his excitement during one of the seminars when he gained an understanding of the social context in which the apostle Paul lived and wrote: "The discussions of the sociology of the Roman world helped me see what Paul said in a way that made sense." [38] Robert Watson lobbied his colleagues to adopt a new reading by Freud for the second year of the course, arguing that, far from promoting sexual libertinism, as had often been claimed, Freud was highly moral and devoted to his medical studies. The text supporting this view was included in the readings for the following year.[39] English professor Richard Wood, an occasional workshop leader, put it this way: "The people who agree to work in Search are members of [widely divergent] departments. They are strengthened, maybe to some degree legitimized, by an officially sanctioned and scheduled review session." [40]

Although the format varied somewhat from year to year, the seminars typically involved a one- to two-week commitment from all staff members and included both workshop sessions for syllabus revision and symposium sessions for close reading and discussion of specific texts. The tedious tasks of course revision—creating calendars, books of readings, introductory materials, study questions, time lines, common writing assignments, etc.—typically were accomplished in an efficient and collegial manner.

The seminars were structured to have a clear focus each year. In 1987 and 1988 the workshops provided the much needed means for instituting the discipline-based tracks in the second year of the course. Thereafter, the focus was related to one or more of the units in the course and the sessions usually were led by a visiting scholar. Several of these leaders were chosen to emphasize a particular concern of the first year of the course. Carl Holladay of Emory University, for example, helped the staff to explore current thinking about biblical criticism, particularly the continuing importance of the documentary hypothesis concerning the sources of the synoptic gospels. Lee Barrett, a professor at the Presbyterian School of Christian Education in Virginia, portrayed Augustine's writings as a point of union between the Greco-Roman world and the

Judeo-Christian tradition and offered suggestions about how to treat Augustine as the culmination of the first year's study. Classicist Susan Ford Wiltshire of Vanderbilt University considered the implications of teaching Aristotle in a course centered on the search for values in the Judeo-Christian tradition. Kenneth Morrell and Livia Tenzer explained to the first-year staff how a major restructuring of the Greek and Roman units could work.

The Douglass seminars improved the quality of the Search course's second year as well. Drawing on the expertise of Rhodes faculty members (including a few who did not teach Search), the second-year staff focused on topics that had proven to be difficult to teach in the previous year or on new topics that would be added to the syllabus. Sandra McEntire led the seminar in studying some feminist readings to be salted throughout the second year. James Jobes worked through some texts on the Scientific Revolution that had been fixtures in the course, and introduced some new ones. In other sessions the staff was made aware of recent developments in American historiography concerning the endurance of the classical republican tradition, was guided through the development of modern philosophy from Descartes to Kant, and was exposed to feminist methods of literary criticism and the ways in which postmodern theorists remain in dialogue with the Western tradition. In addition to learning with and from one another, the seminars allowed the second-year staff to share experiences and teaching tips and generally to "stay on the same page" as far as the purposes of the course were concerned.

Not least of the virtues of the summer seminars was the cathartic opportunity they provided for the faculty. It was in these sessions more than anywhere else that the wider arguments in the humanities visited the Search course. Different readings and strategies of reading emerged as the faculty explored familiar and new texts. Quarrels (mostly of the good-natured variety) would erupt about the meaning of a passage or (and here bickering might ensue) the advantages of jettisoning one reading from the syllabus in favor of another.

If biblical interpretation was the topic, historically minded critics would joust with sociological, literary, or feminist interpreters, and "lay" readers would not hesitate to weigh in with their perspectives. In many ways, these sessions replicated graduate seminars at their best, while being more democratic. Everyone on the Search staff was a scholar in some domain, and the ideas and opinions of nonspecialists were offered confidently and taken seriously. Discussion and argument might oscillate between sobriety and vehemence; but the saving grace of the seminars was that a half hour would not pass without a peal of laughter or some general, exuberant uproar.

A circle of intelligent and committed scholars cannot ponder the best way to teach the Western tradition without their inherent diversity breaking out into disputes about content, pedagogy, and interpretive approaches. Discussions of biblical topics were particularly spirited, and heated arguments could be continued for hours and days: Did early Christianity invent patriarchalism, appropriate it from its cultural milieu, or subvert it? Was Paul's analogy of church and body in I Corinthians liberating, or did it endorse the local status hierarchy? Was the Israelite conception of Yahweh as a god of history (as opposed to a nature god) unique, or could parallels be found in other Near Eastern religions? Time usually passed quickly as the group scrutinized textual passages, debated interpretations, discovered new questions about old material, leaned forward at a specialist's insight—or teased one another with friendly barbs.

Year after year the Search staff found itself reinvigorated by these sessions, which followed closely on the heels of second-semester final examinations, grading, and commencement. Merely congregating with one's colleagues to discuss serious matters would be a worthwhile activity for faculty who, even at a small liberal arts college, are caught up in a hectic routine that keeps them tied down to their academic departments during the year. But coming together to reread and discuss what they put before their students seemed to restore their faith in liberal education, as well as their confidence that treasure had been stored to be discovered by the next year's class of students. The Search course avoided ossification during the 1980s and 1990s principally because of these seminars, which allowed its diverse faculty both to recollect and to renew its unifying mission and, not least, its members' respect and affection for one another.[41]

The Amateur Hour

MICHAEL   NELSON

It is a story that preachers love (I have heard it four times from three pulpits) and it goes like this. The architect Christopher Wren, after working for thirty-five years to rebuild St. Paul's Cathedral in London, took Queen Anne on a tour of the completed renovation. When they were done, the queen delivered her verdict: "It is awful, it is artificial, it is amusing." Wren was thrilled, not devastated. In 1710, *awful* meant "awe-inspiring," *artificial* meant "artistic," and *amusing* meant "amazing."

Amateur is another word that once thrilled but now devastates. The Latin root reveals something of its original meaning: *amare*, to love. Properly understood, an amateur is someone who does something for the love of it. Yet this meaning has been all but lost. To call someone an amateur today is to describe a person of limited competence, a bumbler or trifler.

Dare I say it, then? The faculty of the Search course are all amateurs. No one has a Ph.D. in Search; no such degree exists. Classicists regularly step outside their training to lead colloquia on the Hebrew scriptures; philosophers strain to teach the *Inferno*; theologians march their students though the *Iliad* and the *Republic*; American historians lecture on the Punic Wars. All of them do it out of love. In an age of academic hyper-specialization, in which careers advance by writing more and more about less and less for fewer and fewer readers, no other motive for teaching in the course makes sense.

I hasten to add, without fear of contradiction, that no one in the fifty-year history of Search has been more of an amateur than I—certainly in the modern sense of the word and, I like to think, in the original one as well. Fear of embarrassment prevents me from revealing the full extent of my ignorance when I began teaching first-year Search in 1991. Suffice it to say that although I probably could have eked out a C- on a pop quiz drawn from, say, E. D. Hirsch's *Dictionary of Cultural Literacy*, I almost certainly would have flunked an essay test. Twenty years of studying the American presidency and related subjects had seldom led me into the byways of the Deuteronomistic history or the musings of the Stoics and Epicureans.

What, then, was I doing on the faculty of the Search course? In large part I was there for my own education. I wanted to "learn this stuff," as I put it to myself; I did not want to go to my grave without seriously having read, reflected on, and discussed works such as the *Aeneid*, the *Nicomachean Ethics*, the Hebrew prophets, and Augustine's *Confessions*. I knew from long experience as a teacher and (once upon a time) as a magazine editor that there was no better way to master a subject than to teach it or write about it, and so I resolved to do both with the literature of the classical and biblical world that makes up the first year of the course.

I also knew that Search was the defining academic experience at Rhodes, the soul of the college in some ways. I had learned this while teaching at Vanderbilt University and living in Nashville for thirteen years before coming to Rhodes. My Nashville friends included several Rhodes alumni, and when I would ask them what their college experience had been like, they invariably said the same two things: first, that Search had been the best course they had ever taken, the one that had stayed with them the longest and affected them the most; and second, that they wished they had realized how valuable the course was at the time they were taking it. When I left Vanderbilt for Rhodes, I did so for several reasons—the lure of small classes, the beauty of the campus, a fondness for midtown Memphis, and so on. But high on the list was my desire to teach in the Search course.

My first year as a colloquium leader (I did not dare take on a lecture assignment) was, in some ways, the sort of experience that, while you are having it, you hope you will laugh about someday. I prepared feverishly for each class, trying to keep Jeroboam and Rehoboam straight and thumbing futilely through the *Iliad* to find the parts about Achilles' heel and the Trojan horse, knowing that the most talented group of students I had ever encountered awaited me. (Five of my eighteen Search students from that year went on to earn membership in Phi Beta Kappa.) Professors joke about staying a chapter ahead of their students, but what do you do when despite your best efforts they seem to stay a chapter ahead of you?

What you do is manage, or at least I did, and treasure the odd moment when it seems that perhaps you belong at the head of the seminar table after all. I vividly remember the joy I took when, as a political scientist, I was able to offer insights into King David that might not have occurred to an Old Testament scholar.

You also revel in your status as a fellow searcher with your students. One of our goals in the course is to encourage students to take seriously their own searches for meaning, and one of the things we always tell them in furtherance of that goal is that the faculty are searching with them. During that first year, I didn't have to fake it a bit.

In the fall of 1996 I began my sixth year in the course. I still work harder to prepare for each Search class than for all my political science classes put together. But since that first year I have lectured on Augustine, Homer, and Virgil. I have published the occasional journal article on topics like "Kennedy and Achilles: A Classical Approach to Political Science" and the role mythology played in C. S. Lewis's spiritual odyssey. A few of my students (how little they know, how kind they are) praise me in the course evaluations for my "command of the subject." Equally important, I actually expect to leave this world an educated person. An educated amateur.

The lesson, I think, is that any member of the Rhodes faculty can teach in the Search course. That was the hope of Fred Neal, who directed the course for so many years, and I could easily be entered in evidence as Exhibit A for his case. ("If Nelson can do it, *anyone* can.") The students would not suffer if the course were infused with enthusiastic natural and social scientists—far from it. After all, the issues that engage students as they read biblical and classical texts are the issues that engage the amateur even more than the specialist. As for the faculty—well, if my experience is any guide, they would be personally enriched beyond measure.

5

Influences Beyond
the Walls

JAMES M. VEST

During the decade after World War
II, interest in general education increased markedly in the humanities.
Around the country, many academicians became convinced that undergraduate curricula were too fragmented.[1] "All thoughtful persons are
concerned about the lack of an integrating factor in contemporary life,"
began a 1949 study describing various integrated college humanities
courses that were being offered as a remedy to this predicament.[2] At
church-related colleges in particular, the growing sense of a need for coherence fused with a concomitant desire for values-based education, and
for several of these colleges integrated humanities courses seemed to offer
an opportune means to move beyond "the bewildering present" to an
"intellectual renaissance" in which "all things are possible."[3] The broad-
based approach of the Man (hereafter Search) course seemed highly
promising to such colleges, especially to church-affiliated liberal arts colleges in the South, where in the mid-1950s and thereafter an increasing
number of interdisciplinary course offerings were created, several of
which looked to Search as a model.

Church-related colleges also resisted the growing secularization of
college curricula that had been taking place in higher education throughout the twentieth century.[4] These colleges not only acknowledged a need
to educate an informed citizenry to meet the challenges of contemporary
life but also evinced a strong desire to modernize the church's mission to

and through education. Presbyterian synods in North Carolina and Florida were at the forefront of this effort: in the late 1950s they established
St. Andrews Presbyterian College and Florida Presbyterian (now Eckerd)
College, respectively, with Search-style interdisciplinary courses of study
serving as the centerpieces of their curricula. At about the same time,
Austin College in Texas and Davidson College in North Carolina also
initiated ambitious interdisciplinary programs based on the Rhodes
model, and Hampden-Sydney College in Virginia did so soon thereafter.
In the mid-1960s Millsaps College in Mississippi followed suit. As re-
cently as 1992 the University of the South in Tennessee introduced a
Search-influenced interdisciplinary program.

Five of these programs were established at Presbyterian institutions—
St. Andrews, Eckerd, Austin, Davidson, and Hampden-Sydney. In each
case, the founders were Presbyterian ministers involved in higher education who stayed in contact with one another through established clerical
and academic channels. Much of the impetus for this movement came
from three allied Southern Presbyterian institutions in Richmond, Virginia. Interdisciplinary discussions at Union Theological Seminary and
the adjacent Presbyterian School of Christian Education directly inspired
several of these programs, and the denomination's Division of Higher
Education, also headquartered in Richmond, provided much of the momentum needed to implement and staff them. One of the first fruits of
the discussions affected the Search course itself. In 1944, John Osman
brought to Southwestern at Memphis (hereafter Rhodes) the keen sense
of interdisciplinary fervor he had shared in Richmond with Laurence F.
Kinney who, before coming to Rhodes the same year, taught at the Presbyterian School for Christian Education and was an adjunct professor at
Union Seminary. Kinney ardently pursued the idea of interdisciplinary
reform in higher education with Osman and his fellow seminarians, who
met regularly with Kinney to discuss philosophy and education. Among
them were Leslie Bullock and E. Ashby Johnson, who helped to carry
similar ideas to Presbyterian colleges in North Carolina, Texas, and Florida, where they joined in founding interdisciplinary programs that looked
to the Search course for inspiration.[5]

Soon after Kinney and Osman came to Rhodes and, in 1945, the
Search course was established, the institutional church's active role in fostering interdisciplinary general education programs in the humanities was
determinedly expanded by Hunter B. Blakely, Jr., who from 1950 to 1962
served as head of the Division of Higher Education. In this capacity

Blakely actively cultivated his longstanding interests in educational reform and spearheaded operations that would bring his ideas to fruition at
Eckerd, St. Andrews, and other colleges. He fostered discussions of the relationship between religious values and college teaching in two groups—
the Faculty Christian Fellowship and the Presbyterian Education
Association South—by helping to organize their annual meetings and by
using them as a forum to bring together educators who shared an interest in interdisciplinary teaching.[6] Regional meetings of these groups were
often held at the Presbyterian conference center in Montreat, North Carolina. Fred Neal met Blakely through the Presbyterian Education Association South and soon was recruited to teach in the Search course.
Similarly, at regional meetings of the Faculty Christian Fellowship, Search
course professors such as Milton Brown and Larry Lacy met Blakely,
Rene Williamson of Louisiana State University, and others who figured
prominently in the spread of integrated humanities programs during the
1950s and 1960s.

The interest in cross-disciplinary teaching that yielded the integrated
programs described in this chapter was widespread. Another organization
that promoted similar discussions was the Danforth Associates program.
Founded in 1941 by the Danforth Foundation of St. Louis, this organization strove "to recognize effective teaching and humanize teaching and
learning experiences, sensibilities, and values" by creating values-centered
"interdisciplinary opportunities" in intercollegiate settings.[7] The Danforth program provided funds to foster closer contacts between students
and professors while emphasizing interdisciplinary exchanges and team
teaching.

In several Presbyterian-related colleges, discussions sponsored by these
organizations and furthered by support from Blakely's office in Richmond led to the creation of interdisciplinary humanities programs. As one
professor of humanities at Davidson put it, these programs were natural
outgrowths of the time-honored Presbyterian ideal—*ecclesia reformata sem-
per reformanda* [a reformed church, ever reforming]—and the related
predilection "to reform education as a means for reforming the world."
As another at St. Andrews said, "The Calvinistic tradition has always emphasized broad-based education. Calvin did it in Geneva when he set up
the Academy. Calvin believed in education and Presbyterian thinking has
always been to educate." A third professor, from Eckerd College, stated it
this way: "The story has to be put into the historical context of Presby-
terian-Reformed concern about educating leaders in church and state,

extending back to John Calvin and his Genevan Academy as well as post-Reformation Scotland." Such was the heritage and mission, and the times were conducive in the 1950s for that kind of thinking in Southern church-related colleges.[8]

The Search course at Rhodes provided a ready model for such colleges. Directly or indirectly, it inspired similar programs at several other institutions. Among the most prominent of the interdepartmental courses to have drawn from Search are the Christianity and Culture program at St. Andrews Presbyterian College, the Integrated Studies cycle at Austin College, the Core Program at Eckerd College, the Interdisciplinary Humanities courses at Davidson College and Hampden-Sydney College, the Heritage Course at Millsaps College, and Tradition and Criticism in Western Culture at the University of the South. Although stories of these courses are too vast in scope and protean in nature to be chronicled here in detail, some sense of the formative importance of the Search program may be gleaned from looking at what has been done at these seven colleges. In addition, an appendix at the end of the chapter briefly describes the continuing education (Lifelong Learning) version of the Search course at Rhodes and Search-inspired courses at two churches and one secondary school in Memphis.

Christianity and Culture at St. Andrews College

In 1953 the Presbyterian Synod of North Carolina obtained a $50,000 grant from the Ford Foundation to undertake "a careful study both of its educational problems at that time and of its own responsibility in the field of education."[9] That study proposed a major restructuring and consolidation of Presbyterian institutions in central and eastern North Carolina in order to provide college students with "an opportunity for higher education of superior quality, shaped by Christian ideals and values."[10] The synod determined that a new four-year college should be formed by merging some smaller institutions in eastern North Carolina, including Flora Macdonald College and Presbyterian Junior College.[11] As head of the Presbyterian General Assembly's Division of Higher Education, Hunter Blakely supported the synod's decision and helped it to raise money and secure key personnel, including the new college's first president.[12] Supporters of the plan in Scotland County, many of them Presbyterians, raised several million dollars for the college, and the synod acquired eight-hundred acres near Laurinburg for the new campus. Both the physical plant and the curriculum were designed to be integrative: facilities were to be completely accessible to the physically handicapped and the central curriculum for all four years was to be interdisciplinary. The college to be built around these ideals would be called St. Andrews Presbyterian and would open its doors in 1961.[13]

Robert F. Davidson, who was dean of the young college from 1962 to 1971, wrote that from the outset the curriculum was designed to reflect "in meaningful fashion . . . the relationship of the college to the Presbyterian Church."[14] The educational philosophy at St. Andrews was crystallized around an ambitious program of integrated study known as Christianity and Culture. In this "comprehensive four-year program of general education, designed for all students at the college . . . ," Davidson wrote, "the Hebrew-Christian faith would provide the dominant and integrating principle."[15] As Leslie Bullock, the new curriculum's chief architect, put it, Christianity and Culture was designed to be an interdisciplinary program grounded in the idea of "the relevance of Christianity across disciplines and across time."[16]

The broad outlines for the interdisciplinary course of study at St. Andrews were established at a month-long planning conference in the summer of 1957. A Curriculum Conference at Chapel Hill was convened to provide an opportunity for those who were developing St. Andrews to meet with outstanding educators. Jameson M. Jones, who was Rhodes's academic dean, participated. He recalls the excitement of those heady days when a college was in the planning and its mission and goals were consciously linked to team teaching and interdisciplinary study:

I was asked because they were interested in the way things were developed at Southwestern. They also asked Rene Williamson, a political science professor at L.S.U. who was an avowed Christian professor familiar with our program. . . . We would discuss how to formulate the program for this new college [and] whether there ought to be team teaching in these courses. As we formulated the curriculum, our main concern was for general education, principally for the first two years. We also added a topping-off [experience for students], a finishing-off course.[17]

The results of the conference, summarized in the Chapel Hill Report, were submitted to the fledgling college's trustees in 1957 as an experimental "venture in Christian higher education."[18] St. Andrews should be "a Christian college with a new and vital approach to liberal education" and the four-year required curriculum should be integrative in several ways:

> The Christian faith offers distinctive insights for ordering the curriculum, the architecture and the total community life of a college. . . . Human civilization can best be understood as a dialogue between Christ and mankind. . . . The fundamental distinctiveness of a Christian college should be that it is a community where this dialogue has full play. It must be a community which is attuned by design to the voice of God in Christ and also to all matters of human interest and knowledge, including those not yet related to faith. . . . We emphasize the solemn obligation of the college not to distort liberal education in a narrow, shortsighted effort to "prove" Christianity. Religion can better be tested than proved.

According to the report, a major objective of the proposed Christianity and Culture curriculum was to develop in students "certain characteristics, both Christian and liberal," among them "breadth of sympathy and interests," "intellectual discipline and standards," "communication," "physical fitness," "lively and intelligent Christian citizenship," and "capacity for growth."

The trustees of St. Andrews adopted the plan, and Leslie Bullock, a Presbyterian minister and professor of religion at Flora Macdonald, was placed in charge of implementing it. Bullock knew Laurence Kinney and John Osman from his Union Seminary days and had kept up with them across the years. Under Bullock's guidance, the Search course became the principal model for the heart of the Christianity and Culture curriculum. "We looked at a number of programs," Bullock explained, "but we got more inspiration for ours from Southwestern than from any other, in terms of both format and approach. I had tremendous respect for Larry Kinney and all the Southwestern program stood for."[19]

While the new campus was being built in Laurinburg, Bullock began assembling his staff. The first person he asked to join him was Carl D. Bennett, professor of literature at Wesleyan College in Georgia, whom Bullock knew through the Danforth Associates program. Bennett had studied under Ernest C. Colwell, former president of the University of Chicago, in Emory University's Institute of Liberal Arts, a team-taught program based on the great books. Bullock and Bennett spent two years "dreaming and planning and recruiting for this program" as the campus went up around them. In the fall of 1959 they traveled to Memphis, ob-

served the operations of the Search course, and made mental notes about
what they liked and what they wanted to do differently. "Seeing the interdisciplinary program in place at Southwestern was exciting," recalls
Bennett. "We liked what we saw," adds Bullock, "and wanted to do more,
to create an integrated course of study extending over four years, to spend
more time reading primary sources."

The St. Andrews team soon expanded to include Harry Harvin (history) and David Hawk (sociology). Bennett recalls that these were "seasoned professors, ready for new challenges of looking across traditional
disciplines." When St. Andrews opened its doors in the fall of 1961, another seminary-trained Presbyterian, W. M. Alexander (philosophy and
religion) was on board. Together, the five led freshmen through the Old
and New Testaments and Greek and Roman culture. Six more professors
then were hired to staff the second year of the Christianity and Culture
sequence. Two crucial elements in this process, Bullock insists, were the
freedom a new college enjoyed to put together a team of dedicated professors and the continuing assistance of Dean Robert Davidson, who supported the program fully. For ten years, whenever any academic
department at St. Andrews was considering hiring a professor who might
teach in the Christianity and Culture program, Bullock participated in
the interviews. Happily, Bullock and Davidson observed growing student
interest in the program.[20]

Christianity and Culture entailed four years of course work. Students
were expected to take two-fifths of their courses (four semester-long
courses per year) in the program during each of their first two years, plus
two courses their junior year and one course their senior year. The first
two years were loosely based on the Search course. The freshman program emphasized Bible-related materials and their classical cultural setting. According to Davidson, "Unified by the insights of the
Hebrew-Christian faith, the program included a careful study of the great
literature and philosophy of Western civilization. . . . The Bible itself provided the integrating principle in the freshman course."[21] The sophomore
year extended from the Middle Ages to the twentieth century. Junior year
was devoted to non-Western studies and American studies. The non-
Western studies course required special preparation by the faculty, and
Bennett, who coordinated this part of the program, received a Fulbright
Fellowship Grant to study in India. Senior year offered a capstone course,
led by three or four professors, that was designed to pull together the students' college experiences around a salient theme and to prepare them to

face the future. *Learning for Tomorrow,* edited by Alvin Toffler, cited the capstone course as an example of a forward-looking, future-oriented curriculum.[22] In addition, the entire Christianity and Culture program received special mention in the Danforth Foundation's study of curricular developments in American colleges. *Eight Hundred Colleges Face the Future* saluted the four-year initiative at St. Andrews as "a carefully planned sequence of courses" that could serve as a model to other Christian colleges wishing to "help students reach a considered view on basic issues in the light of the Christian Faith."[23]

For a while St. Andrews offered a program in the natural sciences, called Selected Topics in Modern Science (STMS), that was equivalent to its interdisciplinary humanities program. STMS consisted of two courses taken by all students their freshman year. These courses constituted the science requirement for non-science majors and the foundation of science study for science majors. In them "teachers working in teams [were to] present an integrated sequence of mathematics, physics, chemistry and biology" in ways that consciously linked basic scientific issues to societal concerns.[24] Typical course topics included thermodynamics and kinetics, viruses, and nuclear energy and its effects on living systems. The program was coordinated by G. Tyler Miller, who published widely in the field of environmental studies and helped plan the science center at St. Andrews around a 20,000-square-foot laboratory with moveable furnishings, shared by all the sciences. In the early 1980s, after Miller left St. Andrews, the STMS program declined and its physics, chemistry, mathematics, and biology components were subsumed within the curriculum of the interdisciplinary humanities program. In the mid-1990s considerable discussion took place about reestablishing a science program along the lines of STMS, and in December 1994 the faculty approved reinstituting required core courses in interdisciplinary science, provisionally called Science and the Public Interest.

The general education curriculum at St. Andrews has gone through a series of recastings over the years. According to Lawrence E. Schulz, professor of political science and vice president of academic affairs at St. Andrews, the intermediate phase, instituted in 1974 and called St. Andrews Studies, was more skills-oriented than Christianity and Culture, and the version of the program begun in 1981 and still in place in the mid-1990s, called SAGE (St. Andrews General Education), combined interpersonal and communications skills with content of topical interest. A grant from the National Endowment for the Humanities provided summer workshops to train faculty in this newest program, in which entering freshmen take a course (SAGE 105) that emphasizes writing and critical thinking and introduces them to college life through an exploration of the topic The Individual in Community. According to the SAGE program director, philosophy professor Richard C. Prust, this course attempts "to integrate the student into the [college] community by being the advising group, the venue for working on basic communications skills, something of a social home base, a place to disclose oneself personally through journal writing, and an occasion to get intellectually passionate."[25] All sections of the course assign some readings in common, but each section also contains materials and a topic unique to it—a poet teaches poetry writing, a business professor teaches personal finance, a philosopher teaches the philosophy of romantic love, and so on.

After SAGE 105, a three-term World Cultures sequence takes the student through the end of the sophomore year. In the early 1990s the name of this sequence was changed from Christianity and World Cultures (reminiscent of the original name of the program) to World Cultures. Organized around the concept of "texts in context," World Cultures includes segments on the ancient world, the Old and New Testaments, the Renaissance, the Reformation and Counter Reformation, the Enlightenment, and the modern period. Carl Walters, who taught in the Search course at Rhodes before moving to St. Andrews in 1982, notes that SAGE, although much like Search, emphasizes selected cultural epochs, highlighting "essentials of civilizations at their zenith and societal consequences."[26] A one-semester senior capstone course on personal values and global issues completes the SAGE cycle.

SAGE's founders and those who have taught in the program speak of it with great enthusiasm. "It's the way education ought to be done in a Christian college," says Bullock, "allowing Christianity to be studied in relation to other forms of religious and non-religious expression, not in a cubicle by itself." "I love it," says Schulz, who lauds the program for its long-term benefits:

Students come to appreciate it later than faculty do. They say, "Why take Core courses? What value is it?" We bring back grads who are great ambassadors for the program. They tell of how it helped them in their jobs: breadth of knowledge, thinking through issues, constructing arguments, general culture, writing, critical thinking. It's a great endorsement.

Schulz regards the interdisciplinary humanities program as a defining principle of the college, a key to retaining students, and a priority guiding hiring decisions: "We recruit faculty on this basis. They must be comfortable in this program. We don't hire anyone who is not committed to this idea." Alexander adds, "This program is consubstantial with the identity of the college. It is a worthwhile way of educating students in a church-related college of liberal arts and sciences to become creative, intelligent citizens of character, who will play roles in church, community, and nation."

SAGE was described in the 1995–1996 St. Andrews catalogue in these terms: "SAGE is committed to realizing St. Andrews' mission to be a college for the Church. By providing an opportunity for students to attain a degree of biblical literacy at the same time that they cultivate the critical skills needed to reason about that tradition, we hope to avoid both the fanaticism of an anti-intellectual faith and the cynicism of knowledge without faith."[27] Assessing the evolution of the course since its inception, Schulz says that the original focus of Christianity and Culture is still broadly operative: "Religious questions run throughout the program, questions of faith."

Integrated Studies at Austin College
and the Core Program at Eckerd College

In the late 1950s, E. Ashby Johnson adapted the Search course to life at Austin College in Sherman, Texas. A few years later, in the early 1960s he helped institute a similar, more ambitious program at Eckerd College in St. Petersburg, Florida. Johnson had known Laurence Kinney and Leslie Bullock from his seminary days in Richmond and was familiar with their continuing commitment to interdisciplinary learning. After several years in Presbyterian pastorates and four years teaching philosophy at King College in Bristol, Tennessee, Johnson served as chaplain at Austin from 1956 to 1957 and as professor of philosophy and religion from 1957 to 1960. He was named as Austin's director of instruction in 1958. In this role, Johnson obtained a grant from the Ford Foundation to create a course at Austin modeled on the Search course at Rhodes. He also designed the program and assisted Austin's president, John D. Moseley, in securing faculty approval for it.[28]

Johnson enthusiastically admits his personal and programmatic debt to the Search course: "For me and the programs in which I was involved it is clear that Southwestern had the most immediate impact." He explains the personal connections that linked him with Kinney and Osman and fueled his interest in cross-disciplinary learning:

My friendship for Larry Kinney extended back to our Richmond days (1938–1942) and with John Osman even farther (1934). Before either of us became involved in higher education, John got me interested in what was happening at the University of Chicago and St. John's College, Annapolis. I had a number of sessions with Dan Rhodes and with Taylor Reveley at Southwestern. Before I came to try my hand at curriculum shaping at Austin I had picked up from the Man course and the Memphis Adult Education Program a hearty respect for interdisciplinary scholarship, tutorial instruction, and "Great Books" methodology.

Austin's experimental effort "to introduce a synthesis of knowledge and analytical thought" was christened Basic Integrated Studies (BIS).[29] In the fall of 1958 it began modestly, as a one-year pilot program for about a quarter of the entering class. It soon was expanded to two years. The BIS program made use of existing courses when necessary but relied extensively on new team-taught courses and directed study.

Johnson believes that several circumstances made BIS possible at Austin, especially the solid backing of President Moseley and the fact that the venture was initially perceived by faculty, even those who were fiercely committed to their academic departments, as unthreatening because it was presented as "experimental." Moseley pushed BIS, touting it as furthering the "integration of learning." Others associated with the program thought of it as advancing the "interrelatedness of knowledge," or referred to it more prosaically as "The Big Picture."[30]

Basic Integrated Studies embraced the total academic program of the first and second-year students who enrolled in it. Two other innovative aspects of the program were planned but never implemented: a two-year introduction to the natural sciences that would provide the foundation for a major in physics, chemistry, or biology; and a comparable two-year program in linguistic principles that would help students become fluent in specific languages. "The biggest contribution I made," Johnson claims, "was to get out early in the game. The faculty . . . could [then] settle down and salvage what was best in the program."

In 1961 Basic Integrated Studies was renamed Basic Studies and was required of all students. BS, as it was inevitably called, consisted of four semesters integrating history, religion, and philosophy, plus a senior capstone colloquium. During the 1960s the existing faculty gradually adjusted to "the teaching demand of courses in which they were not so much specialists as participants in reading primary materials and asking questions" about them,[31] and more than a dozen new faculty members were added, providing renewed vigor for the program.

Around 1970 the Basic Studies program was renamed Heritage of Western Man; it also was redesigned in an attempt to underscore the relevance of ancient cultures to the present. The program was again renamed Heritage of Western Culture in the mid-1980s in response to growing dissatisfaction with the label *Man*. In 1988 professors and administrators who served on the original planning team were invited back to the college for a special Homecoming convocation celebrating the program's thirtieth anniversary. Ashby Johnson, then at Eckerd College, was honored for his part in creating the courses along with fellow program founders Lee Scott, then at Denison University, and Charles Kennedy, then chair of the religion department at Virginia Polytechnic Institute. Students from the two original experimental groups, also invited back for the event, participated in a special alumni colloquium on the influence of the program on their academic lives, and an alumni breakfast was organized around the theme of "old BS stories."

From the mid-1980s to 1995, the Heritage of Western Culture program consisted of three semester-long phases, which all students took after they completed an interdisciplinary freshman course on critical thinking, communication skills, and information management. The first phase, Roots of Community, was taken during the spring semester of the first year. It focused on Western concepts of community from antiquity to the Renaissance and Reformation. The second phase, taken during the spring semester of the sophomore year, was called Models for Scientific Thought. Taught by faculty members in biology, chemistry, and physics, as well as the humanities and social sciences, this course considered major paradigmatic shifts in science from the seventeenth century through the twentieth century, as illustrated by Newtonian and Einsteinian physics, Darwinism, plate tectonics, and molecular biology. In the third phase, taken during the fall semester of the junior year, professors in the humanities and social sciences led students through an interdisciplinary study of The Individual and Society in the Modern World, that is, from the Enlightenment to the present. These three courses involved both lectures and discussions, and the first and third phases included two-week minicourses in individual professors' areas of interest. By the mid-1990s all phases of the Heritage of Western Culture program were paying increased attention to diverse voices within the Western tradition as well as to non-Western parallels and differences.

Dissatisfaction with the first phase's attempt to crowd too long a chronological span and too many themes into one semester led to substantial changes in 1995. Although continuing to emphasize premodern materials, the faculty approved a number of new team-taught courses with more focused content and less reliance on mass lectures. The three courses, from which each student chose one, were Who Owns the Past? a course concentrating on biblical and classical materials; Love, Power, and Justice, involving readings and issues from the Middle Ages and Renaissance; and Cultural Interactions, an inquiry into the origins and early development of Latin American civilization.[32]

"Our commitment to general education has remained strong, and this interdisciplinary cycle is an essential part of that commitment," reports Academic Dean David W. Jordan, who is responsible for staffing the Heritage program and for coordinating its freshman phase. Jordan adds: "New faculty are hired with this commitment in mind, and career development funding is available to prepare new faculty during the summer to teach in this team venture. [Since the time of] Ashby Johnson, there has been a component on religion and a values dimension in this program, at some level. We believe that an understanding of such considerations is essential to growth, and this program continues to have a central philosophical or religious dimension, encouraging students to examine religious traditions."

In 1960 Ashby Johnson was invited to join the faculty of Eckerd, a new college being established in St. Petersburg, Florida, at which the interdisciplinary humanities program was to be the heart of the curriculum. The president, William Kadel, and the academic dean, John M. Bevan, were recruited by Hunter Blakely through his contacts in the Faculty Christian Fellowship and the Presbyterian Educational Association South. "Hunter Blakely was the spirit behind Florida Presbyterian College," said Bevan. "He sensed that Florida was on the brink of a tremendous population explosion and decided the time was right to create a Presbyterian college there that would grow with the region and would last."[33] To fulfill this vision Blakely involved both the Office of Higher Education of the Southern Presbyterian Church and its counterpart in the Northern

Presbyterian Church, a venture that would serve as a model for cooperation as the two denominations moved toward official merger during the next two decades. For his part, Bevan hired several professors for the new college's interdisciplinary program whom he knew through Faculty Christian Fellowship and allied organizations, among them Keith Irwin in philosophy and religion, Burr Brundage in ancient history, and John Dixon in art history. In 1959, the new faculty came together in St. Petersburg to hammer out the curriculum, with assistance from others who shared their interdisciplinary vision. One of them was Fred Neal, who had recently been invited to join the Search program at Rhodes; another was Robert F. Davidson, who had taught humanities at the University of Florida and was soon to become dean at St. Andrews.[34]

In 1960 Kadel and Bevan invited Johnson to come to Eckerd to direct the Core Program that would be required of all students, including the basic Western Civilization and Its Christian Heritage course and the interdisciplinary senior capstone course on Christianity and contemporary issues. "We were building from the ground up," says Bevan, "assembling a faculty who were coming from different backgrounds to lay out this new program with which they identified personally. . . . We needed someone who could bring people together, who could listen and lead toward consensus." Johnson was that person. "The development of Basic Integrated Studies [at Austin College] was a major factor in my being invited to be a member of the founding faculty of Florida Presbyterian," Johnson recalls. At his suggestion members of the new staff at Eckerd visited Rhodes to observe the Search course. Johnson served as director of Eckerd's Core Program from 1960 to 1968 and continued to teach in it until he retired in 1983.

During his ten years as dean, Bevan based faculty hiring decisions on the expectation for interdisciplinary teaching: "When employed, it was clear professors would participate in this program and not just pursue their specialties. The whole faculty had to be committed to this project." According to Johnson, all of the original faculty embraced the concept enthusiastically, as did most of the newcomers. The time the faculty spent honing the integrated curriculum was, says Johnson, "a uniquely challenging and rewarding experience." Administrators also were involved in interdisciplinary teaching. For example, the capstone course, initially called Christian Faith and Great Issues, was coordinated by the college's chaplain, Alan Carlsten, who came to Eckerd in 1961 from Dartmouth College and modeled the course in part on the Dartmouth Great Issues series. Speakers, including Episcopal bishop James Pike, were brought to campus as part of the program.[35] After Carlsten left, the capstone course assumed different forms under different leaders and eventually came to be known as the Judeo-Christian Perspective course, or JCP. According to Bevan, the interdisciplinary program as a whole served to develop in students a creative "curiosity about religion, and raise the issue of a commitment to a philosophy of life focused on faith."

Interdisciplinary studies became one of the most distinctive features of the Eckerd curriculum. As originally designed, it encompassed three of every student's four years at the college: two courses during each of the first two years plus the senior capstone course. All segments of the Core Program included general lectures and discussion sections of twelve to twenty students. The program involved the faculty and subject matter of the natural and social sciences as well as the humanities.

As the program matured, changes occurred on several fronts. "One of the most important additions to the Core Program was the junior-year Asian Civilization course, added around 1963," says William Wilbur, professor emeritus of history and chronicler of the program at Eckerd. "Bevan had from the outset wanted to bring the Oriental dimension into the program and early on added [three] faculty members who were native Chinese. That program collapsed in the 1970s because of the financial crunch at that time. Now we are . . . trying to restore the Oriental component."[36] In the 1970s, too, the Western civilization course went through what Wilbur described as a major "revision along *gestalt* lines" that deemphasized some of its historical dimension.

Over the years, the Core Program has encountered some hostility from faculty who believe that their academic careers rest on their contributions within their own disciplines. But, Johnson argues, "the continuing experience of scholars being compelled to plan curriculum across disciplinary lines has provided a framework for creative dialogue in spite of these problems." Indeed, the Core Program has produced important scholarly spinoffs. Bevan recalls articles by members of the Eckerd faculty in publications such as the *Christian Scholar* that grew out of their experiences in interdisciplinary teaching.

Two Eckerd alumni who came to Rhodes as professors look back with pleasure on their experiences in the Core Program. Bette Ackerman, a psychologist, remembers being attracted to Eckerd because of the program. "The fact that administrators . . . as well as every professor in the college all taught in this course made me feel part of a community," she recalls. "My first term I was taught by the dean of students, an anthropologist by training, who was personally involved with student adjustment to college living. There was an intense feeling of a common purpose, of belonging. . . . [The Core program] was the vehicle through which the message 'growth and change are good and necessary in living things' was delivered. It was a strong influence in my life."[37] According to chemistry professor Bradford Pendley, the senior Judeo-Christian Perspective course actively incorporated ethical and practical reflections on contemporary issues:

We met three times per week: twice in small discussion groups and once when all the seniors met for a focus lecture. The lecture was normally given by an invited speaker and dealt with issues that we would discuss the next week in our smaller groups, [where we were encouraged] to make strong moral arguments on particular topics. . . . This course challenged me to refine and reexamine my own opinions about a variety of contemporary issues.[38]

Pendley says that the view of education as a team effort that was inspired by the Core Program influenced his decision to come to Rhodes. Both Ackerman and Pendley regard the program as an unusually effective means of unifying knowledge·and bridging the gap between the theoretical and the practical.

In the mid-1990s the Core Program was still going strong.[39] All Eckerd faculty were still teaching in the core, and its director continued to interview all prospective faculty to explain the program and ascertain how they might contribute to it. Every entering student was enrolled in a yearlong course, now called Western Heritage, that covered *Gilgamesh* to Machiavelli in the fall and the Renaissance to the present in the spring, to a rhythm of one lecture and two discussion sessions each week. During their second and third years, students were required to select one course each semester from a series of "perspectives" courses—interdisciplinary efforts, spread throughout the curriculum, dealing with aesthetics, cross-culturalism, environmentalism, and social relations. During the senior year they took the Judeo-Christian Perspective course, which investigates selected contemporary issues. In that course the seniors read materials as diverse as Presbyterian doctrinal statements, papal encyclicals, contemporary fiction, and political speeches. According to Thomas Oberhofer, the director of the Core Program, Eckerd's interdisciplinary curriculum continued to uphold the college's covenental relation with the

Presbyterian church, providing students an opportunity to encounter the Judeo-Christian tradition in such a way that they can accept or reject it, but not ignore it.[40]

Davidson College's Program in Interdisciplinary Humanities

The principal link between the Search course and the Interdisciplinary Humanities program at Davidson was Daniel D. Rhodes, who taught in Search for seven years in the 1950s as the R. A. Webb Professor of Bible and philosophy before accepting an offer in 1960 to establish an expanded version of the course at Davidson. The Presbyterian-affiliated liberal arts college near Charlotte, North Carolina, had much in common with Rhodes College, and its administration was prepared to introduce a two-year interdisciplinary program similar to the Search course, but larger in scope.[41] In the late 1950s, Dean of the Faculty Frontis W. Johnston had attended professional meetings dealing with innovations in humanities programs and had observed the Search course while visiting the Rhodes campus. Supporting the idea of an interdisciplinary program at Davidson, Johnston agreed to help launch and staff one. The college's president, D. Grier Martin, promised all necessary start-up moneys, provided the faculty approved the venture.[42]

According to Rhodes, the terms of his employment at Davidson were tied to these plans. He was hired for the interdisciplinary position of professor of philosophy and religion with the explicit understanding that he would help expand the curriculum within the Bible and religion department and also would lay the foundation for a two-year interdisciplinary humanities program.

Upon moving to Davidson in 1960, Rhodes addressed both challenges. He found the second to be by far the more daunting. The interdisciplinary enterprise had to be approved by the faculty as a whole and the first year of the program had to be planned and fully staffed, all in a relatively short time. The process of recruiting faculty members from appropriate departments and of convincing the rest of the faculty to support the program was laborious and sometimes discouraging. Among the most common complaints of faculty opponents were that such an enterprise would distract faculty members from departmental responsibilities, that it would be a hodgepodge of superficial information, that it would skim off the best students, that it would divert too much time from students' majors, and that scheduling for the program, which was designed to meet every day of the six-day class week, would disrupt the rest of the curriculum. These objections, along with related issues concerning graduation requirements and departmental staffing needs, had to be acknowledged, confronted, and laid to rest before the faculty's approval could be obtained. Looking back on that demanding and sometimes rocky initiatory phase, Rhodes recalls:

In the winter of 1960-61, the Dean and I talked with individual faculty members, asking whether they would be interested in participating in such a program. The result for the first-year program: 1 professor from classics; 1 from history; 1.5 each from philosophy and from religion. The Dean would make sure that we had an appropriate professor in literature, and we would be free to invite professors of art and music to give some lectures. This was what we needed.

Finally, in the spring of 1961, after hearing, as Rhodes put it, "a report that was as specific as possible but still general," the faculty allowed the project to proceed. The motion to create the Interdisciplinary Humanities program, to be known as The Western Tradition, passed by a very slim margin.[43]

Philosophy professor Daniel Rhodes, surrounded by students at his birthday party.

The cluster of professors committed to the new program at Davidson—including Rhodes and Max Polley in religion, George Abernathy
in philosophy, George Labban in classics, J. A. McGeachy in history, and
Richard C. Cole, who was brought to Davidson as professor of English
for the express purpose of helping to develop the program—met frequently during the next year. They discussed the purposes to be realized
and the methods to achieve them, then drew up a syllabus that specified
reading assignments, study questions, testing strategies, term paper topics,
and all the other elements of the twelve-credit, first-year course that was
to be inaugurated in the fall of 1962. In doing so they consulted with colleagues who were formulating the Christianity and Culture program at
St. Andrews and the Core Program at Eckerd.[44]

Rhodes laughingly recalls the staff's enthusiasm and its oversized expectations for the course work that students in the program could handle:

During the summer of '62, when the first-year faculty was trying desperately to
bring a syllabus into final form, we thought we should spot-check the reading
assignments that we expected freshmen to master overnight. We had agreed that
two hours of preparation could be legitimately required. So for about two weeks
I picked out specific assignments and asked all Humanities faculty members to
read a given assignment and report back the next day. The results were even more
dramatic than we anticipated. Suddenly a considerable amount of "essential" material was declared deletable. In light of this, we went through the whole syllabus
judiciously using a paring knife. Even so, at the end of the first year we had to
revise the syllabus again in light of some remaining unrealistic expectations.

The Davidson faculty had determined that the humanities program
would satisfy graduation requirements in each area of the curriculum except mathematics and science. Students would receive twenty-four credit hours for the complete program, nearly one-fourth of the hours
required for graduation. The highest academic space on campus, the
Dome Room of the Chambers building, was renovated to accommodate
the lectures for the program. Ninety-six of the roughly 250 entering students enrolled in the first-year course in the fall of 1962. Interdisciplinary
Humanities at Davidson had begun.

The entire Western Tradition program was based on the presupposi-
tion "that synthesis can and should accompany analysis, even at the freshman and sophomore levels; that the past, present, and future are
inextricably intertwined; and that the life and achievements of Western

man can and should be seen in meaningful patterns."[45] The first-year course was divided into units on prehistory and ancient Near Eastern civilizations, the Hebrews and the Old Testament, the Greeks, the Romans and the New Testament, and medieval Europe. The Hebrew unit focused "upon the people who gave the West the Old Testament, in which God is revealed as Lord of human history." The unit entitled The Roman Period and Christian Beginnings was intended to demonstrate "how the Romans were indebted to the Greeks and the Christians to the Jews; how the Romans developed the arts of war and peace, government and law; how the Christian Church emerged from Judaism and proclaimed its faith in Christ as Savior." The Medieval unit portrayed the period's "serious attempt to synthesize the Greco-Roman and the Judeo-Christian traditions into a Christian Europe."

The second-year team—Malcolm Lester and Bradley Thompson in history, Samuel Maloney in religion, Frank Bliss in English, Philip Secor in political science, and Earl MacCormac in philosophy—followed a similar plan of action in proposing its first offering in the fall of 1963. The second year began with the Renaissance and Reformation and continued to the present. It was easier to recruit professors to teach in the second-year program than the first. As time went on and Western Tradition proved its worth, others joined the ranks and new professors were hired with the understanding that a portion of their teaching would be in the humanities program.

Thus the Interdisciplinary Humanities program at Davidson—nicknamed "Humes"—took shape, partially on the Rhodes College model. "My experience in interdepartmental work began at Southwestern," Daniel Rhodes acknowledges. "The approach taken at Davidson was similar: historical, interdisciplinary, and Western with general lectures and small discussion groups. [But] I had wanted a more fully developed program than the one year [and twelve credit hours] we had at Southwestern."

The pace was intense in Humes: six days per week, 180 class meetings per year. Half the sessions were mass lectures, half were discussion circles of sixteen. The first year was particularly demanding. Polley recalls that the staff spent an hour or two every afternoon discussing how best to present the materials the following day. Participating professors found the pace taxing to the point of physical exhaustion. Yet all of the original staff members remained with the program, providing it with a needed sense of stability and even a certain mythos. They viewed themselves as pioneers in an endeavor that was draining but ultimately rewarding.[46]

Rhodes, who served as chair of the first-year humanities course from 1962 to 1980 and continued to teach in it until he retired in 1984, took particular delight in the teamwork inspired by the humanities program in its early days and in meeting objections from critical or even hostile colleagues who were not teaching in the course:

In its early years the program took a good bit of criticism from some members of the science faculty who objected that it was too broad or that it would take time and effort away from one's major. But things quieted down when sometime in the 1970s the chairman of the Physics Department, who also chaired a faculty committee concerned with student academic achievement, announced in a faculty meeting that students who took Humanities earned higher scores on GRE's than those who did not.

Gains from the Interdisciplinary Humanities program may be measured in terms of personal growth as well as in test results. Students rose to the challenge of Humes as best they could, and the program inspired a sense of camaraderie among many of them. "It was a common experience for freshmen, working through it together," says Polley, who describes a group of six students who struggled through the humanities program in its early years and who, after graduating, gathered each summer with their families to meet and discuss texts from the syllabus: "The six, who called themselves 'The Survivors,' had studied together, suffered together, and grown together through this course, and they wanted to perpetuate the sense of accomplishment that had come out of that experience; these summer reunions continued for years."

Faculty in the program were challenged to grow in similar ways. Soon after the program began, Davidson received a grant from the Duke Endowment to permit staff members to travel abroad to enhance their preparation for teaching in it. "It was a wonderful boon that enriched our teaching" says Polley, who used a Duke grant to travel with his family to course-related sites in France, Italy, Greece, and Yugoslavia. "It brought the course content to life for me and anchored it in geographical and social reality. I took slides that I showed in class, and came to appreciate associations among the sites and the periods we studied."

The Interdisciplinary Humanities program has seen many changes over the decades, some due to calendar revisions, others because of pedagogical shifts. In 1968 Davidson changed from a two-semester to a three-term calendar, and Humes became a six-course rather than an eight-course program. Content was "squeezed" and some historical and religious materials were reduced or eliminated. In 1988 the college returned to the semester system, and the humanities program was reduced to a five-course sequence, forcing additional cuts in historical and religious materials. The college's reduction in graduation requirements, from thirty-six courses in the 1960s to thirty-two courses in the 1990s, explains some of the changes, as do alterations in distribution requirements. Other changes in the program reflected shifting academic predilections. For example, the first semester of the first year was redefined as The Classical World, while the second semester was recast as The Judeo-Christian Tradition and the Medieval World. In this reorganization, says Polley with a note of regret, "Athens was indeed separated from Jerusalem."[47]

In 1992, Davidson's humanities program entered its third decade under the leadership of political science and humanities professor Brian J. Shaw. Still known as The Western Tradition, the multi-course interdisciplinary cycle remained a distinctive feature of a Davidson education, satisfying graduation requirements in religion, philosophy, history, literature, and English composition. Its major problem, according to Shaw, has been staffing. "At the present time, academe does not reward interdisciplinary endeavors," he laments.[48] "This kind of teaching is so time consuming," adds Polley, "that it may leave little time for scholarly publication or for advancing in one's discipline. It's tough on younger colleagues who sometimes discover that teaching in this kind of program doesn't help get tenure or help get jobs elsewhere." Physics professor Robert Manning, who has taught in the program since 1971 and was formerly its coordinator, comments, "It's often best to recruit newly tenured faculty for this course since it is increasingly difficult to find younger faculty who are willing and able to participate." For those who do teach in Interdisciplinary Humanities, Manning adds, "This is the best faculty development program there is. It provides a chance to be with other faculty members I'd never see otherwise, and I grow all the time."[49]

Looking to the future of the humanities program, Shaw foresees more sensitivity to women's issues and women writers. Manning anticipates an increased use of computerized learning exercises to assure students a strong sense of historical perspective. In 1995 Manning was named the college's first distinguished professor of humanities. An astronomer who uses examples drawn from history and art in his science lectures, he speaks with enthusiasm about adding a new emphasis to the humanities program during the next two years through a series of lectures on "cosmology," which he defines as "any civilization's attempt to understand its purpose by understanding nature."

Just as Rhodes College inspired Davidson College to inaugurate its Interdisciplinary Humanities program, so has Davidson returned the favor. Robert Llewellyn, a Rhodes philosophy professor who has helped to coordinate the Search course since the mid-1980s, took courses from Daniel Rhodes as an undergraduate at Davidson and was intrigued by the idea of interdisciplinary humanities: "I very much wanted to be a part of the program at Rhodes—for my own education." Donald Tucker, who has taught in the Search course since 1971, was formerly a professor of Spanish at Davidson, where he was invited to teach in the humanities program. Although he was prevented from doing so by his departmental responsibilities, his acquaintance with Daniel Rhodes and with the Davidson program led him to become involved in Search. French professor James Vest, another Davidson alumnus associated with the Search course, had Rhodes as a colloquium leader as a first-semester freshman. "The Humanities program attracted me to Davidson and stimulated my thinking through half my time there," says Vest. "It had a profound effect on the way I see the world, the way I view learning as a cooperative venture. I'm glad to be continuing that tradition with my students."

Hampden-Sydney College's
Interdisciplinary Humanities Program

Hampden-Sydney College, an all-male Presbyterian-affiliated institution in Virginia, instituted an interdisciplinary humanities program in 1967. When first created, it was called Humanities; one year later the name was changed to Western Man, then in 1991 to Humanities: Western Tradition. According to professors John Brinkley, Hassell Simpson, and Owen L. Norment, who were involved in the program at its inception, the idea for the course was brought to Hampden-Sydney by W. Taylor Reveley, a Presbyterian minister with a Ph.D. from Duke University who had taught in the Search course at Rhodes from 1956 until 1963, when he left to become the president of Hampden-Sydney.[50] Brinkley, himself an Episcopalian, emphasizes the significance of Presbyterian teaching-clergy in the formation of Hampden-Sydney's Humanities program and the importance of the Search course as a model for it: "Presbyterian ministers who were trained in their academic disciplines were a driving force for establishing this interdisciplinary approach in lieu of existing requirements. We looked at the programs at Southwestern and at Davidson, but it was the Southwestern syllabus that had the most influence on our program."

The new Humanities initiative, approved by the faculty in 1965, was put in place in the fall of 1967 and was required of all entering students. The first year was a ten credit-hour double course that covered the period prior to the Renaissance; the six-hour, second-year component brought the students up to the present.

From the outset, according to Brinkley and Norment, the greatest problem the course had was recruiting faculty. Within a few years, sentiment for discipline-based requirements resurfaced among faculty and students. In the early 1970s, a separate composition course for entering students was reinstituted. At about the same time the first-year Humanities sequence was made optional, allowing students to choose between it and a two-term Western civilization sequence offered by the history department. The second year of the Humanities program disappeared altogether, and the first-year course was reduced from five to three days a week, with a corresponding reduction in credit hours. Chronologically, the course now ended with John Milton.

In the mid-1990s, the first year of Humanities: Western Tradition was still in place at Hampden-Sydney, with approximately 40 percent of all entering students electing to take it. The number of lectures was reduced to two (both on art history) each term; all the other class meetings were in discussion groups of up to eighteen students taught primarily by faculty from classics, religion, philosophy, and English. An effort was made in 1994 to reinstitute the second-year component when Dean of the Faculty J. Scott Colley offered a prototype interdisciplinary course called Modernity. This experiment proved successful and has rekindled interest in the Humanities program among students and faculty alike. "The interdisciplinary initiative currently enjoys strong administrative support," says Norment, who hopes that the Modernity course will become a staple for future years, thus partially filling the gap left by the loss of the second year of the program.

At the outset, the Humanities program at Hampden-Sydney was primarily theological and philosophical in focus. The Christian component has remained prominent, according to Norment and Brinkley, as has the emphasis on primary texts from the classical tradition. Students read portions of the Old and New Testaments, Augustine, Aquinas, Dante, Luther, and Calvin, as well as Homer, Virgil, Plato, Aristotle, and the Greek tragedians. "This program gives students an overview of really crucial foundational documents, ideas, and people in the Western tradition: who we are and where we come from," says Norment. "We can't understand ourselves or our world without it." He adds there has been considerable discussion about instituting a non-Western component in the course.

Humanities program director Patrick Wilson, who taught in a great books program at Notre Dame before coming to Hampden-Sydney, would like to see a second-year course that includes more treatment of science, political theory, and perhaps Eastern traditions. "I'm dead set on this program," Wilson commented.

Students are engaged in active learning at an early stage in their college careers. They have to grapple with their own views about issues of ethics, religion, heroism [as they encounter] readings that have captured the imaginations of students for hundreds, even thousands, of years, readings that deal with the central issues of human nature. They will take what they learn with them through life. Students see relationships between fields of study that they don't encounter in other courses. Faculty benefit in having regular discussions with people outside their discipline in staff meetings and in insights gleaned from rereading these texts.

Millsaps College and the Heritage Program

In the mid-1960s, shortly after becoming academic dean at Millsaps, history professor Frank Laney asked the faculty of the Methodist-affiliated liberal arts college in Jackson, Mississippi, to undertake a comprehensive review of the curriculum. A subcommittee on "Innovative Programs" chaired by English professor Robert H. Padgett, and another on "Traditional Programs" chaired by Magnolia Coullet, professor of ancient languages, collected materials from schools all over the country, including information on Rhodes's Search course, then two decades old. The two subcommittees cooperated in bringing to the faculty a proposal for a four-course interdisciplinary program that would provide students with an alternate way of satisfying core curriculum requirements. The courses were:

1. a course for entering students, first called Man and Western Civilization and Culture but ultimately named The Heritage Program, that would fulfill many of Millsaps's traditional literature, history, religion, philosophy, and fine arts requirements;

2. an interdisciplinary science course for non-science majors;
3. a non-Western Studies course to complement the Western emphasis of the Heritage course;
4. a senior capstone course focused on twentieth-century issues.

Most of the proposed courses were conceived as year-long efforts bearing six to fourteen credit hours. For financial reasons, each course was developed independently by different faculty teams. The Heritage Program progressed most rapidly, partly because many of Millsaps's younger faculty were eager for educational innovation and cross-disciplinary learning, but also because it was presented to the faculty at large as an option not required of all students.[51]

After securing faculty approval, Laney acquired a grant from the Danforth Foundation to begin developing the Heritage Program. Among the Millsaps professors who were intimately involved in establishing the program were religion professor T. W. Lewis, who subsequently taught in it for nearly thirty years, Lee Reiff, also from religion, Madeleine McMullan from history, Bob Bergmark and Michael Mitias from philosophy, Bill Rowell from art, Jonathan Sweat from music, and English professor Padgett, who served as the program's director from its beginning in 1966 to 1975 and taught in it until 1992. Padgett's keen interest in music and the fine arts helped shape the special character of the program.

The Heritage Program was implemented as an alternative to traditional disciplinary requirements in history, religion, philosophy, fine arts, and English. The program consisted of two courses, each extending across two semesters: the Cultural Heritage of the West (fourteen credit hours) and English Literature and Composition (four credit hours). Together, the courses constituted 60 percent of a student's normal first-year course load. Students met in both large lectures and discussion groups of fifteen or fewer. Integrated into the program were a number of theatrical, artistic, and musical events. The Cultural Heritage of the West satisfied half of the college's six-hour requirement in religion because the Judeo-Christian tradition, viewed in historical perspective, was a prominent feature of the course.

From the beginning, lectures and laboratory experiences in music, art, and theater were integral parts of the Heritage Program. A three-year federal grant, awarded in 1967 under Title III of the Higher Education Act, allowed special "co-curricular" artistic performances, open to the entire community, to be part of the program. Students were required to attend the performances and were encouraged to incorporate them into their compositions and class discussions. The performers included sitarist Ashish Khan, the Guarneri String Quartet, the New York Pro Musica, and the Beaux Arts Trio. The program's cultural impetus even took it to surrounding states: for example, one field trip brought students to Memphis in 1970 to hear Joan Sutherland and Marilyn Horne in the Metropolitan Opera touring production of Bellini's *Norma*.

A unique role in the formation of the Heritage Program was played by Tom Jolly, a professor of ancient languages at Millsaps who had taken the Search course when he was a student at Rhodes in the late 1940s. Although Jolly left Millsaps in 1965 to join the classics department at his alma mater, he stayed in close contact with the emerging Heritage Program and proved a valuable resource, supplying the planning committee with syllabi and other information about the structure and operations of the Search course and advising it on Greco-Roman culture. Jolly also was influential in developing the Heritage Program's artistic component, taking his inspiration from the artistic and musical interests that John Henry Davis had brought to the early years of the Search course and lending his personal expertise concerning music and sound systems to assist in the selection of recordings and equipment for the "art and music lab" component of the Millsaps program.

Under Padgett's leadership, the Heritage courses also met the college's freshman English composition requirement in new and experimental ways. The original intent was "to augment the student's analysis and appreciation of major works of our western literary heritage and to develop . . . skills in written and spoken expression through frequent writing assignments and class discussion."[52] According to Padgett, we "had read enough 'My Summer Vacation' themes and argument themes based on pure assertion without adequate support from experience or research. I thought that by giving them the *Iliad* or *Oedipus Rex* or Dante's *Inferno* to write about they could be more productive."[53] One writing assignment required studying the Greek myth of Orpheus in Cultural Heritage and Tennessee Williams's *Orpheus Descending* in English composition, then seeing a campus production of the Williams play. This approach occasionally had its problems, Padgett admits, "but I do think the students wrote better overall from having something worthwhile to write about."

Over the years, the Heritage Program expanded, enrolling more students and addressing new concerns. In 1976 the college received a grant

from the Phil Hardin Foundation to support a full-time program director. Richard Freis, who held that position from the mid-1970s until 1991,
brought a philosophic vision and thematic coherence to the program.
Freis assembled a team of young professors to take Heritage into the late
1970s and through the 1980s—Charles Sallis, history; Steve Smith, philosophy; Elise Smith, art history; Leroy Percy and Richard Mallette, English. Mallette later alternated with Freis as director and helped to
strengthen the art labs and tighten the focus of the discussion sections.

Since the late 1980s, the Heritage Program has expanded topically to
include postmodernism, feminism, and multiculturalism. In addition,
three more courses have developed from the program's founding vision.
The interdisciplinary science course was finally inaugurated during the
1980s, and Nonwestern Studies was included in a 1992 curriculum revision. The senior capstone course in twentieth-century issues was in ges-
tation at the time of this writing.

In 1995, the Heritage Program at Millsaps enrolled 120 of approximately 330 entering students in discussion groups of fourteen or fifteen
each. It was a double course for freshmen offering an interdisciplinary alternative to four core requirements in the humanities, covering the ancient, premodern, modern, and contemporary periods. According to the
program's director, historian David Davis:

The Heritage course preserves a Western focus within world perspectives. In an
effort to answer the question "What is Western civilization?" students are exposed to differing perspectives—including Southwest Asia, China, India, and
Africa—to challenge them to explore what is shaping Western culture. At appropriate points, materials on Islam, Hinduism, and Taoism are introduced. Africa
is studied from the standpoint of how things were there before and after contact
with European colonizers and in light of Chinese exploration of East Africa.[54]

Recruiting faculty for the Heritage Program is not hard, Davis explains, in part because the Millsaps administration is highly supportive and
also because the departments of philosophy, English, religion, history, art,
and classics are committed to supplying faculty on a rotating basis. "Those
who teach it want to," says Davis. "For first-year faculty, it's great. They
get to know other faculty and students. It's a learning field: they see how
art and literature and music fit in with their own professional interests."
Because faculty members rotate through the program on a three-year

cycle, there is less of a sense that teaching in it keeps them away from their disciplines. Some have discovered enriching new perspectives on their disciplinary research through teaching in the program.

"Tradition and Criticism in Western Culture" at the University of the South

As recently as 1992 a two-year program of similar character to the Search course was inaugurated at the University of the South in Sewanee, Tennessee, an institution closely related to twenty-eight dioceses of the Episcopal Church. Sewanee's chronologically organized interdisciplinary sequence, known as Tradition and Criticism in Western Culture, was designed for the four semesters of a student's freshmen and sophomore years. It was not required, but instead offered an optional way for students to fulfill several requirements in English, history, the arts, and philosophy and religion. History professor W. Brown Patterson, a member of the program's teaching staff and, as dean of the college, instrumental in its inception, explained that the university was "trying to provide the kind of program which Rhodes College has long offered" but one uniquely tailored to Sewanee's particular needs and to the strengths and interests of its humanities faculty.[55]

The Tradition and Criticism program grew out of a thorough revision of the curriculum that was approved by the faculty in May 1990. This revision included a call to explore "the possibility of an interdisciplinary program for freshmen and sophomores in the humanities . . . [which] would incorporate classic texts from western civilization and encourage the discussion of important ideas and themes from the past in relation to modern political, social, moral, and cultural problems."[56] A seven-person planning group was created by Dean Patterson to implement the proposal. Under the leadership of philosophy professor James F. Peterman, the group examined interdisciplinary humanities programs at Rhodes, Columbia, Davidson, Earlham, Millsaps, and Occidental.

The planning group's report recommended creating a program that would examine "important works of the Western tradition in their historical context" in four successive courses, designated as the Ancient World, the Medieval World, the Early Modern World: Renaissance to Revolution, and the Modern World: Romantic to Post-Modern. Each course would have its own team of four faculty members drawn from seven departments: English, fine arts, history, music, philosophy, religion, and theater. Lectures in each course would be given to all of the students in common (around eighty), and discussions would be held in sections of no more than twenty students. Upon completing the program students would receive credit for general degree requirements in the areas of philosophy and religion, literature, history, and the arts.

This proposal was adopted by the faculty in the spring of 1991. A detailed course description and reading list were constituted at a three-week seminar that summer and finalized during the next academic year. Pamela Royston Macfie, a member of the English department, was appointed director of the program and William S. Bonds of the classical languages department was appointed associate director. The name, Tradition and Criticism in Western Culture, was chosen to show that Western culture has been marked by diversity and conflict from the beginning.[57] Although the primary emphasis remained on the Western tradition, the plan was "to include discussions of nonwestern influences on Western culture and of recent philosophical and social scientific debates about the ways in which the Western tradition sometimes misrepresents its own character as well as the character of nonwestern traditions."[58] Tradition and Criticism was approved in 1992 for a three-year trial period. Its first-year sequence was launched in 1992–1993 and the second-year sequence began in 1993–1994.

In addition to important texts, which are read in their entirety whenever possible, the program stressed historical events and artistic creations of established cultural significance, "monuments" that have shaped and reshaped Western civilization. First year students read Genesis, Exodus, *Antigone*, the *Republic*, the *Aeneid*, selected letters of Paul, the Gospel of John, Augustine's *Confessions*, Bede's *Ecclesiastical History*, *Beowulf*, the letters of Abelard and Eloise, and Dante's *Inferno*. The second-year syllabus included works by Pico, More, Luther, Shakespeare, Descartes, Milton, Voltaire, Rousseau, Dickens, Marx and Engels, Nietzsche, Freud, Eliot, and Fitzgerald. Each reading was to be studied for its aesthetic and argumentative structure, its vision of the world, and the interplay of text and context. A distinctive feature of the program was its special attention to the arts, including ancient architecture and sculpture, the art of the early Christian empire, pilgrimage churches, Giotto, Masaccio, Leonardo, Michelangelo, Rembrandt, Romanticism, Impressionism, and modern and postmodern works. Musical components included Handel's *Messiah*, Mozart's *Don Giovanni*, Beethoven's Ninth Symphony, and Wagner's *Tristan and Isolde* .

A strong emphasis on writing lay at the core of the new enterprise. During the first two years of Tradition and Criticism's existence, students would write analytical or interpretive essays appropriate to each of the four principal curricular areas represented in the program: philosophy and religion, literature, history, and the arts. Students were required to bring initial drafts of their essays to writing workshops directed by the faculty. In 1994 writing assignments became more interdisciplinary in nature, such as comparing spatial representations in Dante with those in medieval churches or drawing analogies between literary images in *The Great Gatsby* and motifs in Wagnerian opera. Through the summer workshops staff members continued to revise the content of the course as well as their expectations for student essays, with an eye to improving specific aspects of writing. English professor William E. Clarkson authored a pamphlet called "Preparing Essays for Humanities Classes" that was used as a guidebook in the program and at other colleges as well, including Rhodes.

As an expression of its status as an Episcopal university, the Tradition and Criticism program paid special attention to the Judeo-Christian tradition in all four semesters. Although no specifically Anglican texts were assigned, the program emphasized the Old and New Testaments and the spread of Christianity, medieval theology and religious literature, Protestant and Catholic Reformations, the idea of God in seventeenth-century philosophy, the evangelical revival of the eighteenth century, and nineteenth- and twentieth-century challenges to traditional Christian beliefs. The Judeo-Christian tradition was treated historically rather than dogmatically, and the "monuments" studied were used to demonstrate the inclusive and multifaceted nature of Christian faith and practice.

During the three-year trial period, a series of evaluations was conducted and several problems were identified. These ranged from malfunctioning equipment to staffing difficulties to students' complaints that the connections between disciplines were hard to grasp, the readings too demanding, and the improvement in their writing not as dramatic as expected. Even so, the overall sentiment was positive enough for Director Macfie to recommend continuing the program on the grounds that it "emphasizes the subjects, texts, and values that have traditionally been at the center of our undergraduate curriculum . . . in a focused and coherent way, and, ultimately, it challenges students to define the relevance of our curriculum to contemporary issues and controversies."[59] The faculty approved the Tradition and Criticism program unanimously in December 1994 and the administration committed itself to insuring adequate staffing and technical support, as well as additional assistance for the summer workshops.

Conclusion

The Search-influenced programs at St. Andrews, Austin, Eckerd, Davidson, Hampden-Sydney, Millsaps, and the University of the South represent a variety of interdisciplinary endeavors spanning several decades. Yet some common threads link them. Several of the programs originated in the postwar ethos, in which the challenge of responding to totalitarian ideologies soon merged with a sense of expansive confidence. The idea of trying something new became adequate incentive for reform, especially when it conformed to a sense of essential educational mission. New ideas about teaching and learning made sense in the era that created colleges such as Eckerd and St. Andrews, brought John F. Kennedy to the White House, and gave impulse to Vatican II. The sense of a new beginning, a conviction that all things converge, and a feeling that "we can do anything" spawned innovative approaches to matters as mundane as fulfilling academic requirements and as heady as restructuring learning and teaching to meet the demands of a new era.[60]

For church-related colleges the impetus to innovate went beyond the traditional thrust of general education. Such colleges were especially concerned with exploring the relationship between religion and academic study. As one professor in the Search course saw it, here was a grand opportunity to develop the person, not in the context of a limiting academic specialty, but for the full expression of each individual's God-given potential.[61]

The period from the mid-1960s to the mid-1990s brought challenges radically different from those in the previous two decades. Technological advances, the spread of specialization and individualism, the war in Vietnam, political scandals, and assassinations of prominent leaders of the "can-do" generation brought a tumultuous end to the postwar optimism. Student unrest in the 1960s and 1970s paralleled and sometimes spawned intellectual upheavals within the academy. New intellectual movements, such as semiotics, deconstructionism, liberation theology, feminism, and multiculturalism, challenged the curricula of interdisciplinary humanities programs, as did emerging new cross-disciplinary fields grounded mainly in the social sciences and fine arts, including women's studies, American studies, urban studies, and film studies. These challenges were particularly felt by programs committed to the Judeo-Christian heritage, as that tradition increasingly came under suspicion and attack for perceived hegemonistic, androcentric biases.

The 1960s and 1970s also took a toll on the organizations that had had the greatest influence on the founding of most of the interdisciplinary programs chronicled in this chapter. In 1963 the Presbyterian Education Association South went out of existence after a half-century of service to integrated studies. The Danforth Associates program suffered a similar fate: in the early 1970s annual meetings became biennial, then were phased out altogether in the early 1980s. In 1968 the *Christian Scholar*, which had given voice to the interdisciplinary humanities movement in church-related colleges, changed its name to *Soundings*, reflecting more secular times. In the mid-1980s higher education itself came under ideological attack from several sides, and disciplinary demands reasserted themselves, creating staffing difficulties for interdisciplinary programs.

Taken together, these forces account in large measure for the reduction in the place that interdisciplinary humanities courses have occupied in curricula since the 1960s. Many such programs began on a grander scale than the twelve-hour requirement at Rhodes. Austin College's Basic Integrated Studies represented a total two-year involvement for some 25 percent of entering students. Eckerd created double courses for each of the first two years of study and single courses for the final two years. The program at St. Andrews also encompassed all four years. Davidson offered a double course spanning two years, and Millsaps projected a four-year program, with one year devoted to science. In general, depending on the college, these courses occupied 20 to 50 percent of the students' total academic experience, compared with around 10 percent at Rhodes.

In every case except Rhodes, however, the size of these programs has been reduced. Eckerd's Core Program, as of the mid-1990s, entails one course during the first year, plus one course per semester for the next two years and one course during the senior year. Davidson's four-semester program consists of four single courses. At Hampden-Sydney, where the second year of the program was phased out entirely for a time, a single topical second-year course reemerged in the mid-1990s. At Millsaps the Heritage courses constitute a double-course load spread over two semesters. The St. Andrews program now involves five semester-long courses. Search, meanwhile, continues as a twelve-hour sequence, for reasons that are explored in chapters 3 and 4.

In view of, on the one hand, continuing trends toward disciplinary demands and specialization and, on the other, forceful intellectual and popular challenges, one may wonder how labor-intensive interdisciplinary courses such as those at Rhodes and elsewhere have survived at all, or how similar programs could be attempted or even contemplated in the future. A partial answer may be found in this chapter. In most cases significant accommodations have been made to new trends in terms of course scope and content. Most of the interdisciplinary humanities programs have been reduced so as to be a less preponderant part of the student's education. In every instance the courses have been revised or reconceived to include previously underrepresented perspectives. The name changes across the decades, moving away from titles such as Man and Christianity and Culture to more neutral cognomens such as Search and Tradition and Criticism, also reflect these trends.

Yet more than mere compromise has been at work. Perhaps because they are so firmly grounded in diversity, interdisciplinary humanities programs have proven resilient, flexible, and able to incorporate concerns for other cultures, for the fine arts, and for developments in the natural and social sciences. Perhaps because of what they are—team-taught, collaborative ventures whose nature is to include rather than exclude—these courses have indeed managed to "weather the storms of curricular confusion and the cacophony of views about teaching."[62] Their integrated approach to learning about the self and the world has helped them not only to adjust and endure but, in most cases, to thrive. Thus the tradition of a holistic, values-centered investigation of the humanities, as a way of facing the future, has persisted in varied and modulated forms for a half-century and found some of its most innovative expressions in the interdisciplinary curricula derived from the Search course at Rhodes College.[63]

Appendix:
Offspring of the Search Course in Memphis

The Search course and Rhodes's adult education program began at the same time, largely through the efforts of the same person: John Osman. One of the undergraduate course's founders, Osman inaugurated the college's Division of Adult Education in September 1944. The purpose of this division was to help "mature men and women orient themselves to the changing situation of our civilization" and "become fitted for more useful service in business, industry, and church."[64] Integrated humanities was an essential part of that experience: serving as "the unifying principle in the course of study, it gives the Division of Adult Education an integrating center to its program, and makes for unity and direction in the intellectual experience of the student."

A cross-disciplinary lecture course called The Great Centuries was one of the offerings when the new adult education division opened its doors in September 1944. In 1945–1946, Osman and Laurence Kinney taught a discussion course called The Great Tradition. The next year Osman initiated a full-blown great books course entitled Freedom and the Books: A New Education for Adults. That program continued for many years. "Osman and his colleagues set an intellectual standard that attracted an impressive array of community leaders," comments Sally Thomason, director of Special Studies at Rhodes from 1985 to 1995. "Among them were Ed Meeman, editor of Memphis's evening newspaper, the *Press-Scimitar*, and Edmund Orgill, future mayor of Memphis."[65] With the help of a grant from the Ford Foundation in 1953, the adult education division became a training center for discussion leaders in great books programs throughout the Mid-South. Leaders of more than six hundred great books discussion groups were trained through the division.

In 1954 Granville Davis was hired as executive director of the renamed Memphis Adult Education Center at Rhodes. As director (and later dean of continuing education) and as chair of the college's history department until his retirement in 1980, Davis developed his deep interest in interdisciplinary learning. Throughout his time at the college, he served as a member of the Search course staff and was a mentor to many younger faculty members who were beginning to teach in that program. Conversely, the educational objectives of the Search course influenced Davis's perspective on continuing education for adults.

In 1976, in response to public interest, the Search course became a bona fide offering of Continuing Education, under the leadership of Fred Neal. It was offered in the evening, taught by regular members of the Rhodes faculty, and spread over a four-year cycle with a comprehensive syllabus of readings. Many alumni who had taken the course as undergraduates enrolled in the evening version, bringing to it a deep appreciation of interdisciplinary learning based on personal experience.

The evening program continued until 1985, when the entire continuing education division was reorganized. The division, now called the Meeman Center for Lifelong Learning, charted new courses under the leadership of Sally Thomason. The Search course began a four-year cycle in 1986. Robert Watson, who held advanced degrees in history and theology, codirected the program with Neal. As many as forty adults at a time took the evening version of Search, in which Rhodes professors Milton Brown, Horst Dinkelacker, Robert Patterson, James Jobes, James Roper, Douglas Hatfield, Steven McKenzie, Larry Lacy, Robert Llewellyn, Richard Wood, Donald Tucker, Robert Watson, and Valarie Ziegler helped teach. Thinking back on his time as codirector, Watson recalls, "It was a joy working with Fred Neal. He is open-minded, catholic in the broadest sense of the term, a gifted church historian."[66]

In 1990 the directorship of the Special Studies Search program passed to Watson and then, in 1991, to political science professor Daniel Cullen. Under their leadership, adult students were able to follow the main lines of the college course with a faculty that now included Ellen Armour, James Clifton, Gail Corrington Streete, Robert Entzminger, Stephen Haynes, Carolyn Schriber, and James Vest. Cullen introduced several changes to the evening program's structure:

My hunch was that an adult audience, willing to devote an evening out of a busy week to continuing education, would not be averse to study and discussion in greater depth. Consequently, the Greco-Roman Unit (which was where I entered the cycle) became a yearlong affair, and we found time for more topics in history, philosophy, religion, and art. The response was gratifying and confirmed my hunch. Several classes on art and architecture were particularly popular.[67]

Cullen came to delight in the healthy spirit of camaraderie that developed among members of the group, some of whom had been together in the course for years. "One evening a class member brought in his personal collection of Roman coins," he recalls, "having been stimulated by the previous week's lecture on the emperors. Other students had visited classical sites and recalled how they had seen a certain statue or painting during their travels." Cullen was particularly impressed with the wealth of learning and experience the adult students brought to the course and the pleasure they derived from their time together: "I marvel at the way people with very strong moral, social, and even aesthetic convictions allowed themselves to roam quite freely among alien thought, beliefs, and perspectives. This was a group to whom nothing human was really alien. In that spirit of encounter, that openness to difference, one significant goal of the course was met."

One other Rhodes adult educational venture was firmly anchored in the Search course tradition. In 1955, a decade after the course had been introduced into the regular college curriculum and adult enthusiasm for liberal learning had been demonstrated by the success of the evening Great Books series, Granville Davis and Laurence Kinney created a program designed specifically for active business people. Firm believers in the value of liberal learning in developing enlightened leaders, they launched the Institute for Executive Leadership, a daytime adult education program that promoted directed discussion of great readings. The stated goal of the program was to help "oncoming business leaders" to develop a "toughness of mental fibre, a warmth and depth of human feeling, and an awe and appreciation for the universe and its realities" that would help them to cultivate the "imaginative capacities and mature judgment required for major decision-making and 'statesmanship' in business." In its cross-disciplinary readings and in the format of its discussions, the institute resembled the Search course. As of 1995, more than 130 businesses and civic organizations had participated in the Institute, which enrolled an average of eighteen to twenty participants each year.

In 1994–1995, the fortieth year of the institute, time constraints of working people forced a modification from its traditional nine-month schedule. The institute was restructured as a twelve-week program offered twice a year, with each semester preceded by an opening retreat. The basic premise remained: a search for values through reading and discussing great works of literature and philosophy and applying them to the lives of working men and women. Over the years, the leadership of the Institute for Executive Leadership included Search course stalwarts Larry Lacy and Llewellyn Queener, working with banker Wayne Pyeatt, civic leader Selma Lewis, and Special Studies director Sally Thomason. In 1993 the National University Continuing Education Association Division of Humanities, Arts and Sciences, presented the P. E. Frandson Award for Continuing Excellence to Thomason and Lacy for their work in conjunction with the Institute.

The Search course also spawned offspring outside the confines of higher education. Since the early 1960s, versions of the course have proliferated in Memphis. These include classes offered by one of the city's leading preparatory schools and two churches.

An interdisciplinary humanities course for high school seniors was instituted at Memphis University School in the mid-1960s under the leadership of Leigh W. MacQueen, William R. Hatchett, and William T.

Sullivan, all of them Rhodes alumni. "Our course was modeled on the concept of the Man course," says MacQueen, and it was intended to be "a culminating experience drawing together strands of study and broadening the students' horizons." For MacQueen, Senior Humanities proved "a viable and fascinating kind of course, . . . stimulating to those who take it or teach it. It causes people to look into new areas, areas with which they may have had little contact."[68] James Russell, head of the English department at M.U.S. and coordinator of the integrated Humanities program from 1965 until 1992, reflects with enthusiasm on the stimulation for students provided by such a course and the renewal that it brings to teachers:

There was always room for experimentation. In the 1970s, for example, the Humanities course at M.U.S. was modified to include topics in anthropology, with readings from Margaret Mead and others, investigating the nature of being human. That was topical and exciting. But the course never lost its basic chronological approach and its integrated cross-disciplinary thrust.[69]

Other adaptations of the Search course have been offered through Memphis churches. One such program was launched by Rhodes philosophy professor Robert Llewellyn in the mid-1970s for the Covenanters' Class at Idlewild Presbyterian Church, where two dozen adults took the class. "For a year we followed the syllabus for the Old Testament and New Testament units in Search as Sunday School material for that class," Llewellyn explains. "In another year, we did the *Odyssey*, the *Aeneid*, and Job as a mini-course using the course readings, augmenting them with Niebuhr's *The Responsible Self*, a book that I came to appreciate as a result of my own efforts preparing for my duties in Search. This version was consciously derived from the Search course."[70] Search continues to appeal to adult learners, often numbering close to one hundred, in a Sunday morning version taught since 1992 at Calvary Episcopal Church by Robert Watson, occasionally assisted by Mikle Ledgerwood and other members of the Rhodes Search course faculty. Watson speaks with appreciation of the "loyal constituency" of adult participants in that program, many of whom encounter interdisciplinary humanities there for the first time.

On Diversity and Conflict

ELLEN T. ARMOUR

Courses like Search tend to arise out of a perceived need to bolster traditional Western values in response to increased social fragmentation. But, once born, courses take on a life of their own. Resisting social fragmentation is not why I teach in the Search course, for example. I greet claims that our time is more fragmented than others with skepticism. Social unity is always more easily seen in hindsight than in the present. Moreover, fragmentation is not such a bad thing, especially for those who experience it as an opportunity for growth. Finally, I would be quite uncomfortable with any suggestion that answers to contemporary problems lie in nostalgic returns to "the tradition."

Having said all that, I believe that texts and ideas from the past are well worth studying, both in their own right and because they can provide a critical perspective on the present. I also think that Search can help students prepare to live in the world beyond Rhodes's cloistered campus. Students who graduate from liberal arts colleges these days join an increasingly diverse work force. They cannot count on longevity with a particular company or in a particular career. The two things they *can* count on—and therefore need to become comfortable with—are change and diversity. Students also need to be able to think critically and stay open to new perspectives.

In the Search course, I try to help students learn that diversity is not a recent invention. Examining the ancient Greeks, Romans, Hebrews, and early Christians gives students a sense of historical change as a series of fits and starts, often marked by conflicts whose resolutions yield both gains and losses. Since their access to this history comes through the primary texts that reflect it, I try to teach students to read critically and carefully—that is, to attend to what texts say and to what they leave unsaid in order to discern the interests and aims of their writers and editors.

One of the distinctive features of the Search course is its focus on religion. As a scholar trained in religious studies (I specialize in contemporary philosophy and theology), I think the study of religion as a cultural phenomenon can be particularly effective in bringing students to appreciate change and diversity and develop critical thinking skills. At the same time, the focus on religion—especially through the Bible—presents some special challenges to meeting these goals. Students sometimes find it hard to grasp the difference between academic study of the Bible and church-school study. My approach to getting them to discern and appreciate the difference is to describe the Bible as, among other things, a window into the world that produced it. Gaining access to that world requires that one ask not, "What does this text mean for me?" but rather, "What did it mean for those who produced it?" It also means realizing that the Bible is not a book that says the same thing from cover to cover. Instead, it is a library containing a variety of genres of literature and views of deity, all reflecting a wide range of historical perspectives and interests. (The word *bible* is itself from the Greek *biblia*—that is, books.) Thus, the Bible contains bumps, bruises, and warts that may trouble contemporary readers.

Students are aware that the Bible is often invoked by partisans on all sides of contemporary conflicts about values. Because the Search course focuses on the roots of modern biblical religions, it offers students the opportunity to gain some historical perspective that can help them to evaluate politically motivated appeals to biblical texts.

For example, the story of the destruction of Sodom and Gomorrah is often cited as evidence that biblical religion and homosexuality are incompatible. Situating this story in its historical context can help students to assess that claim. Most modern scholars argue that the story condemns the men of Sodom for violating the code of hospitality. Under that code, one was obligated to care for any stranger who asked for shelter. The men of Sodom went beyond neglecting a guest's needs, which would have been bad enough, and actually threatened the guest's well being. That ancient peoples would attribute the destruction of a city to such a violation may seem extreme to modern readers, but, as I remind students, the absence of ancient versions of Holiday Inn and Motel 6 meant that travelers' lives depended on the reliability of the code.

Students are sometimes reluctant to subject religion to critical reflection. Whether they identify themselves as religious practitioners or not, they are used to thinking of religion as purely a matter of private belief. Examining biblical texts in historical context helps them to see that, then as now, religion is a public site in which conflicts over social values are played out. Ancient Israel's struggle to define, forge, and maintain a distinctive identity constitutes a major theme of the Bible. Because Israel's political identity was intimately enmeshed with its religious identity, political struggles were reflected in religious struggles. Israel eventually came to define itself as the people in covenant with Yahweh, but that identity was not established without conflict. The texts of ancient Israel contain numerous and frequent prohibitions against worshiping other gods, especially the gods (and goddesses) of ancient Canaan. Those prohibitions show students that religion was a crucial site of Israel's struggle to define itself.

Sometimes, too, sediment from historical battles about identity affects present conflicts. Students know that New Testament texts are sometimes invoked in support of anti-Semitism. My job is to try to show them that, for example, the imprecations against "the Jews" in John's gospel reflect an intra-Jewish struggle for identity. Christianity began as an apocalyptic sect within Judaism. It became a separate (and predominantly Gentile) religion over many decades, mostly as a result of conflicts between Jews who followed Jesus and Jews who did not. Remembering that most of those whose views are reflected in early Christian writings considered themselves Jewish (as did Jesus) challenges any citation of those texts in support of anti-Semitism.

Students also are aware that biblical texts are still invoked to oppose greater equality between men and women. The texts of the ancient world, in which women were considered property, show students how deeply the roots of misogyny run in the West. Yet careful study also uncovers countercurrents to misogyny in these texts. For example, when we study the New Testament, I try to engage the students in what biblical scholar Elisabeth Schüssler Fiorenza calls "subversive remembering." I point to evidence that women were important and active participants in the early Jesus movement. As the course follows Christianity's emergence as a religion in its own right and then as a powerful institution, I try to help students see the gains and losses that came with those achievements. To be sure, Christianity gained a unity of doctrine and clarity of authority that encouraged its growth as a major world religion. But much of the diversity of interpretation that had characterized early Christianity was lost. Moreover, women were systematically denied access to position and power in the process.

Some students are troubled when they learn that the Bible is not what they thought it was. Coming to terms with its diversity of viewpoint, its bumps and bruises, and its political legacies can be disturbing. My hope, however, is that students will find that biblical religion and the world it reflects are richer and more interesting than they had imagined.

I also hope that the course will offer students some degree of comfort with diversity and conflict. If they and I have done our work well, students may even emerge with some tools—the ability to think critically, to engage in considered debate about issues of importance to them, and to appreciate other cultures and other perspectives that will serve them well in their own diverse and everchanging lives.

Critical Reflection in the
Western Tradition

JAMES JOBES

One thing that initially attracted me to Rhodes in 1964 was the chance to teach in the Search course, a course that resembled in significant ways the program of "great books" seminars that was the main feature of my undergraduate curriculum at St. John's College in Annapolis, Maryland.

I see several important differences between the Rhodes and St. John's programs. First, the St. John's seminars, continuing through four years, occupy roughly twice as much class time as the Search course, and so can address much more material.

Second, at St. John's the seminars are regarded as the heart of the curriculum, and the rest of the curriculum is coordinated with them; the Search course is integrated with the rest of the Rhodes curriculum in only a few ways. For example, a student at St. John's will, while reading Plato for seminar, also study ancient Greek and ancient Greek mathematics (which has important connections with Plato) in two other classes.

A further difference is the tendency at St. John's to limit the amount of attention given to the historical context of books and to the circumstances of their composition. This approach seems to stem from a fear of slipping into reductive historicism, that is, into writing off ideas as mere products of their historical circumstances and, consequently, as not deserving the modern reader's serious attention. As I see it, significant losses result from this abstraction from context, greater losses with some books than with others. I think that by and large the Search course manages to give appropriate attention to context without getting trapped in the very real hazards of reductionism. For instance, reading Biblical texts in historical context and with attention to the possibility that multiple sources have been blended in them greatly enriches the texts and resolves many perplexities but does not require or even invite the reader to explain everything away.

One significant difference between the St. John's and Rhodes programs is that each St. John's seminar has two or three faculty leaders, whereas a Search colloquium has only one. Contrary to what one might expect, having multiple leaders seems to encourage student participation in discussion. Moreover, it goes some way toward insuring that multiple viewpoints are considered. Nevertheless, Search colloquia, while at a disadvantage, usually manage fairly well in these respects.

An especially important similarity between the Search course and the St. John's program is an approach to the books studied that is at once respectful and critical. This approach judges that good things may be found in the Western tradition (as well as mistakes that it would be good to recognize) but also holds that aspects of the tradition should be appropriated or rejected only upon critical reflection. The hope is that students will be changed by this process of reflection, finding better support for their current beliefs or being led to changed beliefs. Of course there is no guarantee that critical reflection will always change our beliefs for the better, but it seems the best course available to us.

A practical problem arises in trying to encourage critical reflection about the Western tradition in an academic program. A responsible effort to understand works of the tradition often leaves little time in class to reflect critically on them. St. John's may be more effective than the Search course in fostering critical reflection, because understanding and reflecting on the tradition is the primary focus of the whole curriculum, with more time spent on the project than the Search course can devote to it and with greater emphasis on the project in the whole life and spirit of the college than is found at Rhodes. Nevertheless, the Search course does appear to lead a good many of its students to significant critical reflection, both at the time they are taking it and also, as we learn from graduates, at later times in life.

The project of critical reflection on the Western tradition is challenged today both by certain would-be supporters of the tradition and certain critics of it. Both are driven in part by some very real problems and concerns, but both seem to me to be off the mark.

Some champions of the Western tradition, who see it as something to be simply inculcated into students, overlook or play down two of its important features. First, although some ideas are fairly pervasive in the tradition, it also is marked by diversity, tension, and conflict, so that even the would-be traditionalist must end up, with or without deliberate choice, as an adherent of one set of alternatives out of many. Not only are there significant differences among the main strands of the tradition; such differences may also be found (along with significant similarities) within a single strand, as we can see in the relationships of Plato to Homer, Aristotle to Plato, Job to some earlier parts of Hebrew Scripture, Locke to Hobbes, Hume to Locke, and Nietzsche to Mill. Second, critical reflection is itself a fairly widespread feature of the tradition, so that to reject it is untraditional. One thinks, for example, of the critical stance of Jeremiah, Socrates, and Jesus. Moreover, since critical reflection seems our best bet for getting things right, rejecting it is unwise.

Some critics of the Western tradition see it as not merely seriously flawed but as so corrupt, benighted, and harmful that it is best rejected altogether in favor of new ways of thinking. I agree that the tradition is seriously flawed. For one thing, some points made by feminist critics are compelling—a severe male and patriarchal bias infects more than one strand of Western tradition. But it also seems to me that some of the strongest impulses and most effective resources for criticizing the tradition come from within the tradition itself, as we see in the civil rights movement's invocation of the Exodus, of prophetic calls for justice, and of such New Testament texts as Galatians 3.28 ("There is no longer Jew or Greek, there is no longer slave or free. . .").

Further, there are good negative reasons to pay attention to the thought of the past rather than to disregard it in favor of a completely fresh start. Awareness of past errors should put us on the lookout for ongoing influences of those errors, and, again, the critical process that leads to discovery of past errors may at the same time point the way out of those errors to a more adequate understanding. Finally, I see a great deal more good in the Western tradition than do many of its radical critics, though I know no responsible way to argue briefly for my view.

None of this is to deny that much can be gained both from trying to come up with novel ideas and viewpoints and from the study of non-Western traditions. But it seems to me that the project of critical attention to the Western tradition that is common to St. John's and the Search course at Rhodes is a good place to start.

6

A Week in Search

DAVID WELCH SUGGS, JR., '95
and
JAMES W. TURNER, '95★

*I*magine Kelly, an eighteen-year-old
first-year student at Rhodes. She is from Paragould, Arkansas, and was valedicto-
rian of her senior class. She is no stranger to thinking about life beyond the weekend's football game or homecoming dance: she was active in the youth ministry at
First Methodist Church, and she also went to the Arkansas Governor's School,
where she encountered many ideas that she had never heard of before, as well as a
number of outrageous, iconoclastic individuals from all over the state. Because Kelly
wants to be a doctor, she plans to major in biology at Rhodes. Other than botany,
she is not sure what she wants to take during her first semester.

The summer before Kelly comes to college, she finds an explanation of the
Search and Life programs (one of which she must choose) in her preregistration
packet. Search, she reads, is a four-semester interdisciplinary course that combines
elements of the Bible with other aspects of Western culture, including literature, history, and philosophy. Students enrolling in Life, on the other hand, take four one-
semester classes from a list that consists mainly of religious studies courses.

Like the majority of her classmates, Kelly decides that the Search course is
something she wants to explore. She thinks she knows the Bible pretty well, and
her introduction to philosophy at AGS has piqued her interest in that subject.

★ In completing "A Week in Search," we were ably assisted by the following Rhodes
students: Jacob Abraham '96, Amy S. Hall '96, Rachel Kelly '96, Van Savage '96, Andrew
M. Veprek '97, John Weeden '97, and Nowell York '98.

Some of her hometown friends at Rhodes say that Search is usually more inter-
esting than Life, even though it can be harder.

By the middle of March, Kelly is a different person: the first year of college
tends to do that. Taking botany has cured her of any desire to major in biology, so
her career plans are on hold. She did fairly well on her midterms, she is dating a
sophomore from Colorado, and she has not talked to her parents in two weeks.

Kelly's decision to take Search has had some interesting repercussions. She does
not always jump in on the wide-ranging discussions in class. Sometimes she feels
self-conscious talking about issues she has not entirely settled for herself, and some-
times she thinks that discussions of religion and philosophy work better outside the
classroom. Still, she has found much to ponder in reading Seneca, Socrates, and
Homer, as well as in rereading the Bible. She had never thought of studying the
Bible as a work of literature, with its own history and poetry. Doing so has pro-
vided a new context for the work of faith she had always thought the Bible to be.

In class, many of Kelly's fellow students raise the same questions that occur to
her, and although the class gets tedious from time to time, she usually looks for-
ward to going. While doing the readings at night, she finds herself wondering just
what she believes, after all.

Although Kelly is fictional, her experiences resemble those of many
first-year students at Rhodes. By the middle of the second semester, students enrolled in Search have been confronted with a multitude of questions about their culture, values, and religion. Some, of course, will have
begun to tackle these questions already, on their own. Others will be
shocked and a little dismayed at the heterodoxy that seems to arise from
examining cultural and religious issues in an academic setting.

With this amalgam of faiths, philosophies, and ideas, students find
Search to be a singular educational experience. They register for their
colloquium sections without knowing anything about the professors, except for advice they may have heard from older students. And, of course,
they know almost nothing about the other first-year students in the class.
As such, they find themselves studying material that few of them have encountered before and in a way that often does not come easily.

We visited several first-year Search colloquia during the third week of
March 1995, listening to the discussions that took place. By that time in
the academic year, students are comfortable with each other and with
their professors. But the material itself remains unsettling, forcing students
to think about religion and culture in new ways.

Monday, March 20

Twenty-five minutes past 11:00 on a Monday morning is the middle of the morning rush at Rhodes. Classes will not begin for another five minutes, so the halls and walkways of the college sustain a steady flow of students and professors. Some students stumble blearily to their first class of the day, while others hurry from earlier classes at opposite ends of the campus. A lapsed-time photograph would show a colorful blur streaming across the limestone and slate buildings that form a quadrangle in the middle of campus, with smaller streams heading for Buckman Hall south of the quadrangle or for Hassell Hall to the northeast. Administrators and student tour guides take particular pride in a recent *Parade* magazine report of a student survey that named Rhodes as the most beautiful college campus in the country.

The refectory, known colloquially as the Rat, is a particularly chaotic spot: one crowd issues forth in a rush, clutching sandwiches and plastic cups filled with soft drinks, trying to make it to class before D hour starts at 11:30. Pushing against them are those newly released from C-hour classes, with a chatter arising from shouted greetings, questions about upcoming exams, and gibes about the events of the previous weekend.

Now, in late March, spring has made its presence known: a thick coat of pollen rests on cars and windowsills while unusually warm temperatures cause the running track by the gymnasium to shimmer in the late morning sun. Most of the sororities held their date parties during the previous week, and spring break, two weeks before that, is already fading from memory. The NCAA Division I men's basketball tournament, currently in full swing, is another topic of student conversations, particularly among fans of top-ranked Arkansas.

Palmer Hall is the oldest building on the Rhodes campus, dating back to the college's move to Memphis in 1925. The second floor houses a number of classes, primarily in English, French, Spanish, and philosophy. Several Search colloquia also meet here, including that of Ellen T. Armour of the religious studies department.

A few minutes before class begins, a slow but steady stream of men trickles into the classroom, dumping backpacks carelessly onto the four tables arranged in a square in the middle of the room and sharing spirited analyses of either the basketball tournament or the various parties of

Saturday evening. Wiping lips and chins from the water fountain outside, they spread themselves along the square at equal distances from each other. The conversation subsides as they shift their attention to their backpacks, leaning back in their seats. With preregistration for the fall semester in full swing, several look at the course listings, sighing and shaking their heads.

Suddenly, a group of five women bursts in, talking animatedly and laughing as they find seats. Tina sits back in her chair and gathers her hair in a ponytail while she jokes with Elise about a spring break trip to Daytona Beach. Two others discuss a mutual friend at another college who is coming to visit Rhodes.

Gabe and Gina talk quietly across a corner of the square, speaking of another absent friend who, Gina says, "has never left his high school football mentality." Waving his hands animatedly, Gabe tells Gina about being in the Detroit airport at 6:00 that morning, having had no sleep at all.

More people enter and fill the remaining seats; a hush falls over the room, although the professor has not arrived.

Religious studies professor Ellen T. Armour clarifies a point for her first-year Search students.

Buckman Hall is an imposing structure that sits in magnificent isolation along North Parkway. It is the newest classroom building on campus, having been built in 1991 to house the departments of economics, political science, and international studies, along with the computer and language laboratories. Buckman is in the same collegiate gothic style as its neighbors, making it look as old and venerable as any building on campus. Its classrooms are of all shapes and sizes, and the long, narrow seminar rooms on the third floor are often host to the twenty-student Search colloquia.

Greek and Roman studies professor Livia Tenzer's class is one of them. With five minutes remaining before D hour begins, the first two students venture in, taking seats across from each other at the seminar table in the center of the room. Each whips out the *New Oxford Annotated Bible* that is required for Search. Today's assignment is from the Gospel of John, and both students flip to the appropriate passages. At the same time, they retrieve their Search study guides, which contain review questions and supplemental information.

Four more students enter and seat themselves around the table, which gives the class the appearance of a board meeting: students and the professor face each other around the table and speak freely and directly to each other. Two more women, apparently sorority sisters, enter and continue to chat about the previous weekend's formal.

Tenzer, in her second semester at Rhodes, bolts in and checks the clock. She is animated and has an air of being perpetually harried.

Robert Patterson's colloquium in Palmer opens with the professor passing out chocolate bunnies in celebration of the birth of his granddaughter. Individual students approach him to consult about paper topics as the class rustles from the traffic coming in.

In the early minutes of the period, the festive chaos continues as some students hand in rewritten papers and Patterson passes out study sheets for the upcoming "take-home" exam. In this variation, students take the assignment home with them, study and discuss it among themselves, then spend an allotted amount of time writing their answers. Once they begin working on the exam, they are bound by the Honor Code not to consult books and notes or to discuss their answers with others.

John asks how this kind of test differs from an assigned essay. Patterson explains that the test will have a topic on which the writer must take a position, as opposed the more familiar essay assignment that allows the student to choose a theme as well as a thesis. Mary Alice wants to know if she may research the exam questions in the library; Patterson encourages her to do so.

Armour walks into her colloquium and sits down, meticulously arranging her papers on the table in front of her. As Susan whispers to her neighbor that she has not gotten into a biology class she needs, Armour begins class with the usual housekeeping matters: she is still grading the

class's recently submitted papers, and her exam questions will be distributed on Wednesday.

Armour continues by explaining the take-home format of the test,
emphasizing that once the students begin writing, they are on their own.
She also tells them that she will be available all week for meetings. Several students perk up at this, scribbling in weekly planners while watch-
ing her attentively.

Gail Murray, a professor of history, enters her Buckman classroom
quietly and sets down her materials. She draws up two columns on the
whiteboard, titling one "Synoptic Gospels" (that is, Matthew, Mark, and
Luke) and the other "John's Gospel." She then hands back graded papers,
instantly captivating the class. Most flip immediately to the end to see
how they have done and begin comparing grades.

Joanna and Tracy enter late, find seats, and confer with neighbors
about their papers.

Tenzer notices aloud that a few students are absent; as if on cue, three
more straggle in together. Currently finishing her doctoral dissertation on
Seneca at Stanford University, Tenzer admits privately, "I myself am
searching for an understanding of the reading. I'm expecting some help
from the students who have had more religious instruction than I have."

The Search faculty is drawn from nearly half of the departments at
Rhodes. Some have taught Search for many years, but others are new not
only to Search but to Rhodes. Patterson has taught in the course for some
twenty years, Armour for four, Murray for two, and Tenzer is new. Professors have a great deal of freedom in how they choose to structure their
colloquia, and their own perspectives occasionally come into play during
discussions.

Tenzer's students, hearing her turn her attention to upcoming assignments, listen intently and transcribe her admonition to finish the paper
before starting on the weekend's exam. One can hear sighs of relief when
she announces, "There will be no class on Friday. Call it a sort of 'working holiday' to take the test."

Armour asks, "Do you think the Gospel of John is different from
Matthew?" The class turns to John's gospel in unison, looking up when
Jenny, a tall woman with long hair, leans her cheek on her hand and says,
"There's no birth narrative." She looks as though she is trying to appear

bored, flipping through the pages of her Bible. Several students eye her and turn pages in perfect mimicry.

Armour tries again. "How does John's point of view tie in to what you have considered Christian throughout most of your experiences, if any, with the religion?"

"This is a lot more of what I've seen in church," answers Jenny.

Nodding her head, Armour rolls her felt-tipped marker in her fingers. "Pay attention to the differences you see between John and the synoptic gospels, but also to its similarity to other things we've read. Think of this in terms of what evolves into popular Christianity. Remember that Christianity starts as an apocalyptic sect within Judaism, and then it becomes a Greco-Roman religion. Does this make sense?"

Armour's mini-lecture appears to be the cue for most students to begin taking notes. She moves to the whiteboard, saying, "I want you to think of John in light of the questions we've considered about the other gospels." She writes:

Who is Jesus? Why is he significant?
What does it mean to be his follower?

Sebastian looks at the board and adjusts his tie, appearing deeply interested.

Armour breaks the class down into groups of three to consider these questions, as well as the significance of the story of Mary, Martha, and Lazarus, which is found only in John. Group members rearrange their chairs into small clumps in varying tones of excitement and trepidation.

Tenzer offers her students some background on John's gospel, differentiating it from the synoptic gospels and noting some of its prevailing themes. She tosses out a few questions for discussion as students scribble furiously. The class stirs when Jody tries to make a connection between the Gospel of John and the Roman Stoic philosophers. Tenzer nods her head, adding a quick review: "What is the role of logos in Stoicism?"

After several students murmur, "Reason," Tom poses a question of his own: "So is John trying to make God reasonable, or is he redefining reason in terms of God?"

Emily, clad mostly in black, picks up the thread, and she and Tom pursue the discussion with a few comments from others. They appear to be regular sparring partners in Tenzer's colloquium and present a study in contrasts. Emily sits on a side of the table that seems to consist mostly of brooders, turning pages and taking notes but rarely participating in discussion. Tom's side of the table is comparatively chatty; he is dressed neatly and speaks with eloquent precision.

Patterson turns his class's discussion to Jesus' relationships with women, including the scene with the Samaritan woman at the well and the story of Mary, Martha, and Lazarus.

"The fact that Jesus had these interactions with women suggests something about the context of the Christian community in which John was writing," he says. "It was one in which women probably had a role of much greater esteem and importance than in the later Catholic hierarchy. They were not only church members, but they were also ministers, deacons, prophets—full participants in the Christian life of John's community."

Gretchen takes issue with part of Patterson's statement. "Aren't Mary and Martha still dependent on men for help?" she asks. "Don't they play a submissive role?"

"You have to consider the context and history in which the gospel was written," answers Patterson. "Anyone coming in direct contact with Jesus was regarded with great importance and favor, and the fact that these women had that kind of contact brings respect to women as a whole. Their playing a role at all in the gospel story is significant. This is not a tract for 'women's lib,' but, rather, it's an assertion of equality with men in their importance and opportunity for life with Jesus."

Carl then asks about the story of Mary anointing Jesus' feet, in which Jesus overrules Judas's objection that the money for the oil would have been better spent on the poor. It's not the kind of reaction, he says, that he would expect from Jesus. "It sounds like he doesn't care about the poor—like he's worth the luxury of the oil. It sounds almost selfish."

Patterson responds that the gospel was written in a community seeking to honor Jesus and to demonstrate that he is worthy of great esteem—to honor him as the "real thing."

Also, Patterson points out, the episode is not quite as self-serving as it may appear on a first read: Jesus is protecting Mary from the anger of the disciples and is demonstrating that one must be willing to serve others' interests over one's own in order to inherit the kingdom of God.

"How does the Gospel of John deal with the question of Jesus being

God incarnate, and how does this differ from the other gospels?" asks Murray.

One by one, different students point out the seven signs in John, with Jesus changing the water into wine a particular favorite. Murray notes these in the "John's gospel" column on the whiteboard. This prompts most of the class to reproduce the chart in their notes, while discussion turns to the differences in the various gospels' portrayals of Jesus' baptism and his relationship with John the Baptist.

As the class progresses, almost everyone contributes to the discussion, often talking at the same time. Murray quietly gets up to close the classroom door against noise from the hallway as another question arises: Was the author of the Gospel of John familiar with the synoptic gospels when he wrote his own account?

Faith, who is wearing a cross necklace, and Cerise argue vehemently that John and the synoptic gospels were written independently of each other, while other members of the class are just as convinced that John was written much later and incorporates elements of the other gospels. Murray clicks the cap back on her marker and lets the discussion range freely.

The different groups in Armour's colloquium concentrate on their assignments. Most seem absorbed in the text, while a minority glance carelessly around the room. The loud hum of the air conditioner breaks the silence. Sam chews gum slowly as he looks through his own Bible, running a finger up and down the open page. Sebastian makes notes hurriedly in both Bible and notebook, while Andrea gnaws on the edge of her pen. Tina digs in her backpack and, not finding what she wants, pokes Elise on the shoulder and whispers. Elise pulls out a tube of Chapstick and hands it over as other students lean back, apparently finished.

Elise, Tina, and Samantha seem amused by John's gospel. "What's the deal with the woman who had five husbands?" asks Samantha.

"This one describes Jesus in different ways than the others, or at least I think so," volunteers Tina.

Elise asks Samantha for her opinion. Samantha seems a little discomfited, but they continue to work through the questions Armour has written on the whiteboard.

Tina continues, "It seems like the text is implying that if you follow Jesus, he'll always be there for you." The group eagerly finds other evidence to support this claim in the text.

Elise then asks, "What do you make of this eternal well of life?"

"I don't know."

"Everybody ready?" drawls Armour after a few minutes, prompting nods and shuffles as the groups rearrange themselves around the table. When everybody settles down, the five trios each report on their discussions about the text.

Tenzer's class becomes much more engaged as the discussion turns to early Christian parallels in Greek and Roman philosophy. Whenever a link to the Romans is suggested, students perk up and explore every possible avenue, but there is less interest in the nuances of the Gospel of John.

Tenzer lectures for a few minutes, stopping occasionally to extract comments from the class, much like pulling teeth. Chuck, a stocky football player, draws attention to the theme of how a person may be permanently transformed. He makes his point quickly, and Tom and Emily pick up the thread in a fast-paced dialogue. The class seems to defer to the pair's opinions, since they appear to be most comfortable with the material.

Armour stands back to look at the reassembled class. "What's the status of Jesus in John's gospel?" she asks.

"It seems like it's saying Jesus is God," volunteers Anna. Jenny pipes up, "He's not considered a prophet in here."

Playing with a pen, Denise comments, "The prologue is kind of like Genesis as far as saying, God equals creator." "It's like saying Jesus is the word of God," suggests Frank.

Armour waves her hands and starts to address the flurry of comments. "Yes, remember the synoptic gospels did not talk about Jesus as God incarnate. You're right about Jesus as 'Word of God.' Remember the Greek term for 'word,' *logos*? That's the term John is using here," writing the Greek word on the board. "Where have we heard it before?"

"It means reason, doesn't it, so it's sort of like Seneca?" Sebastian half-says, half-asks.

Armour nods as Amy says "ah" dramatically. The students scribble furiously in their notebooks, some glancing at Amy and smiling among themselves.

"What about the parallels with the account of creation found in Genesis 1?" Armour asks.

"It sounds like the creation idea is like putting things in their proper place," answers Sebastian.

"Do you think this is like the Stoic view of the relationship between divinity and cosmos in any way?" asks Armour.

Emily, one of Tenzer's students, says something that appears to challenge the doctrine of the Trinity. With just a few minutes left in class, the more religious students do not rise to the provocation (as they probably would have done, say, a half hour ago), and so Tenzer is left to wrap up the discussion and emphasize a few key points. Class ends promptly at 12:30, and most students noisily pack up their bags and make for the door, heading almost in unison toward the Rat. A few remain to discuss their papers with Tenzer.

The discussion in Murray's class is still heated when Jonathan looks at the clock and nudges his neighbor. Both collect their books, prompting a chain reaction as Murray reminds everyone about the take-home test that is due on Monday. One by one, students file out until there are only two left. The pair retrieve French books and quiz each other on vocabulary in preparation for an impending test.

Armour hurriedly shifts the discussion to the question of what it means to be a follower of Jesus. Papers shuffle around the room as students arrange their notebooks and flip through their Bibles.

"It seems like you're supposed to worship truly in spirit, I mean truth," Elise ventures.

Armour writes this on the board, nodding. Chris adds, "It seems like people expect Jesus to do miracles and stuff, and Jesus is really tapped into God's power."

The period draws to a close, and a buzz arises as bags are packed and papers filed. Armour agrees with Chris's comment, competing with the clock for attention. "There is a close connection between Jesus and God in this gospel, and this closeness is unique to John."

As the students begin to head out, the professor exhorts them to consider the mysterious nature of religion implied in the reading assignment for Wednesday, which involves comparing all four gospels' accounts of the crucifixion. Students appear rejuvenated as they leave, resuming discussions about the weekend and about tests in other classes that are coming up this afternoon.

Wednesday, March 22

At the beginning of every year, at any place on the Rhodes campus, one can hear first- and second-year students complaining about the exorbitant prices of their materials for Search. Since the course does not center on one or two textbooks, students find themselves with armfuls of books ranging from the Bible to the *Epic of Gilgamesh*, from Plato's *Republic* to the *Confessions* of St. Augustine.

With this canonical avalanche comes a thick, red, faculty-produced tome with an engraving of an ancient map on the front. This comb-bound book, which usually falls to bits after the first year, is the Search study guide, containing not only the schedule of topics and readings for the entire academic year but also two-page companions to each assignment. Students usually discover that the study guide proves extremely useful when preparing for tests.

Today's assignment bears the title "The Passion Story," rendered in the study guide in the sort of ornate typeface that professors with newly acquired software use to demonstrate their technical expertise. The rest of the page contains an introductory paragraph about the day's topic, separate checklists of "Persons, Places, and Things to Note" (such as Caiaphas, Golgotha, and Peter's denial) and "Things to Look For" ("different interpretations of Pilate's motivations and role," "how the gospel writers interpret Judas's actions," etc.), and three essay-style "Questions for Reflection." The third of these questions asks the students to "[c]ompare and contrast key elements of Jesus' suffering, death, and appearances after death with those of other characters whose deaths we have read about in this course. Was Jesus' death ultimately heroic? Why or why not?" The idea is that students will use the checklists to guide their comprehension of the passion narratives and use the reflection questions to begin thinking about what they have read, with particular attention to how each day's assignment fits into the context of the entire course.

The study guide represents Search in its commonality: although different professors emphasize different aspects, every first-year colloquium uses it. In contrast, there is no study guide for second-year Search, only a readings book from which individual professors choose selections according to the disciplinary emphasis of their colloquia and their own styles of teaching.

Indeed, second-year Search is a substantially different course from the first-year experience. Students in the second year choose an area of emphasis—a philosophy, literature, history, politics, or religion "track"—and, usually with faculty from the appropriate discipline, they study selections ranging from the early medieval period to the present. Because the material differs somewhat from one track to the next, the second-year course lacks some of the unity that distinguishes the first year. By the time students are sophomores, with their academic interests coming into focus, they seem to prefer it that way.

Jenny and Amy enter Armour's classroom together talking about a test they have in biology the next day. Weighing just as heavily on their minds, though, is the weekend's Search test. "I'm so glad it's a take-home," says Amy. "I couldn't handle another test on Friday."

It is apparent, as he walks in with Gina, that Gabe is having another difficult day: he dropped his keys in his hot chocolate earlier this morning when he was already late for class.

Jamie, who was absent on Monday, hurriedly flips through his Bible and looks tense. He appears to be cramming for class. It is clearly a Wednesday: in the middle of the week, there is little respite from the relentless grind of class work.

In Murray's class, Cerise complains that her classmates keep changing their seats, and it's beginning to confuse her. Chris enters singing "Saturday night, I'm feeling all right," obviously not overly concerned about the upcoming test.

Murray walks in with another student discussing the weather, a popular topic in Memphis this freakish spring. It is already quite warm this morning, resembling June more than March.

Tenzer bustles in with a stack of test sheets, saying, "We might as well give these out." As the stack makes its way around the room, she gives advice on budgeting time and organizing answers, but the class seems absorbed by the test itself. Intent expressions indicate that answers are being formulated already.

Tenzer begins the day's discussion by posing a question: "Why is it called the 'Passion' story?" The class is stumped, so she continues with a smile, "You all ought to take Latin. *Passio* means 'suffering.'" She admits to the colloquium that her class preparation included her first reading of the gospel stories.

After class, students express a mixed reaction to this statement. "I can't believe that she has never read the Bible," gasps Jerrilyn, who grew up in a very religious family. Other students, however, seem relieved that Tenzer teaches the text simply as a sequence of narratives. In class, she emphasizes the differences among the early Christians, reviewing the various conceptions of Jesus as "the Messiah, Anointed One, King, and Son of God."

Rhodes students represent a variety of scholastic and religious backgrounds. Twelve percent of the Class of 1998 graduated from "religious" high schools and more than 30 percent from "independent" schools, according to the college's admissions office. Many independent schools include some form of religious instruction, and most religious schools require Bible study as part of the standard curriculum.

The religious identities of the first-year students are even more diverse. Rhodes is affiliated with the Presbyterian Church (U.S.A.), and 15 percent of the class members identify themselves as Presbyterian. The same percentage are Methodist, 12 percent are Catholic, 10 percent are Baptist, and almost 9 percent are Episcopalian. Other students belong to the Church of Christ, the Disciples of Christ, and the Church of God in Christ. In addition, six members of the 423-person class are Hindu, three are Jewish, and two are Muslim.

Almost a quarter of the class either expressed no religious preference on their application forms or, in a very few cases, checked one of the other twenty-four possibilities that were listed. Being at an age when many are questioning the beliefs passed on by their parents or seeking new ways to express those beliefs, a substantial number of Rhodes students are truly in a "searching" period, both intellectually and spiritually.

Regardless of personal belief, many students are disinclined to speak out about religion in class. One's beliefs are widely considered to be a private affair. Although the campus is politically conservative in the main, in-class statements of faith and letters to the campus newspaper that contain Christian rhetoric are often greeted by some other students with disdain or incredulity.

Armour is a few minutes late, and the students chatter loudly. "Maybe we'll be out for the day," says Matt excitedly.

Armour enters apologizing for her lateness and explains that the closest copier decided to break down despite her best efforts to make it work. She sets down her effects and, while adjusting her glasses, tells the class that it will break up into groups again to look at the passion narratives in the different gospels. Forcefully, she throws out a piece of paper that was presumably a casualty of her attempts to conquer the copier.

Discussion in Tenzer's classroom has begun in earnest. Jesus is first considered as a God, then as a tragic hero as students compare him with previously studied Sumerian, Greek, Roman, and Jewish examples of both roles.

In the discussion of Jesus as god, Jerrilyn is extremely engaged—she is obviously quite knowledgeable about the texts. The rest of the class's imagination, however, is sparked by the invocation of the other cultures. One after another, students draw connections between Jesus and the exploits of Greek heroes and Babylonian deities.

Tenzer looks pleased by the fast-paced discussion. When it comes around to the New Testament, she asks, "So is Jesus a god, or a hero, or both, or neither?"

Margaret has already taken the lead in Murray's class, raising a tough question from the study guide about the Last Supper. "Do you believe Jesus was aware of his impending arrest, or did the authors write that back in?"

The class fumbles for an answer—some tap on their notebooks, others look puzzled. She probes further: "He said in Mark that they won't always have him with them, though the poor will always be with you."

After some time, Brian says, "The Pharisees wanted to kill him, so he must have had some suspicion that he would die."

Reid adds, "The question just comes down to 'What do you think?' All you have is the gospels."

"Four gospels is all the text we have," Margaret agrees.

"Are you trying to say the passion narratives differ?" asks Ron, befuddled, as he runs his hand through his hair.

At this point hands go up all around the room, and students begin to break in on each other. Murray calms the class down to allow the discussion to proceed.

The students then bring up the Crucifixion-eve scene in the garden of Gethsemane. Chris comments, "It seems that the general fear is death."

"He was human, also," Hal says.

Margaret connects the thoughts: "That's why they bring up the fear when he prays."

Armour says it is time to count off in groups, but first she asks if anyone did not finish the homework. Obviously, she explains, one member's lack of preparation will hold back a group's discussion.

Terry and Donna timidly raise their hands. Armour tells them to start reading the homework on their own. They begin to leaf through their books.

According to Armour, "The homework is done by most students most of the time, [but] the assignments are intense sometimes."

After people have their group numbers, Armour instructs each group to compare the account of Jesus' Crucifixion in John with the account in one of the synoptic gospels. "Try to determine their most salient differences and connect them to the distinctive viewpoint of each gospel," she instructs. "Look also for what they have in common."

After the groups arrange themselves in the four corners of the room, Armour asks them which two gospels they have selected to compare, making sure that all four are covered well. Various students chorus "Luke and John," "Matthew and John," and "John and Mark" until, satisfied, she tells them to begin their discussions.

Armour leaves the room to copy the test she wants to distribute at the end of the class. A light murmur begins throughout the classroom and quickly evolves into a loud discussion. A range of opinions and thoughts is heard from the different groups:

"John still has all this weird stuff about how Jesus thinks John is his right-hand dude."

"The woman at the well is only in Mark, I mean John."

"Matthew had the curtain story."

"I don't think the apostles understood him in that one."

"John doesn't go into detail about carrying the cross."

"Matthew shows everybody believing in Jesus; I thought Mark was different in that respect."

The solitary studiers look humbled, quietly taking notes as they read the assignment.

Tina seems exasperated in her group. She pushes her chair away from her peers and says authoritatively, "I think that we have enough differences, let's get some similarities."

"In John they didn't wash him before the Crucifixion," Jenny says softly, fingering her book. "For some reason I thought that was important."

Armour returns with a thick stack of papers. Her entrance is almost unnoticed as the discussions continue around the room. After she is settled, she starts walking from group to group, checking the answers students have listed.

Armour likes this class, and feels that her students have really gotten into the material. "They're an engaged group. They have improved a lot since last semester. They've never had closed minds."

Two groups have finished, and their conversation strays to other things:

"I'm going to tell your boy about what I've been hearing."

"Arkansas has been playing hideously; California's going to take it."

Murray's class has shifted its discussion to the death of Jesus. She asks why the Passion is described as the pivotal event of Christianity.

Scott makes an attempt: "They were trying to prove that Jesus is the Son of God."

"And that his death had a purpose," adds Meg.

Murray challenges them: "How does the Passion story prove this?"

Chris responds, "He overcomes his death."

Andrea develops the idea: "Jesus used stories to explain resurrection. Yet the gospels have different accounts of the resurrection."

The discussion goes on, shifting from topic to topic until time runs out while they are talking about Pontius Pilate's role in the Crucifixion.

Discussion in Tenzer's class ranges freely over a number of topics: the political maneuverings preceding the Crucifixion, the Last Supper, and comparisons of Jesus with Moses.

Most students seem truly to enjoy these freewheeling discussions. Later, Tom offers his take on the situation: "The readings predicate thinking, not just cursory synopses. Reading the text will not help your Search grade, but analysis and reflection will."

As class winds down, Tenzer compares Socrates to Jesus. The students are struck by the appropriateness of this comparison for the final exam, coming up in about five weeks, and scribble notes furiously.

She reminds them about the Monday lecture, to be attended by members of all Search colloquia. Bags are packed and the powerful attraction of lunch draws students out of class as Tenzer wishes them good luck on the weekend's test.

Armour approaches Tina and Terry and nods approvingly at the notes they have outlined.

Gina and Gabe compare the endings of John and Matthew. Andrea develops a nosebleed and holds the tissue to her nose while she pores over her open Bible.

"Matthew has a big deal about that, something like you can save others but you can't save yourself—I don't know," confesses Sarah to Jim.

Armour continues to circulate around the room, waving her hands as she talks about the gospels. Gabe and Gina remember a song they had to learn about the disciples when they were children.

"Well, you guys have had a fruitful discussion. You seem to have this all down pretty well," Armour says as she begins to pass out the tests. She reminds them that their responses are due Monday at class time.

Dead silence prevails during the quasi-religious act of receiving the tests, but then the students leap to shove all in their backpacks and leave talking and excited.

Students make plans to study with one another before Sunday night and several linger in the classroom to ask Armour questions about the test's grading scale.

Search does not meet on Friday, this being the "working holiday" that was originally scheduled to be the in-class test day. Of course, college students being college students, Thursday night did not find large numbers of people preparing for the test. By the weekend, though, much of the conversation in the Rat and around first-year dorms concerned people's progress on the exam.

The exam is scheduled to take ninety minutes, with the questions varying from colloquium to colloquium and covering most of the New Testament. For example, the first question on Patterson's edition of the test requires his students to consider one of two topics, either the delay of the Parousia (the end of the age) or the nonresponse of most Jews to the preaching of the Gospel, and to discuss how early Christians changed their understanding of these matters, or developed a variety of understandings, during the first century.

"In your essay," the question reads, "include specific reference to the understandings found in Matthew, Mark, Luke, John, Paul's letters, and James."

Noah's answer includes these paragraphs:

The Parousia, or Second Coming of Christ, was anxiously anticipated by those who interpreted the sayings of Jesus to convey the message that he would return before the death of his own earthly generation. As decade after decade passed, however, these hopes were reinterpreted to impart a life of continual readiness. The impact of the Parousia's delay can be seen within the early Christian writings, as their understandings of the imminent nature of this event transformed over the course of the first century.

The Apostle Paul expected the Parousia imminently. The relatively brief period since the ministry of Jesus and the current conditions of persecution and oppression which were foretold in his teachings, suggested to Paul that the new world was about to come into being. "I consider that the sufferings of this present time are not worth comparing with the glory about to be revealed to us" (Romans 8:18). "I think that, in view of our impending crisis, it is well for you to remain as you are"—an excerpt which applied to virgins and demonstrated the immediacy of the Parousia (1 Corinthians 7:26). . . .

Over the course of the first century, the Christian understanding of the Parousia changed from an imminent happening, to an event that would gradually occur. The reinterpretation advocated a life of continual readiness, as the Parousia became more and more delayed. Eventually this delay invested all of Christianity with hope. . . .

(Welch writes): *While working on this project, Jim and I spent a good deal of time reflecting on what first-year Search meant to us, three years after taking it. We were not in the same colloquium, but being roommates and friends, we studied for tests together and often argued about what we were reading and thinking during the course.*

The two of us come from entirely different backgrounds. Jim is from Marvell, Arkansas, where he graduated from high school with a class of twenty-eight and was the only person to leave the state for college. I grew up in suburban Atlanta, attending one of the leading prep schools in the country and receiving a healthy dose of conservative Christian instruction along the way. I had two years of Bible classes there and was exposed to any number of sermons and Christian focus groups.

Search began as a review for me, enabling me to revisit many questions that I thought I had settled, while the course exposed Jim to a myriad of new material and new ways of thinking about the Bible and the world. Studying together for tests, along with another friend who is the daughter of a Methodist minister from southern Illinois, enabled us to discuss our feelings and views in an environment in which our grades became the least of our worries.

Indeed, studying and discussing religious issues without having my less-than-orthodox viewpoints and objections met with condescension or hostility led me to a fuller understanding and acceptance of Christianity, so much so that I studied philosophy at Rhodes and seriously considered going to seminary. Studying the Bible, particularly in conjunction with the Stoics and the Greek philosophers, wrought intellectual changes in me that manifest themselves every time I read a text or hear a sermon.

(Jim writes): *During much of my time in the Search course, I exhibited the wide-eyed wonder of someone pulled from Plato's cave. As my eyes adjusted to the light, however, new forms of thinking emerged in me.*

I found expressed in those ancient texts the basic human desires for order, understanding, a place in the cosmos. The pursuit of these desires became the focus of my studies in economics: not the traditional avenues of calculating utilities and production possibilities, but rather a concern for what people really want and what they are willing to do to get it.

In addition, progressing that first year of Search through Plato, the Hebrew prophets, the Stoics, and the early Christians, I began a renovation of my own views of morality and what it means to be Christian. I do not believe that the renovation will ever end. Thus, the Search course achieved its end in me: I will forever be a seeker. For two years, Welch and I and many of our friends retraced the steps of those who have walked through Western civilization before us. Now we walk with them.

Search and the New Colloquia

KENNETH MORRELL

"Come on then and let's follow where the behests of the gods lead," Anchises urges the refugees from Troy in Book 3 of the *Aeneid*. "Appease the winds and head for the Gnosian kingdoms. / They are not far. Let Jupiter be with us and the third dawn will see the fleet on Cretan shores." As Anchises, the father of Aeneas, eventually discovers, interpreting oracles is not without its hazards. He has just misunderstood the oracle of Apollo and is about to lead the Trojan refugees to Crete, where a plague will frustrate their attempt to found a city.

As the Search course contemplates its direction for the next fifty years, I have been reviewing the most recent dispatches from the Pythia (the oracle of Apollo) to see what the future may hold for the course. Having run across an interesting entry with some reference to Rhodes, I thought I would risk trying my hand at an interpretation. The oracle and translation read:

> ὦ ʹΡόδιοι, τί κάθησθε; ἑκόντες λείπετε τείχη
> καὶ σκηνὰς καὶ βύβλινα; μανθάνετ' ἔσχατα γαίης
> ἑσσάμενοι ὑάλου καὶ χαλκοῦ ἀγλαὰ ὅπλα.

People of Rhodes, why are you sitting around? With good will leave the walls and tents and things of papyrus behind; inquire about the ends of the earth having clothed yourselves with shining arms of clear stones and copper.

My experience teaching Search, brief as it has been, tells me that neither the students nor the faculty are sedentary, so the oracle's opening statement must be hinting at the "settled" nature of the course. For some years, faculty members and students have done most of their work in small colloquia, wrestling with an ambitious but limited range of printed texts and topics, and have paused occasionally to meet as one large group for a lecture. Although discussion sections and lectures have long been and will likely remain the mainstays of college courses, the information itself, usually in the form of texts and pictures, is undergoing a transformation that will undoubtedly call for modifications in the long-established formula.

The "walls" mentioned by the oracle might be classrooms. Students would, I am certain, like to abandon the classroom more frequently for a spot under the trees. But when dealing with the Pythia, I hesitate to be too literal, especially when she goes on to mention "tents and things of papyrus." If we are correct about the oracle's opening admonition, we should perhaps look more closely at the most settled aspects of the course: the colloquia themselves, the lectures, and the texts. Along with strengths, each has its problems and limitations.

The shortcomings of colloquia include a chronic lack of preparation by a few recalcitrant students, the reluctance of some other students to express their views spontaneously in a group of their peers, and the constraints the classroom and class period place on the range and depth of discussion. Lectures, too, have their faults. The professorial monologue, conforming to "classical" rhetorical practice, may not be the best way to convey information or serve the needs of the class. Finally, the texts often prove intractable. In making every effort to choose readings with care, identify the most readable and lucid translations, and create accompanying guides for study, we inevitably struggle with the cost of books, the availability and format of texts, and the year-to-year fluctuations in the reading assignments.

The oracle begins to make better sense if we understand the "walls" as both a concrete reference to the classroom and metaphorical allusion to conceptual barriers. *Skenas* (σκηνὰς), the word I have translated as "tents," could refer to lectures if we assume the Pythia was thinking metonymically of the raised platform behind the orchestra in the theaters of ancient Greece, another possible meaning of the word, from which actors declaimed to the assembled throng. Finally, since papyrus was the most widely used medium for published texts in the ancient world, the Pythia's "things of papyrus" could refer to printed materials in general.

Abandoning papyrus can only mean a turn toward electronic texts, a topic of some interest to Apollo, the god (we now know) of computer technology. During the last two decades, Apollo has undoubtedly observed how the information on which the study of ancient Greece is based has begun to migrate from printed to electronic form. Manuscripts, inscriptions, collections of papyri, infrared photographs from satellites, images of vase paintings, exhaustive bibliographies, and more are all available on-line. Computers have also begun to redefine the way faculty and students interact. For example, with much of the corpus of ancient Greek literature and thousands of images instantly accessible from computer networks, lectures in Search may start to resemble nonlinear discussions in which the participants can explore topics and ideas as they arise rather than follow the lecturer's script.

Now we come to the last of the Pythia, which admonishes us to clothe ourselves with the "arms of clear stone and copper." If our interpretation is not completely off the mark, we need to look again at the word for "arms." In Greek opla (ὅπλα), from which the word *hoplite* (heavily armed soldier) derives, generally meant *arms* and particularly *large shields*. But it could also refer to the tackle or rigging of ships, especially the lines or ropes. If Apollo has *lines* in mind instead of *arms,* he might be trying to describe the "information highway." If so, my revised translation of the oracle would read:

People of Rhodes, why do you remain in one place? Willingly leave
    the classroom walls
and lecture platforms and printed texts behind; inquire about
    the ends of the earth
having clothed yourselves with shining lines of optical fiber and copper.

How will Search appear in Apollo's new format? Here are a few predictions.

First, as students begin to use computer networks and encounter a wider selection of electronic texts and visual and audio information about antiquity, the place that certain texts now occupy and the perspectives on past and present cultures derived from them are likely to become more fluid. At the time of the course's inauguration, in the era of the New Criticism championed by former Rhodes professors Robert Penn Warren and Allen Tate, each text held a privileged position, often regarded as standing above and apart from the society in which it was created. With

access to more artifacts from ancient Athens, students will have the resources to interpret Sophocles' Theban plays, for example, as part of more
complete and variable composite images of Greek culture. For one student the plays may become the basis for understanding hero cult; for another they may appeal as documents reflecting the changing position of
Thebes in the political struggles of Athens during the fifth century B.C.E.
As important and interesting as the New Critics' emphasis on irony and
the imagery of darkness and light as they pertain to Oedipus's self-knowledge may be, students will be able to move beyond the limits of the texts
themselves.

Second, the instructor will become a guiding master-academic for his
scholarly apprentices, who will have greater range to explore topics of
more personal interest. The hour-long colloquia will begin to resemble
the staff meetings of a research group, during which students will report
on their findings rather than respond to preassigned questions. Discussion
will overflow the spatial and temporal limitations or the classroom and
class period and continue on-line, where participants can follow more
than one conversational thread simultaneously, contributing at their own
pace. Once the discussions leave the "walls" and enter the electronic environment, they can include other interested participants, not just from
the campus but also, potentially, from around the world.

How will all this affect the students? They will have to assume a
greater sense of ownership in the Search course and view it even more
than they do now as a vehicle for their own search for understanding.
Rather than merely examine and master the questions others have raised
and tried to answer, they will join as fellow pilgrims those who have gone
before, needing not fear the plague, although viruses of another sort will
remain a hazard. Instead of simply reading about the exiled Trojans' de-
tour to Crete, they will be able to travel there electronically, meeting on-
line the inhabitants and fellow travelers.

7

The Future of the Search Course

MICHAEL NELSON

I began this book by marking the arresting contrast between the endangered status of Western civilization courses as a species and the robust health of one of its longer-lived specimens, the Search course at Rhodes College. Readers may already have drawn conclusions from the preceding chapters about why Search is thriving; in this chapter I will offer some observations of my own. Readers may also wonder what it will take for Search to continue to thrive. This, too, is my concern, especially in the areas of content, faculty, and technology. Specifically,

- How will the Search course deal with issues of course *content* that are being raised, in some cases, by scholars in the humanities who have strong and often contrasting opinions about traditional approaches to the teaching of general education courses in Western civilization and, in others, by students whose response to such courses is shaped less by ideology than by personal concerns and experiences?
- How will Search recruit *faculty* members, most of whom are strongly encouraged by graduate training and the pressures of a forbidding academic job market to specialize in their disciplines, to teach ably and enthusiastically in a multidisciplinary freshman and sophomore course?
- How can Search make good use of the new opportunities offered by

personal computers, CD-ROM, the Internet, and other forms of educational *technology* without losing its character as a course that teaches students to immerse themselves deeply and critically in the
enduring texts of the past?

Content

During its first two decades, from 1945 through the mid-1960s, the
Search course rode a longstanding and rising tide of general education
courses in Western civilization at American colleges and universities. The
two world wars had each brought the United States into alliance with
Great Britain and other European nations, reminding many Americans of
their Old World roots, both intellectual and personal. But the Cold War
with the Soviet Union that followed World War II had a different effect
on Western civ courses, according to the historian Gilbert Allardyce.[1] The
combination of the Soviet explosion of a hydrogen bomb in 1953 and
the *Sputnik* launch in 1957 provoked such widespread anxiety about
American education as to prompt a hasty turn away from general education and toward academic specialization. In addition, the global rivalry
with the Soviets in the emerging nations of the Third World diverted
much scholarly attention from Europe to Asia, Africa, and South America. Responding to these changes, many colleges and universities ceased to
require Western civilization courses of their students. "When compulsion
stopped," Allardyce found, "enrollment dwindled, and across the nation,
one after another, Western Civ courses were decommissioned like old
battleships."

Allardyce's study was published in 1982. In 1984 National Endowment for the Humanities chair William J. Bennett offered a different explanation for the declining interest in Western civ and other humanities
courses, one grounded in the anti-Western and libertarian pressures that
had been aroused by the campus protest movements of the 1960s.[2] Bennett began his widely publicized report, "To Reclaim a Legacy," by de-
claring that educators "too often have given up the great task of
transmitting a culture to its rightful heirs." Blaming "a collective loss of
nerve and faith on the part of both faculty and academic administrators
during the late 1960s and early 1970s [that] was undeniably destructive
of the curriculum," Bennett issued a wide-ranging indictment of: colleges
and universities for failing to require more humanities courses of their
students; humanities departments for assigning the teaching of general

education courses to inexperienced or part-time faculty; and politically radical humanities scholars for labeling the traditional approaches to their subjects as, alternately, "handmaidens of ideology" and devoid of "inherent meaning because all meaning is subjective." What students needed, Bennett concluded, was "access to the best that tradition has to offer," namely, "such principles as justice, liberty, government with the consent of the governed, and equality under the law," all of them "descended directly from the great epochs of Western civilization—Enlightenment England and France, Renaissance Florence, and Periclean Athens."

Bennett's report struck a responsive chord among editorial writers and other opinion leaders, as did Allan Bloom's *The Closing of the American Mind*, a polemic on the subject of (to quote its subtitle) "How Higher Education Has Failed Democracy and Impoverished the Souls of Today's Students" that led the nonfiction bestseller lists for more than six months in 1987.[3] Bloom, a University of Chicago philosopher, argued that colleges and universities had embraced "relativism" and abandoned their responsibility to give students "the good old Great Books approach, in which a liberal education means reading certain generally recognized classic texts, just reading them, letting them dictate what the questions are and the methods of approaching them." Like Bennett, Bloom laid much of the blame for the decline of humanities education on a sixties-spawned combination of political pressure from faculty activists on the humanistic left and acquiescence from timid colleagues and administrators.

Supporters of Bennett and Bloom (known to their critics as the "Killer Bs") seemed to find grist for their mill everywhere they looked. In 1988 conservatives jeered when Stanford University revised its Western civilization requirement to assure that a wider range of authors would be studied and that "substantial attention" would be given to "the issues of race, gender, and class." Far more provocative than any substantive change in the Stanford curriculum was the chant of "Hey hey, ho ho, Western culture's got to go" that briefly accompanied a Jesse Jackson-led campus demonstration. In 1990 "P.C." entered the national vocabulary as shorthand for a congeries of "politically correct" attitudes and practices that supposedly had become the new academic orthodoxy concerning race, gender, sexual orientation, and other cultural matters.

Defenders of the changes that were taking place in the humanities were slow to respond to their critics. As the literary scholar Gerald Graff, who identifies himself as one of the "academic radicals" he describes, noted in 1992, "having trained themselves for two decades to speak in voices that would be resistant to co-optation by the dominant discourses, academic radicals find themselves almost without an idiom in which to contest the misrepresentations being made of them. . . . Thus the right has been able to co-opt the rhetoric of democracy and populism, and turn labels like 'elitist' and 'authoritarian' against the academic left."[4]

Graff was right: the jargon-ridden, self-referential responses of academic radicals to their critics in pamphlets such as the American Council of Learned Societies' *Speaking for the Humanities* and anthologies such as *The Politics of Liberal Education*, edited by Darryl J. Gless and Barbara Herrnstein-Smith, have reached the general public mainly through the caricatures of conservative writers like Roger Kimball and Dinesh D'Souza.[5] Yet the radicals remain influential within the humanities community itself. Their argument, loosely translated, generally goes something like this: the history of Western civilization is in large measure a history of oppression—of women, who have been degraded; of ethnic, racial, and cultural minorities, who have been enslaved or exploited; and of non-Western peoples, who have been made subject to imperialism and colonialism. White males have been the main villains in this historical drama, and the so-called "great books" of Western civilization (almost all of them authored by white males) have been, in the philosopher John Searle's phrase, "the official publications of their system of oppression."[6] Bennett, Bloom, and other conservatives want humanities education to serve as a vehicle to "transmit" (a word that Bennett, in particular, uses a lot) this system to future generations of students, thereby assuring their assent to the political and economic establishment. Instead, the radicals argue, education should liberate students by unmasking the oppressors and lifting up the voices of the oppressed.

The Search course has not been immune to this national debate, nor has it sought to be. Rhodes is, to be sure, a church-affiliated private liberal arts college in a conservative region of the country. But it is not, say, St. John's College, a Bloom and Bennett-approved bastion of academic traditionalism. Members of the Rhodes faculty range widely in their opinions about what Graff calls the "culture wars" in higher education. More to the point, as the "perspectives" essays in this book show, instructors with very different views teach side by side in the Search course. James Jobes, for example, writes admiringly of "the tradition" that Gail Corrington Streete vows to teach through a "strategy of subversion." Both Larry Lacy and Ellen Armour want their students to study the Bible critically, but for Lacy it is the "New Testament critics' . . . naturalistic assumption that miracles do not occur" that needs to be examined, while for Armour it is the Bible's "diversity of viewpoint, its bumps and bruises, and its political legacies."

The Search course *has* been free, however, from the vitriol and extremism that has characterized the national debate. Its faculty's response to change has been incremental and consensual, not dramatic and angrily fought. Nearly every one of Bennett's recommended authors—from Homer, Aristotle, and Sophocles to Marx, Nietzsche, and King—appear (or, rather, continue to appear) on the Search syllabus. Yet, as James Vest and Daniel Cullen show in chapter 4, it was just after Bennett issued his report in 1984 (and just before Bloom published his book in 1987) that the Search faculty, responding to feminist concerns but operating by consensus, changed the name of the course from Man to The Search for Values. Subsequently, and again by consensus, writings by women such as "The Martyrdom of Perpetua and Felicitas" and Christine de Pizan's *Book of the City of Ladies* joined the familiar works of male writers (and Simone de Beauvoir) on the syllabus, and new excerpts from existing texts that deal with important female characters were assigned, such as Book 3 of the *Iliad* (Helen) and the Book of Ruth in the Old Testament. In addition, other writings were added to the syllabus to vivify some of the historic conflicts within the Western tradition. Gnostic and Arian writers took their place alongside the orthodox church fathers, for example, making the presentation of early church history seem less like the unfolding of Christianity and more like a struggle among contending Christianities.

Why has the Search course at Rhodes thrived in recent years instead of either atrophying, as similar courses have on many other campuses in the manner described by Allardyce, or becoming a storm center, like the humanities curricula debated by Bennett, Bloom, and their adversaries? The reasons are several yet one; for all their variety, each has to do with the institutions of the course.

One such institution is external to the college, namely, the Bellingrath-Morse Foundation and its stipulation that to continue to receive the abundant financial support pledged by its founders, Rhodes must require students to do two years of course work in the Bible and Bible-related material. The Search course meets this requirement in part by devoting much of its first year to the Hebrew scriptures and early Christian writings and the greater part of the core readings for its second year to Jewish and Christian theological and ecclesiastical texts.[7] A practical effect of this policy is to remove an inherently contentious issue from the table—namely, the amount of religious material that should be included in the course. To be sure, the faculty spends a great deal of time discussing which biblical and other Judeo-Christian writings should be assigned and how they should be presented on the syllabus. But the Bellingrath-Morse requirement performs in such discussions the same function as the control rods in a nuclear power plant, limiting the explosive potential of the inherently combustible material. The requirement also keeps Search from succumbing to one of the stranger trends in modern higher education—the virtual disappearance of close study of the Bible from courses that avow to present the enduring and influential texts of Western civilization.[8]

Leadership by consensus—specifically, Search director Douglas Hatfield's willingness to allow the faculty to talk through curricular matters until, often in response to his adroit efforts to "summarize the discussion," a consensus forms—is another vital institution of the Search course. Fred Neal's style of leadership served the quarter century begun in 1958 well. As Neal often said, he invited discussion on all questions concerning the course, but at the end of the day he made the decisions, or at least decided who would make them. Such a style would not have seen Search through the potentially divisive issues of the 1980s and 1990s. Too many faculty members felt too strongly about too many things for any one of them to decide important matters for the whole.

Because it is the main forum in which consensus-seeking discussions take place, the annual Douglass Seminar is a third institutional prop of the Search course. The week of daylong sessions at the start of the summer, usually preceded by the labors of small working groups near the end of the spring semester, affords the Search faculty ample time to sort through all the issues of course content and design that need to be resolved for the coming academic year. A more important consequence of bringing the faculty together for a week may be the renewing of social and intellectual bonds that almost always takes place, along with the initiation of new instructors into the collegial norms of the course. Even at a relatively small college like Rhodes, few forums—and even less time—exist for faculty members to discuss at length the issues that concern them as scholars and teachers joined in a common enterprise. Not surprisingly, almost everyone leaves the Douglass Seminar with a strong sense of renewal, accomplishment, and enthusiasm for the course.

Finally, and perhaps most important, the teaching of the Search course is considerably more decentralized than in the past. The history, literature, philosophy, religion, and, now, politics track system that has been used in second-year Search since 1989 mandates a common core of readings but no common lectures; it also leaves ample latitude for instructors to supplement the core with texts of their own choosing. Faculty members in the first year of the course still teach a common syllabus, but with considerable freedom to do so in their own ways. The proportion of first-year class meetings spent in common lectures has dropped steadily from two-thirds to half to a third to a fourth, and the essay portions of tests now are written by individual instructors in response to what they and their students have been discussing in colloquia.

Decentralization of teaching in the Search course came about less because the faculty wanted it (almost to a one, for example, faculty members enjoy hearing their colleagues lecture) than because students increasingly prefer the small-group setting and discussion format of the colloquia to the large, impersonal setting of the lectures. Yet without the relative autonomy that decentralization has afforded to each instructor, the variety of approaches that they take to the materials of the course would necessarily be constrained. Issues that are matters of individual choice would have to be dealt with legislatively, creating friction where none now exists and jeopardizing the faculty's ability to continue to deal amicably with those policies that are already on its agenda.[9]

The solid institutional base that has been formed for the Search course by the Bellingrath-Morse requirement, consensus leadership, the Douglass Seminars, and decentralization augurs well for the future of the course. Habits of civility and mutual respect are not formed easily, but once they are the chances that whatever issues of course content arise will be dealt with in an atmosphere free of suspicion and acrimony increase dramatically. This is true even for those issues, no doubt the majority, that will arise in the future but that, because of the cloudiness of crystal balls, cannot yet be foreseen.

Some of the issues of content that will face Search in the future, however, are readily identifiable because students are raising them in numbers that soon will approach a critical mass. One is the students' desire for a non-Judeo-Christian component in the course. This desire, although longstanding, is almost certain to grow both because of the college's commitments to "globalize the curriculum" and diversify the student body and because of the national economic and demographic changes that underlie these commitments. A second issue arises from the students' concern for relevance in the curriculum. In the 1960s the banner of relevance was waved on behalf of social and political issues; nowadays it is more likely to be invoked in the name of personal concerns and ambitions. Either way, students want the curriculum to speak to their own time and situation. The third issue that almost certainly will face the Search course has less to do with what students want than with who they are. Students who enter college in the late 1990s have grown up taking for granted a wide range of technological innovations, from walkmen to the Internet, that even the most recent generations of students (not to mention faculty) have come to late or not at all. They are enormously skilled at processing information in some ways, but reading a difficult text and listening carefully as a lecturer spins out a complex argument are less and less likely to be among them.

Just as Search's institutional base equips it well to deal with matters such as these when they arise, so does the rich half-century history of the course. Fresh as the issues of relevance, non-Judeo-Christian study, and teaching strategies may seem, each has appeared before in some form and has been dealt with in ways that were either successful and can be revived or unsuccessful but for reasons that can be avoided. Elements of a useful approach to relevance, for example, may be found in two aspects of Search's past. The first was the understanding, which accompanied the change in the course's name in 1986, that the "search for values" under consideration was not only the West's, but also each student's. The faculty's desire to cover as much material as possible in the limited time available has usually meant severely subordinating the latter purpose to the former; perhaps it is time to bring the personal search for values closer to the foreground. Second, an earlier experiment with miniseminars built into the regular course calendar, in which students signed up to study a special topic with a Search instructor different from their own, was by all accounts successful.[10] One could readily imagine new modules that explore the ancient roots of modern concerns—how biblical texts have been used in debates on homosexuality, for example, or, following the classicist Donald Kagan, how exploring the origins of ancient wars sheds light on how modern wars may be averted.[11]

The failure of the short-lived effort to include a brief unit on Buddhism in the early 1970s may offer clues about how to bring a non-Judeo-Christian perspective to the course. The unit failed partly because the faculty had insufficient time to prepare to teach it and partly because, as an overwhelmingly Eastern phenomenon, Buddhism was severely disconnected from the rest of the course. It is not much of a stretch to think that, with adequate faculty preparation, a unit on Islam, an important Western religion, would be both timely and interesting to students.[12]

The use of nontextual materials in the Search course is another experiment that was tried and failed for reasons that may be studied profitably today. The founders of the course wanted to bring art, artifacts, and music to their students but were thwarted by logistical and equipment problems. The final section of this chapter deals with the new technologies of teaching and learning at some length; suffice it to say that many of the earlier problems have been overcome, even as new ones have arisen.

Faculty

More than any other course in the college curriculum, Search needs talented and enthusiastic faculty to teach it. This is true not just because the issues of course content discussed above have become increasingly challenging and thorny, but also because Search occupies so large a share of a student's course of study at Rhodes. Students vary widely in their backgrounds and, more important, in their interests in the humanities when they first arrive on campus. Conversations with admissions officers and students indicate that, in contrast to St. John's and one or two other schools, few students are drawn to Rhodes because of the Search course; the requirement simply does not figure in their calculus of college selection. Yet Search, as they often discover during summer preregistration, occupies more than 10 percent of the credit hours they will take toward graduation. Not surprisingly, attitudes that range from "This better be good" to "How can I slide by?" are widespread among first-year students when they enter the course. Unless the faculty ignites their interest, Search will be endured rather than embraced by many of them.

Yet, on the face of it, talented and enthusiastic instructors of the kind needed to excite students in the Search course are not in wide supply in higher education. No one enters graduate school for the purpose of teaching a course such as Search; nor does anyone have a Ph.D. that comprises classics, religious studies, art, music, philosophy, comparative literature, political science, and Western history from ancient Mesopotamia to the present.

To make matters worse, national trends in higher education are not in Search's favor. Many humanities scholars, especially younger ones, are hostile to the very idea of the Western civilization course. Many, too, were trained in graduate programs that, in their efforts to mimic the sciences in hope of gaining the respect and status that scientists enjoy, increasingly encourage disciplinary and even subdisciplinary specialization—the very opposite of what a multidisciplinary course like Search requires. As the literary critic David Bromwich wryly observes, "It is made out to be a scandal that advanced students in English today may have read only a few plays by Shakespeare. [Yet i]t has been a long time since even the most eminent professional philosophers or historians were expected to have read all of Hume or Kant or Thucydides or Gibbon."[13] Even for that growing number of humanities scholars who are intrigued by cross-disciplinary theoretical issues in, for example, cultural studies or gay and lesbian studies, the incentive not to range too far outside one's field is heightened by the relentless tightness of the job market.

To be sure, the faculty of the Search course has served it extremely well in recent years. One measure, however imperfect, is the students' formal end-of-semester evaluations of their courses and instructors, measured at Rhodes by the Educational Testing Service's Student Instructional Report (SIR) questionnaire. As recently as the late 1980s, students in Search rated "the quality of instruction in this course" four-tenths of a point below the quality of instruction in the college's other courses—3.9 compared with 4.3. By 1995, the average score of the Search staff on that question had risen to 4.6, one-tenth of a point higher than the itself remarkable college-wide average of 4.5 for courses other than Search.[14]

The reasons for Search's recent success, however, are dismayingly idiosyncratic—a former director, Fred Neal, who recruited from the existing college faculty with the ardency and skill of Jason rounding up heroes to seek the golden fleece; a former associate dean, Robert R. Llewellyn, who like Joseph in the court of pharaoh quietly protected the course from a sometimes hostile dean; and, in the late 1980s and early 1990s, a new dean, Harmon Dunathan, who was enthusiastic about Search and devoted considerable energy and resources to improving it.

In contrast to the strong institutional base it has built to confront issues of course content, Search is bereft of strong institutions to see it through the coming challenges of faculty recruitment. Individual deans may choose to take an interest in Search, but as an institution the dean's office includes no enduring mechanism to support the course. This, more than any conscious decision, may explain why the director of the course sometimes is left out of the hiring process for new faculty who might teach in Search.

Other of the college's institutional practices, again unintentionally, may discourage faculty recruitment for the course. Tenure and promotion procedures involve assessments from the tenured members of each candidate's department but not his or her senior colleagues in Search; similarly, the annual review process includes department chairs but not the Search chair. The criteria for faculty-development grants apply only to research in one's discipline; they do not support research that, in the spirit of the Search course, takes one beyond the discipline. The instrument used for student course evaluations is riddled with questions that are inappropriate for a team-designed course such as Search.

What can be done to help prepare the Search course to recruit and sustain talented, enthusiastic faculty members in a generally unfriendly academic climate? Taking the right approach to hiring will be important—namely, assessing a prospective faculty member's ability and interest to teach Search during the recruitment process rather than conscripting faculty after they have been hired. To this end, the Search director should always be formally involved in relevant hiring decisions. In addition, both as a way to make teaching in Search more appealing and in the interests of accuracy, those who teach regularly in the Search course should have the words *and Humanities* added to their titles, as in Associate Professor of Philosophy and Humanities. Such a reform, in addition to its practical benefits, would bring the status of the Search course into line with its prominence in the curriculum.

An even more fertile recruiting field for Search is the existing faculty of the college, especially in the natural and social sciences. Inviting such faculty into the course offers several obvious advantages. One is almost tautological: by broadening the talent pool from which the Search faculty is drawn, the chances that the course will be taught enthusiastically are bound to increase. Another is that the more Rhodes faculty members who have taught in the course, the more likely that the issues and information that students encounter in Search will be invoked, applied, and extended throughout the curriculum. Finally, humanists concerned with issues of power, status, race, class, and gender might be better informed if they were exposed to the research that actually has been done on these subjects by social and, in some cases, natural scientists.

Would, say, psychologists and biologists be willing to teach in Search? Many scientists were attracted to Rhodes and colleges like it in the first place by the liberal arts ideal, which they prefer to the narrow specialization of the university. But they are naturally apprehensive about teaching material that is unfamiliar to them. One partial solution is already in place, at least embryonically—namely, to invite prospective Search instructors to join in the Douglass Seminars. Another, even better approach would be to arrange a one-year reduction in teaching load, from three courses per semester to two, for faculty members who are willing to sit in on the Search course in preparation for teaching in it.

In one area, issues of course content and faculty recruitment overlap: preserving the multidisciplinary nature of the Search course. Professionalization is a temptation that was resisted during the first half-century of Search's history, but it is a temptation nonetheless; the norms of specialization and deference to specialized training run strong and deep in higher education. Because, as noted earlier, no one is an expert in Search, a natural tendency exists to carve up the course into smaller segments in which different faculty members are expert, such that the Old Testament unit becomes a mini–Introduction to the Hebrew Bible course designed by the biblical scholars, the Greek and Roman unit becomes the preserve of the classicists, and so on. To take such an approach would be not only unwise pedagogically, destroying the thematic integrity of the course, but also would actively discourage social and natural scientists from joining the Search faculty. They would be stigmatized as amateurs in the modern, disparaging sense of the word, not valued as amateurs in the classical meaning of those who do something for the love of it.

Technology

Technology-inspired innovations are coming to humanities education; on that, all agree. Too much has changed in American society for teaching and learning not to be affected. Because of the cumulative effect of television, personal computers, CD-ROM, VCRs, camcorders, e-mail, the Internet, and other recent inventions, writes Sven Birkerts, "the way that people experience the world has altered more in the last fifty years than in the many centuries preceding ours." Bemoaning the changes he describes, Birkerts adds that "our culture has begun to go through what promises to be a total metamorphosis . . . [t]he displacement of the page by the screen."[15] The classicist Jay David Bolter agrees, but more cheerfully: "The printed book seems destined to move to the margin of our literate culture. . . . What will be lost is not literacy itself, but the literacy of print, for electronic technology offers us a new kind of book and new ways to write."[16] With barely concealed glee, English professor Richard A. Lanham suggests that "[t]he real question for literary study now is not whether our students will be reading Great Traditional Books or Relevant Modern ones in the future, but whether they will be reading books at all."[17]

Those who celebrate technological innovation in education are convinced that, without dramatic change, the humanities will atrophy. "We cannot preserve Western culture in pickle," Lanham argues. "It must be recreated in the technologies of the present." Such technologies are increasingly fast-paced and interactive. The book, in contrast, is neither. It requires the reader to work slowly through a closely-reasoned argument, an image-packed poem, or a complex story in which each page must be mastered in sequence before the next can be understood. As such, it stands as a barrier between modern students and learning. "To defend the book just for the form of the codex book," Lanham concludes, "is to focus on the box and not the contents."[18]

What would a more appealing box look like? In the style of modern consumer technologies, advocates argue, it would be electronic and rich in visual and aural stimulation. Kenneth Morrell reports that when it comes to ancient Greece, for example, "manuscripts, inscriptions, collections of papyri, infrared photographs from satellites, images of vase paintings, exhaustive bibliographies, and more are all available on-line." It also would be interactive. "Electronic text is, like oral text, dynamic," notes Bolter.[19] Students who read, say, the *Iliad* or the *Odyssey* on their computer screens are able to change the text any way that suits them, in keeping with the tradition of the ancient bards who, in the centuries before the Homeric epics were written down, used to vary their recitations in accordance with each audience's response. Or, to use an even more arresting example:

Imagine a student brought up on computers, brought up interacting with text, moving it around, playing games with it. Now let her . . . sift a dubious classic like *Love's Labor's Lost*. Imagine her charting the rhetorical figures, displaying them in a special type, and then diagramming them, and cataloging them, and then, using a cheap program now available, making hyptertext animations of how they work. She'll use a . . . voice program to suggest how certain lines should be read. . . . Or make it into a film.[20]

The very qualities of fast-paced, interactive educational media that excite their champions horrify their critics. In the humanities, unlike the

sciences, Birkerts argues, information "is a means less to instrumental application than to something more nebulous: understanding. . . . In these
disciplines the *process* of study may be as vital to the understanding as are
the materials studied. . . . Part of any essential understanding of the world
is that it is opaque, obdurate. . . . Say what you will about books, they en-
code this sense of obstacle, of otherness." In contrast, "the multimedia
packages substitute transparency for opacity." Birkerts does not doubt that
the student who approaches Shakespeare through interactive software
may learn a great deal about the vagaries of Elizabethan politics or how
the Globe theater was built. But, he wonders, "will this dazzled student
find the concentration, the will, to live with the often burred and prick-
ly language of the plays themselves? The play's the thing—but will it
be?"[21] As for Homer, can manipulating the text take the place of closely
reading it? After all, it was the fixed, written version of Homer's poems
that pervaded fifth-century Athens and, consequently, helped to shape the
Western tradition.

The interactivity that proponents of the new technologies celebrate
involves more than texts. Through the Internet, they argue, the constraints of time (the sixty-minute class), space (the classroom walls), and
people (the students and their instructor) are dissolved. Discussions of
course materials can continue around the clock, involving not just those
on the class roster but also willing academic experts around the globe,
whom students can readily invite to respond to their opinions and answer
their questions. In such discussion groups, advocates have found, students
who sit silently in class sometimes participate actively.

As with electronic texts, however, critics express reservations about
on-line discussions. Some of these are practical: Where will students (and
faculty) find the hours to participate? Will, as some suspect, they drain it
from time better spent studying and reflecting on the assigned readings of
the course? Another concern is pedagogical. Should students be encouraged to think that transmitting messages from the solitude of their computer terminals is a substitute for joining discussions in the company of
their fellows?

Reading and discussion are not the only traditional components of
education affected by the new technologies; so is writing. Hypertext, a
term defined by its inventor, Theodor Nelson, as "non-sequential writing with reader-controlled links," allows students to write in a nonlinear
fashion.[22] A hypertext offers the reader numerous ways to read, exploring
alternate byways of written and, in hypermedia form, oral and visual text.

In its more modest incarnations, hypertext serves as a series of enhanced footnotes, sidebars, pictures, appendices, and indexes, expanding and illustrating the writer's presentation. In a "paper" about, say, Beethoven's late string quartets, the writer may extend readers the opportunity to click on an icon and hear a recorded passage or take an animated tour of early nineteenth-century Vienna. Taken to an extreme, however, hypertext shatters expository writing altogether, offering a riot of pathways through the material, including some that readers can create by altering the author's text. Myron Tuman is among those who argue that hypertexts "are not really texts at all, not documents prepared by authors to convey a distinct world view to readers. [Instead] they are systems for storing and retrieving information"—the thousands of photographs from Ken Burns's Civil War television series, for example, without Ken Burns to arrange them in an intelligible sequence.[23]

The challenge for the Search course, as for humanities education in general, will be to navigate between the zealous Scylla of educational technology's uncritical advocates and the curmudgeonly Charybdis of those who wish that the whole thing would just go away. The latter danger is real because all of the new technologies require faculty to master unfamiliar skills (often in hope of catching up with their students) and to redesign old approaches to teaching. But what is the alternative? Lanham is right: the humanities cannot be taught as if nothing has changed in the larger society. At the very least, some of the old wine must be poured into the new wineskins that modern students are accustomed to using. And why would we want it otherwise? It was, after all, part of the founding vision of the Search course to supplement printed texts with exactly the sort of art, artifacts, and music that now can readily be downloaded into the classroom, computer lab, and dorm room.

The former danger, however, that of going overboard, may be the greater one, partly because of the missionary excitement that enthusiasts always bring to their causes and partly because of all the unreservedly good uses to which the new technologies already are being put. In the medical world, for example, the on-line system Medline brings information to doctors much more quickly than its venerable printed predecessor, the periodical *Index Medicus*, ever could. Law libraries are moving rapidly from print to screen in their efforts to keep up with changes in case and statutory law. Electronic texts for natural and social sciences courses, updated frequently by their authors in response to new research and events, may soon replace cumbersome, quickly outdated textbooks.

But if the humanities are not of a different genus from their professional and scientific colleagues, they are a different species. Few would follow Lanham in heralding the day when "[e]lectronic media will change past literary texts as well as future ones."[24] For a student to understand the West's search for values, or to conduct a personal search for values in dialog with the Western tradition, means reading and thinking deeply about the works of the past in their historical form, then discussing them in the company of fellow searchers. Along that line, Tuman asks forty-year-old proponents of moving from the book to the computer to consider how well interactive technologies would have served them if they had not first been educated in the traditional, print-based way.[25] Similarly, impressive compilations of information in hypertext are no better a substitute for students writing critical and analytical essays than simply turning in their bibliographic note cards would have been in the old days. The purpose of writing assignments is to help students learn to express themselves intelligibly and to draw informed conclusions and defend them with evidence and arguments, not merely to build piles of data in cyberspace. Nor can on-line be allowed to supplant face-to-face as the primary setting for teaching and learning. Liberal arts colleges cannot endure, nor should they, if they do not provide students close personal instruction by a faculty whose concern and attention extends not just to their intellectual accomplishments but to their full flourishing as human beings.★

Conclusion

Writings that have "The Future of . . ." in their title are best known for the hilarity with which they may be read years (often an embarrassingly few years) after they are published. No doubt I have unwittingly added to the sum of laughter that awaits readers in the third millennium. Still, we who live in awareness that the future awaits have little choice but to anticipate what it will be like and how we want to shape it. To the extent that the future is, at least in part, the trajectory of the past as it passes through the present, such an exercise may even be useful.

★ As part of our initial response to recent technological challenges and opportunities, we have established an electronic Home Page for the Search course on the WorldWideWeb, at the following address: http://www.humanities.rhodes.edu.

Useful, but not straightforward. In no case are the matters that I have discussed in this chapter simple ones. The faculty of the Search course enjoy institutions that have helped them to deal amicably and creatively with, for example, the issues of course content. Yet in the larger academic community these issues are so charged with partisan vitriol as to make one wonder how long any institution can resist succumbing to disabling rancor, victory for one ideological extreme or the other, or the abandonment of the Search-style course as a general education requirement. As for the Search faculty, their teaching is as able and enthusiastic in the late twentieth century as at any time in history. But with the trends in graduate training and the academic job market what they are, nothing guarantees that the faculty of the course will remain so indefinitely. Finally, the issues of how and how much of the new educational technologies that loom on the Search course's horizon should be used seem to lend themselves to no better solution than the dismayingly imprecise Goldilocks formula: not too much, not too little, just right.

With all that said, I am optimistic about the future of the Search course in a way that only close study of its history allows. As this book has shown, throughout its fifty years, Search has had ups and downs too numerous and varied to mention. The students who have passed through the course have had a wide range of experiences, some of them less exalted than others. Yet through the unceasing efforts of dedicated faculty and some administrators to keep up with but not give way to the vagaries of changing times, the course has maintained an integrity, deeply grounded in its history and content, that has enabled it to surmount its worst teachers and its most ill-conceived experiments.

The proof of the Search course's integrity is in the alumni of the college, many of whom say they regard Search as the most important intellectual experience of their lives and wish they could repeat it. I experience the effects of this high regard every time I speak to an alumni chapter. I always bring with me a stack of the course's current calendar, and when I announce that I have done so, I know from experience what I will hear from graduates of every generation: a sudden and collective gasp of pleasure, a squeal of delight. I have come to think of that as the sound of the Search course.

Appendix A

COMPILED BY
MICHAEL NELSON

(Name, department)

W. Raymond Cooper, history
John Henry Davis, history
Alexander P. Kelso, philosophy
Laurence F. Kinney, religious studies
John Osman, philosophy
W. Taylor Reveley, religious studies
Daniel D. Rhodes, philosophy
Granville D. Davis, history
Fred W. Neal, religious studies
Charles Bigger, philosophy
Milton P. Brown, religious studies
Larry Lacy, philosophy
James Jobes, philosophy
Richard A. Batey, religious studies
Julius W. Melton, religious studies
George M. Apperson, history
Darrell J. Doughty, religious studies
Robert G. Patterson, religious studies
Dale E. Benson, history
Robert R. Llewellyn, philosophy
Donald W. Tucker, Spanish
Larry Bone, librarian
Richard C. Wood, English
Horst R. Dinkelacker, German
Douglas W. Hatfield, history
Carl F. Walters, religious studies
Ray M. Allen, dean of admissions

(Name, department)

Robert L. Amy, biology
Bo Scarborough, dean of students
John Bruhwiler, German
Diane M. Clark, music
Julian T. Darlington, biology
Bernice White, English
Elaine Whitaker, English
Robert C. Norfleet, chaplain
E. Llewellyn Queener, psychology
Janet Everts, religious studies
F. Michael McLain, religious studies
Steven L. McKenzie, religious studies
James M. Vest, French
James E. Roper, English
Diane G. Sachs, sociology
Michael Shirley, history
Valarie H. Ziegler, religious studies
Robert M. Watson, history
Jesse Garner, humanities
Ann Moyer, history
J. Steven Musick, chaplain
Carol Devens, history
Mikle D. Ledgerwood, French
Stephen R. Haynes, religious studies
Daniel E. Cullen, political science
Gail Corrington Streete, religious studies
Sandra McEntire, English

Carolyn P. Schriber, history
Lynn B. Zastoupil, history
Michael Nelson, political science
Ellen T. Armour, religious studies
Yehoshua Gitay, religious studies
James D. Clifton, art history
Gail Murray, history
Amy Hollywood, religious studies
Richard A. Martin, English

Rahel Hahn, German
Joseph A. Favazza, religious studies
Kenneth Morrell, Greek and Roman
    studies
Livia Tenzer, Greek and Roman
    studies
Richard Cohen, religious studies
Greg Carey, religious studies
Janusz Duzinkiewicz, history

Appendix B

UNITS AND READINGS IN THE
SEARCH COURSE
(1 9 9 5 – 1 9 9 6)

COMPILED BY
MICHAEL NELSON

The first year of the Search course is organized into three major units on the ancient world—the Hebrews, the Greeks and Romans, and the early Christians. It begins and ends with weeklong units on Augustine's *Confessions*. All first-year sections of the course follow the same calendar of topics and readings.

The second year of the course covers the period from the Middle Ages to the present and is organized chronologically into units on the Middle Ages, the Renaissance and Reformation, the seventeenth century, the Enlightenment, the nineteenth century, and the twentieth century. Students in the second year elect one of five tracks: history, literature, philosophy, religion, or politics. (The last was added in 1996–1997.) All five tracks use many works in common (or equivalent works that instructors may assign from the same author or, sometimes, the same period). Most of these works are included in a staff-produced, two-volume *Readings* book, which all students purchase. In addition, each track (and, in some cases, each instructor within a track) supplements this "core" with readings particular to its discipline.

A complete list of the works assigned in the 1995–1996 version of first-year Search and of the core works assigned in the second year is provided below, along with examples of works assigned in each of the second-year tracks.

In order that students may complete the reading assignments for each week in six to nine hours, most of the longer works are read in excerpt form; others are assigned in full and are studied over several days. For example, six books from the *Iliad* are read and discussed in one colloquium, but the *Aeneid* and the *Odyssey* are read nearly in their entirety and are discussed in three and four colloquium meetings, respectively.

227

FIRST YEAR
INTRODUCTION AND CONCLUSION
Augustine, *Confessions*

THE HEBREWS
Epic of Gilgamesh
Enuma Elish
Brief writings from ancient Canaan and Egypt
Genesis
Exodus
Deuteronomy
Joshua
Judges
Psalms
I and II Samuel
I and II Kings
Amos
Hosea
Isaiah
Jeremiah
Ezra
Ruth
Proverbs
Ecclesiastes
Job

THE GREEKS AND THE ROMANS
Homer, *Iliad*; *Odyssey*
Virgil, *Aeneid*
Thucydides, *The History of the Peloponnesian War*
Sophocles, *Oedipus Rex*; *Oedipus at Colonus*; *Antigone*
Euripides, *The Trojan Women*
Polybius, *Histories*
Livy, *From the Founding of the City*
Sallust, *The Conspiracy of Cataline*
Cicero, *Speeches Against Cataline*
Plato, *Apology*; *Phaedo*; *Republic*
Aristotle, *Nichomachean Ethics*
Lucretius, *On the Nature of Things*
Seneca, *Moral Epistles*; *On Providence*
Tacitus, *Annals*

THE CHRISTIANS
> Daniel
> I Maccabees
> Acts
> Galatians
> James
> Romans
> Mark
> Matthew
> Luke
> John
> Hebrews
> Revelation
> *Martyrdom of Sts. Perpetua and Felicitas*
> I Timothy
> I John
> *Apocalypse of Peter*
> Brief writings by Philo, Irenaeus, Tertullian, Arius, Athanasius

SECOND YEAR
THE MIDDLE AGES
CORE:
> Benedict, *The Holy Rule of St. Benedict*
> Anselm, *Monologium*
> Abelard, *Sic et Non*
> Thomas of Celano, *Life of St. Francis*
> Aquinas, "Sermon on the Creed"; *Summa Contra Gentiles; Summa Theologica;* "Commentary on Boethius's *On the Trinity*"
> Dante, *The Divine Comedy*
> Pizan, *The Book of the City of Ladies*
> Hildegard of Bingen, *The Visions of St. Hildegard*
> Julian of Norwich, *Showings*
> Catherine of Siena, "To Gregory XI"
> Mergery Kempe, *The Book of Mergery Kempe*
HISTORY TRACK:
> Bernard of Clairveaux, *Apology*; Ordericus, *The Ecclesiastical History of England and Normandy*; Eugenius IV, *Seven Sacraments*
LITERATURE TRACK:
> *The Song of Roland; Sir Gawain and the Green Knight; Aucassin and Nicolette;* Chaucer, *The Canterbury Tales; The Cid*

PHILOSOPHY TRACK:

Augustine, *City of God*

RELIGION TRACK:

Bede, *Ecclesiastical History of the English People*; Dionysus the Areopagite, *The Mystical Theology and the Celestial Hierarchies*; Julian of Norwich, *Revelations of Divine Love*

RENAISSANCE AND REFORMATION

CORE:

At least two of the following:

Petrarch, "The Ascent of Mont Ventoux"

Pico, "Oration on the Dignity of Man"

Erasmus, *The Paraclesis*

Cellini, *The Life of Benvenuto Cellini*

Rabelais, *Gargantua*

Marlowe, *The Tragical History of Dr. Faustus*

Machiavelli, *The Prince*; "Letter on the Composition of *The Prince*"; *Discourses on Livy*

Luther, *The Ninety-Five Theses*; "An Open Letter to the Christian Nobility"; "A Treatise on Christian Liberty"

Calvin, "Confession of Faith"; *The Institutes of the Christian Religion*

Sadolet, "Letter to the Senate and People of Geneva"; Calvin, "Reply" *Canons and Decrees of the Council of Trent*

HISTORY TRACK:

Castiglione, *The Courtier*; Battista, *Autobiography*; Marco Polo, *Travels*

LITERATURE TRACK:

Montaigne, *Essays*; Cervantes, *Don Quixote*; Loyola, "Spiritual Exercises"

PHILOSOPHY TRACK:

Shakespeare, *King Lear*

RELIGION TRACK:

The Malleus Maleficarum; Paul III, "The Bull of Institution of the Jesuits, 1540"

THE SEVENTEENTH CENTURY

CORE:

Montaigne, "Of Custom, and not easily changing an accepted law"

Copernicus, *De revolitionibus orbium celestium*

Kepler, *Harmonice mundi*

Galileo, *Siderius nuncius*

Bacon, *The New Organon*

Descartes, *Discourse on Method*

Hobbes, *Leviathan*

Locke, *Two Treatises Of Civil Government*
HISTORY TRACK:
Bossuet, *Politics Drawn from the Very Words of the Holy Scripture*
LITERATURE TRACK:
Moliere, *The Misanthrope*
PHILOSOPHY TRACK:
Descartes, *The Meditations on First Philosophy*; Locke, *An Essay Concerning Human Understanding*; Pascal, *Pensees*
RELIGION TRACK:
John Winthrop, *A Model of Christian Charity;* Thomas Hutchinson, *The History of the Colony and Province of Massachusetts Bay*

THE ENLIGHTENMENT
CORE:
Kant, *The Critique of Practical Reason; Metaphysical Foundations of Morals*
At least three of the following:
Kant, "What Is Enlightenment?"
Voltaire, *The Philosophical Dictionary*
Hume, *Enquiry Concerning the Human Understanding*
Lessing, *The Education of the Human Race; Nathan the Wise*
Rousseau, *A Discourse on the Origin of Inequality; On the Social Contract*
Madison, *Federalist* Nos. 10, 51
Smith, *An Inquiry Into the Nature and Causes of the Wealth of Nations*
Wollstonecraft, *A Vindication of the Rights of Women*
HISTORY TRACK:
Diderot, *D'Alembert's Dream*; Declaration of the Rights of Man and the Citizen; Declaration of the Rights of Women; Hume, *An Inquiry Concerning the Principles of Morals*
LITERATURE TRACK:
Voltaire, *Candide*; Paine, *The Age of Reason*; Diderot, "Supplement to the Voyage of Bougainville"; Goethe, *The Sorrows of Young Werther*
PHILOSOPHY TRACK:
Kant, *Critique of Pure Reason*; J.S. Mill, *Utilitarianism*
RELIGION TRACK:
Feuerbach, *The Essence of Christianity*; T. Huxley, *Science and Christian Tradition*

THE NINETEENTH CENTURY
CORE:
Schleiermacher, *Speeches on Religion Addressed to Its Cultural Despisers*
Coleridge, "The Rime of the Ancient Mariner"
Selected poems by Pope, Wordsworth, and Blake
Malthus, *An Essay on the Principle of Population*

J. S. Mill, *On Liberty*

H. T. Mill, "Enfranchisement of Women"

Darwin, *Origin of the Species; The Descent of Man*

Marx, "Alienated Labor"; "Preface" to *A Contribution to the Critique of Political Economy; The Communist Manifesto* (with Engels)

Nietzsche, *The Will to Power; The Geneaology of Morals; Beyond Good and Evil*

Freud, *The Ego and the Id; Civilization and Its Discontents*

Dostoevsky, *The Brothers Karamazov*

Kierkegaard, *Fear and Trembling; The Sickness Unto Death*

HISTORY TRACK:

Burke, *Reflections on the Revolution in France;* Tocqueville, *Democracy in America*; Kipling, "The White Man's Burden"; Malthus, *An Essay on the Principle of Population*

LITERATURE TRACK:

Tolstoy, "The Death of Ivan Ilyich"; Ibsen, *A Doll's House*

PHILOSOPHY TRACK:

Kierkegaard, *Concluding Unscientific Postscript*

RELIGION TRACK:

Selected poems by Hopkins, Yeats, Eliot, Stevens, Plath, Ashberry; George Eliot, *Scenes of Clerical Life*

THE TWENTIETH CENTURY

CORE:

Sartre, "Atheistic Existentialism"

H. Richard Niebuhr, "The Grace of Doing Nothing"; "The Only Way Into the Kingdom of God"

Reinhold Niebuhr, "Must We Do Nothing?"

Wiesel, *Night*

At least two of the following:

    Bonhoeffer, *Letters and Papers from Prison*

    Gandhi, *Hind Swaraj (Indian Home Rule)*

    Gutierrez, *A Theology of Liberation*

    King, "Letter from Birmingham City Jail"

    Beauvoir, *The Second Sex*

    Fiorenza, "Feminist Spirituality, Christian Identity, and Catholic Vision"

    Rorty, *Philosophy and the Mirror of Nature*

    Foucault, *The History of Sexuality*

HISTORY TRACK:

Orwell, *Animal Farm*; Remarque, *All Quiet on the Western Front*; Hitler, *Mein Kampf*; Churchill, "Speech at Fulton"; Browning, *Ordinary Men*

LITERATURE TRACK:

    Kafka, *In a Penal Colony*; Silone, *Bread and Wine*; Hesse, *Demian*; Wiesenthal, *The Sunflower*; Koestler, *Darkness at Noon*; Sartre, *No Exit*; Mann, *Death in Venice*; A. Huxley, *Brave New World*; Baldwin, *The Fire Next Time*

PHILOSOPHY TRACK:

    Wittgenstein, *Philosophical Investigations*; William James, *The Will to Believe and Other Essays in Popular Philosophy*

RELIGION TRACK:

    Teilhard de Chardin, *Hymn of the Universe*; Weil, *Waiting on God*; Daly, *Beyond God the Father*; Falwell, *Listen, America!*; Nishitani, *Religion and Nothingness*

Notes

Chapter 1

1. Paul Flowers, "Southwestern to Turn Back to Great Basic Books," *Memphis Commercial Appeal*, 1 August 1945.

2. George Marsden, *The Soul of the American University: From Protestant Establishment to Established Nonbelief* (New York: Oxford University Press, 1994), 339.

3. See the early chapters of Laurence R. Veysey, *The Emergence of the American University* (Chicago: University of Chicago Press, 1965).

4. The account that follows is drawn mainly from Joan Shelly Rubin, *The Making of Middlebrow Culture* (Chapel Hill, N.C.: University of North Carolina Press, 1992); Harry S. Ashmore, *Unseasonable Truths: The Life of Robert Maynard Hutchins* (Boston: Little, Brown, 1989); Robert F. Davidson, "Trends in the Humanities in General Education," in *The Humanities in General Education*, ed. Earl J. McGrath (Dubuque, Iowa: W. C. Brown Co., 1949), 289–308; and James B. Conant, *My Several Lives: Memoirs of a Social Inventor* (New York: Harper and Row, 1970).

5. Carol S. Gruber, *Mars and Minerva: World War I and the Uses of Higher Learning in America* (Baton Rouge: Louisiana State University Press, 1975), 243

6. The direct descendant of the War Issues Course at Columbia was a "peace issues" course, soon named "Contemporary Civilization," which began in 1919. "CC" has been a required course for undergraduate students ever since, later joined by "Lit Hum," or "Humanities: Masterpieces of European Literature and Philosophy."

7. Robert M. Hutchins, *The Higher Education in America* (New Haven, Conn.: Yale University Press, 1936).

8. Davidson, "Trends in the Humanities," 303.

9. McGrath, ed., *Humanities in General Education.*

10. Hutchins, *Higher Education in America*, 97.

11. Virginia Woolf, *The Death of the Moth* (New York: Harcourt, Brace, 1942), 180–184.

12. Davidson, "Trends in the Humanities," 307.

13. Quoted in Charles I. Diehl, "Post-War Liberal Education," address delivered at

the March 1943 meeting of the Egyptians, Memphis, Tennessee, Monroe Goodbar Morgan Archives, Rhodes College, Memphis, Tenn.

14. Ibid.

15. The information on which the following account is based is drawn primarily from W. Raymond Cooper, *Southwestern at Memphis, 1848–1948* (Richmond, Va.: John Knox Press, 1949); William Morgan, *The Architecture of Rhodes College* (Columbia: University of Missouri Press, 1989); and numerous articles in the *Southwestern News* and the *Sou'wester*.

16. Morgan, *Architecture of Rhodes College*, 94. In 1994, Rhodes was named the most beautiful campus in America by the *Princeton Review Student Access Guide to the Best 306 Colleges*, ed. Tom Meltzer et al. (New York: Villard Books, 1994), 30.

17. Anne Howard Bailey, "Summa Cum Laude," television script presented by Armstrong Circle Theatre, 17 April 1951, under the title "Honor Student," Morgan Archives.

18. Quotations from John Henry Davis, "*Apologia Pro Vita Sua* (or The Memoirs of an Amiable Trifler)," 1974, Morgan Archives; and James E. Roper, *Southwestern At Memphis, 1948–1975* (Memphis, Tenn.: Southwestern at Memphis, 1975), 88–89.

19. Marsden, *Soul of the American University*, 276–282, 358–359.

20. Charles E. Diehl, "College to Contribute Men and Women of Character, Culture, and Competence," *Southwestern News*, November 1943, 4.

21. Cooper, *Southwestern at Memphis*, 163.

22. Southwestern at Memphis Board of Directors, "Bible Teaching at Southwestern," *Southwestern Bulletin*, July 1944.

23. Cooper, *Southwestern at Memphis,* 116.

24. Veysey, *Emergence of the American University*.

25. Charles E. Diehl, "Religious Educator," n.d., 5, Morgan Archives.

26. "The Official Report of the Hearing of the Charges Preferred by Eleven Presbyterian Ministers against President Charles E. Diehl Held on Tuesday, February 3rd, 1931 By the Board of Directors of Southwestern," printed in *Southwestern Bulletin*, March 1931.

27. Diehl, "Post-War Liberal Education."

28. Ibid.

29. Charles E. Diehl, "Notes for Meeting of Committee on Post-War Liberal Education," 28 October 1943, Morgan Archives.

30. Davis, "*Apologia Pro Vita Sua.*"

31. "Report of Committee Meeting Held With Dr. George A. Works Held on February 25, 1944," n.d., Morgan Archives.

32. John Osman, "The Classic of Classics," pamphlet published by Southwestern at Memphis, n.d., Morgan Archives.

33. "The Great Centuries," program published by Southwestern at Memphis, 1944, Morgan Archives.

34. John Osman, "Southwestern Faculty Offers the 'Great Centuries' Lectures," *Southwestern News*, March 1945, 6–7.

35. Bob Wherritt, "Continue Series of 'The Great Centuries,'" *Sou'wester*, 24 November 1944.

36. Margaretta Clark, "She Borrowed Culture from Greece, but in Government, Old Rome Was Supreme, " *Memphis Press-Scimitar*, 16 December 1945.

37. Margaretta Clark, "Looking Down the Centuries," *Memphis Press-Scimitar*, 18 November 1945.

38. Margaretta Clark, "Mankind and 'The Great Centuries,'" *Memphis Press-Scimitar*, 17 November 1945.

39. Margaretta Clark, "Enemy of Peace: The State Itself," *Memphis Press-Scimitar*, 7 April 1945.

40. See Chapter 5.

41. Jameson M. Jones, former dean and vice-president of Southwestern at Memphis, interview by James M. Vest, Memphis, Tenn., 10 October 1994.

42. Gerald Graff, *Beyond the Culture Wars: How Teaching the Conflicts Can Revitalize American Education* (New York: Norton, 1992), 132.

43. Minutes of the 15 January 1945 meeting of the Southwestern faculty, Morgan Archives.

44. Charles E. Diehl, letter to Theodore M. Greene, 16 January 1945, Morgan Archives.

45. The young William F. Buckley, Jr., had a slightly different and less approving view. After Greene left Princeton to accept a position at Yale, Buckley observed that Greene may have been "a Christian by a great many definitions," but his courses were "completely nondogmatic." Buckley, *God and Man at Yale* (Chicago: Henry Regnery, 1951), 7–8.

46. Theodore M. Greene, "Liberal Education in a World at War," commencement address at Southwestern at Memphis, 10 June 1941, Morgan Archives.

47. Theodore M. Greene et al., *Liberal Education Re-Examined: Its Role in a Democracy* (New York: Harper and Brothers, 1943); Diehl's review of the book, titled "Learned Men State Ideals of Education," appeared in the *Memphis Commercial Appeal*, 23 February 1944.

48. Greene, *Liberal Education Re-Examined*, 70.

49. "Summary of Discussion Held at the Southwestern Faculty Conference with Professor Theodore Greene, January 27, 1945," n.d., Morgan Archives.

50. Minutes of the 3 March 1943 meeting of the Southwestern faculty, Morgan Archives.

51. Minutes of the 5 March 1945 meeting of the Southwestern faculty, Morgan Archives.

52. Charles E. Diehl, letter to Theodore M. Greene, 14 May 1945, Morgan Archives.

53. Untitled "memorandum to faculty" from "the committee," 14 May 1945, Morgan Archives.

54. Minutes of the 23 May 1945 meeting of the Southwestern faculty, Morgan Archives.

55. *Man in the Light of History and Religion: A Syllabus* (Memphis, Tenn.: Southwestern at Memphis, 1945–1946), i–ii.

56. Helen Gardner, *Art Through the Ages*, 2d ed. (New York: Harcourt, Brace, 1936); and Edward McNail Burns, *Western Civilizations: Their History and Culture* (New York: Norton, 1941). The quotation is from page xix.

57. John Henry Davis, "Man in the Light of History and Religion: A Humanities Course at Southwestern," in *Humanities in General Education*, ed. McGrath, 96–105.

58. Ibid.

59. Charles E. Diehl, letter to Gordon Siefkin, 28 September 1945, Morgan Archives.

60. Cooper, *Southwestern at Memphis*, 156.

61. Gloria Ash Minor, letter to author, 23 July 1992.

62. Charles I. Diehl, letter to George A. Works, 1 October 1945, Morgan Archives.

63. *Man in the Light of History and Religion: A Syllabus*, 2d ed. (Memphis, Tenn.: Southwestern at Memphis, 1946–1947).

64. Rhodes is quoted in Charles E. Diehl, "Annual Report of the President," 31 August 1946, Morgan Archives.

65. Tom Jolly, interview by author, 8 November 1994, Memphis, Tenn. See also, Helen Lefkowitz Horowitz, *Campus Life: Undergraduate Cultures from the End of the Eighteenth Century to the Present* (New York: Knopf, 1987), ch. 8.

66. Roper, *Southwestern At Memphis*, 10.

67. "Freedom and the Books: A New Education for Adults, 1946–1947," n.d., Southwestern at Memphis, Morgan Archives.

68. *Man in the Light of History and Religion: A Syllabus*, 3d ed. (Memphis, Tenn.: Southwestern at Memphis, 1947–1948).

69. "Wide Majority Favors 'Man' in Recent Poll," *Sou'wester* 23 March 1950.

70. A. Theodore Johnson, "Report of the Dean," August 1950, Morgan Archives.

71. John Henry Davis, "The Humanities at Southwestern," in *The Humanities in General Education*, ed. James A. Fisher (Dubuque, Iowa: Wm. C. Brown Co., 1960), 55–68.

72. Richard C. Wood, memorandum to James M. Vest, 12 October 1994, Memphis, Tenn.

73. Eugene Botsford, "Freshman Discovers College Means Study," *Sou'wester*, 20 October 1956.

74. The student notes for the 1952–1953 version of the Man course are those of Marcia Culmer Beard. In 1946, writing in his capacity as chair of the Faculty Committee on Religious Life, Kinney had reported that the Man course was the college's most valuable recent attempt "to plow religious truth into the fabric of the educational experience" and that the course was "the crucible where men learn to relate the best thought and action of the ages with the Christian concept of life." Quoted in Charles E. Diehl, "Annual Report of the President," 31 August 1946, Morgan Archives.

75. Marcia Calmer Beard, letter to author, 4 July 1992.

76. Davis, "Humanities at Southwestern."

77. Greene is quoted in "Man Course Is a Revolution in Academics Here," *Sou'wester*, 2 November 1945. Diehl refers to other communications in "Annual Report of the President," 11 September 1945, Morgan Archives.

78. The Davis chapters are cited in notes 57 and 71.

79. Rhodes's efforts are described in "Annual Report of the President," 16 October 1958, Morgan Archives.

Chapter 2

1. *The Bulletin of Southwestern at Memphis 1955–56* (Memphis, Tenn.: Southwestern at Memphis), 24. I want to thank Larry Lacy and Michael Nelson for the assistance they gave me in preparing this chapter. I also want to thank all of my colleagues in the Search course through the years, especially Fred Neal, whose vision and courage preserved the course through very difficult times and who represents for me the model of a humanist, teacher, and friend.

2. Ibid., 65.

3. Ibid., 94.

4. Ibid., 37.

5. *Man in the Light of History and Religion: A Syllabus*, 6th ed. (Memphis, Tenn.: Southwestern at Memphis, 1956).

6. Jameson M. Jones, former dean and vice-president of Southwestern at Memphis, interview by Donald W. Tucker, Robert R. Llewellyn, and James M. Vest, 10 October 1994.

7. *Man in the Light of History and Religion: A Syllabus*, 7th ed., 2 vols. (Memphis, Tenn.: Southwestern at Memphis, 1961).

8. Glenn Munson, registrar of Rhodes College, Headcount and Full-Time Equivalent Enrollment, 1958–59 to 1994–95, memo to the author, summer 1995.

9. Man Official Class Roll, 1964–65, Fred W. Neal papers.

10. *Southwestern News*, January 1962, 8–9; Fred W. Neal, interview by Michael Nel-

son, summer 1994. Neal was named the R. A. Webb Professor of Bible in 1960.

11. William Larry Lacy, interview by the author, February 1995.

12. *Man in the Light of History and Religion: A Syllabus*, 8th ed., 2 vols. (Memphis, Tenn.: Southwestern at Memphis, 1965).

13. Robert L. Calhoun, *What Is Man?* (New York: Association Press, 1939); Samuel M. Thompson, *A Modern Philosophy of Religion* (Chicago: H. Regnery Co., 1955); and Jean Bruller [Vercors, pseud.], *You Shall Know Them*, trans. Rita Barisse (Boston: Little, Brown, 1953).

14. *Southwestern News*, January 1962, 8–9.

15. Bernard W. Anderson, *Understanding the Old Testament*, 2d ed. (Englewood Cliffs, N.J.: Prentice-Hall, 1966); and Howard Clark Kee and Franklin W. Young, *Understanding the New Testament*, 2d ed. (Englewood Cliffs, N.J.: Prentice-Hall, 1965).

16. *Southwestern News*, January 1961, 4.

17. *Man in the Light of History and Religion: A Syllabus*, 9th ed., 2 vols. (Memphis, Tenn.: Southwestern at Memphis, 1967).

18. Hugh S. Brown and Lewis B. Mayhew, *American Higher Education* (New York: Center for Applied Research in Education, 1965), 48.

19. Earl J. McGrath and L. Richard Meeth, "Organizing for Teaching and Learning: the Curriculum," in *Higher Education: Some Newer Developments*, ed. Samuel Baskin (New York: McGraw-Hill, 1965), 32.

20. Brown and Mayhew, *American Higher Education*, 52.

21. Gilbert Allardyce, "The Rise and Fall of the Western Civilization Course," *The American Historical Review* 87 (June 1982), 716–717.

22. Brown and Mayhew, *American Higher Education*, 79.

23. Allardyce, "Rise and Fall of the Western Civilization Course," 716.

24. Brown and Mayhew, *American Higher Education*, 79.

25. McGrath and Meeth, "Organizing for Teaching and Learning," 41.

26. Samuel Baskin, "Summing Up," in *Higher Education: Some Newer Developments*, ed. Samuel Baskin (New York: McGraw-Hill, 1965), 325.

27. Ibid., 321.

28. Lewis B. Mayhew, "The New Colleges," in *Higher Education: Some Newer Developments*, ed. Samuel Baskin (New York: McGraw-Hill, 1965), 19.

29. Allardyce, "Rise and Fall of the Western Civilization Course," 720.

30. *The Bulletin of Southwestern at Memphis, 1957–58* (Memphis, Tenn.: Southwestern at Memphis, 1957), 40.

31. *The Bulletin of Southwestern at Memphis 1963–64* (Memphis, Tenn.: Southwestern at Memphis, 1963), 112; *Southwestern News*, October 1963.

32. *The Sou'wester*, 13 May 1966.

33. Jameson M. Jones, Report of the Dean to the Board of Trustees, Minutes of the

Meeting of the Southwestern Trustees, 19–20 October 1966 Meeting of the Trustees, Morgan Archives.

34. Munson, Headcount and Full-Time Equivalent Enrollment.

35. James E. Roper, *Southwestern At Memphis 1948–1975* (Memphis, Tenn.: Southwestern at Memphis, 1975), 77–78.

36. Margaret McKee, "S'Western Names President—He's 31," *Memphis Press Scimitar,* 29 May 1964; Roper, *Southwestern At Memphis,* 64.

37. Roper, *Southwestern At Memphis,* 64–65.

38. Jones, Report to the Board, 19–20 October 1966.

39. "Faculty Scraps Saturday Classes," *The Sou'wester,* 10 November 1967.

40. *The Bulletin of Southwestern at Memphis 1968–69* (Memphis, Tenn.: Southwestern at Memphis, 1968), 73.

41. Man Official Class Roll 1968–69, Fred W. Neal papers.

42. Munson, Headcount and Full-Time Equivalent Enrollment.

43. *The Bulletin of Southwestern at Memphis 1967–68* (Memphis, Tenn.: Southwestern at Memphis), 52.

44. "Faculty Liberalizes Bible Requirement," *The Sou'wester,* 8 December 1967.

45. *The Bulletin of Southwestern at Memphis 1969–70* (Memphis, Tenn.: Southwestern at Memphis, 1969), 58.

46. Roper, *Southwestern at Memphis,* 67.

47. *The Bulletin of Southwestern at Memphis 1970–71* (Memphis, Tenn.: Southwestern at Memphis, 1970), 53–54.

48. Report of Committee on Institutional Racism, Minutes of the Meeting of Directors, 30 January 1969, Morgan Archives.

49. Ibid., 14.

50. George Arthur Buttrick, *Biblical Thought and the Secular University* (Baton Rouge, Louisiana: Louisiana State University Press, 1960), 4.

51. John F. Wilson, "Introduction: The Background and the Present Context of the Study of Religion in Colleges and Universities," in *The Study of Religion in Colleges and Universities,* ed. Paul Ramsey and John F. Wilson (Princeton, New Jersey: Princeton University Press, 1970), 9.

52. James M. Gustafson, "The Study of Religion in Colleges and Universities: A Practical Commentary," in *The Study of Religion in Colleges and Universities,* ed. Paul Ramsey and John F. Wilson (Princeton, New Jersey: Princeton University Press, 1970), 335.

53. Wilson, "Background and Present Context of the Study of Religion," 11.

54. George M. Marsden, *The Soul of the American University: From Protestant Establishment to Established Nonbelief* (New York and Oxford: Oxford University Press, 1994), 415–416.

55. Ibid., 416.

56. Roper, *Southwestern at Memphis*, 73.

57. Ibid., 74–75.

58. *The Bulletin of Southwestern at Memphis 1970–71* (Memphis, Tenn.: Southwestern at Memphis, 1970), 35.

59. *The Bulletin of Southwestern at Memphis 1964–65* (Memphis, Tenn.: Southwestern at Memphis, 1964), 73. Later the name was changed again to the Department of Religious Studies.

60. See discussion early in this chapter on historical-critical menthods of biblical study.

61. *The Bulletin of Southwestern at Memphis 1967–68* (Memphis, Tenn.: Southwestern at Memphis, 1967), 122–123.

62. Jameson M. Jones, interview by Donald W. Tucker, Robert R. Llewellyn, and James M. Vest, 10 October 1994.

63. Fred W. Neal, interview by Michael Nelson, summer 1994.

64. Ibid.

65. Ibid.

66. *Southwestern News*, October 1964, 1.

67. *The Bulletin of Southwestern at Memphis 1969–70* (Memphis, Tenn.: Southwestern at Memphis, 1969), 20.

68. *Southwestern News*, October 1965.

69. *The Bulletin of Southwestern at Memphis 1969–70* (Memphis, Tenn.: Southwestern at Memphis, 1969), 19.

70. *Southwestern News*, October 1965.

71. *Southwestern News*, October 1963, 11.

72. It should also be pointed out that before the work of revision was completed the most nontraditional member, Darrell Doughty, had left to take a position at Drew University.

73. *Southwestern News*, October 1955, 2.

74. Robert G. Patterson, memorandum to members of the "Man" staff, 17 February 1969, Fred W. Neal papers.

75. Ibid.

76. Ibid.

77. Ibid.

78. Ibid.

79. Ibid.

80. Robert G. Patterson, Man in the Light of History and Religion, an outline of the course, attached to the memorandum of 17 February 1969, Fred W. Neal papers.

81. Robert G. Patterson, memorandum to members of the "Man" staff, 17 February 1969.

82. Robert G. Patterson, autograph emendation of the attachment to the memorandum of 17 February 1969.

83. Robert G. Patterson, Where We Are in the "Man" Syllabus Revisions, memorandum to the staff, 27 February 1970; Fred W. Neal, memorandum to the unit editors of the Man syllabus, 5 May 1970; Robert G. Patterson, memorandum to the members of the Man staff, 6 May 1970, Fred W. Neal papers.

84. *Man in the Light of History and Religion: A Syllabus*, 10th ed. (Memphis, Tenn.: Southwestern at Memphis, 1970).

85. *The Bulletin of Southwestern at Memphis 1970–71* (Memphis. Tenn.: Southwestern at Memphis, 1970), 111, 149.

86. Ibid., 53–54.

87. *The Bulletin of Southwestern at Memphis 1973–74* (Memphis, Tenn.: Southwestern at Memphis, 1973), 54.

88. Robert G. Patterson, memorandum to James M. Vest, 25 October 1994.

Chapter 3

1. *The Bulletin of Southwestern at Memphis, 1974–75* (Memphis: Southwestern at Memphis, 1974), 163. For their invaluable assistance, without which this chapter could not have been written, I would like to thank: Fred. W. Neal, who sat for several interviews and offered constructive criticism of earlier drafts; Elaine Whitaker, who provided insights into Neal's leadership and Granville Davis's teaching; and, for their able work in recovering pertinent documents, Sherry Fields and Margaret Handwerker.

2. *The Bulletin of Southwestern at Memphis, 1984–85* (Memphis: Southwestern at Memphis, 1984), 153–158. In the 1982–1983 and 1983–1984 catalogues this text was part of a section called "Purpose of the College." In the 1981–1982 catalogue, it was the standard catalogue entry for the Man course. The change in location is explained later in this chapter.

3. Daughdrill succeeded William L. Bowden, who had become president in 1970 after John David Alexander left Southwestern to accept the presidency of Pomona College.

4. Robert G. Patterson, et. al., "Year of Challenge: Report of the Committee to Plan for the Eighties Regarding Faculty and Educational Program," May 1977, Morgan Archives.

5. Charles O. Warren et al., "Memorandum to the Southwestern Faculty," 25 May 1978, Morgan Archives.

6. Faculty of Arts and Sciences, *Report on the Core Curriculum* (Cambridge: Harvard University, 1978).

7. The titles of three publications of the era give evidence of some of the motives behind curriculum reform: Ernest L. Boyer and Arthur Levine, *A Quest for Common Learning, The Aims of General Education* (Washington, D.C.: Carnegie Foundation, 1981);

William J. Bennett, *To Reclaim a Legacy, A Report on the Humanities in Higher Education* (Washington, D.C.: National Endowment for the Humanities, 1984); and *Integrity in the College Curriculum: A Report to the Academic Community: The Findings and Recommendations of the Project on Redefining the Meaning and Purpose of Baccalaureate Degrees* (Washington, D.C.: Association of American Colleges, 1985).

8. Charles Frankel, "Why the Humanities?" *ACLS Newsletter* 30 (1979), 17–18.

9. "Deed of Trust," The Bellingrath-Morse Foundation (1 February 1950), Office of the Dean of Academic Affairs, 4.

10. *The Bulletin of Southwestern at Memphis, 1982–83* (Memphis: Southwestern at Memphis, 1982), 8. It appears quite clearly that the language of Bellingrath's deed of trust was modeled after a speech delivered by Diehl in 1943:

From the Hebrew-Christian tradition comes the root principle of democracy, the dignity and worth of the human individual. Made in the image of God and accountable to Him, endowed with reason, conscience, and the power of choice, it is of vital importance that this human being make the most of his abilities and opportunities.

11. "Deed of Trust," 13.

12. *The Bulletin of Southwestern at Memphis, 1976–77* (Memphis: Southwestern at Memphis, 1976), 35.

13. The Presidents and Chairs of the Boards of Trustees of Huntingdon College and Stillman College, letter to Downing (Chair of the Bellingrath-Morse Foundation), 25 September 1979, Office of the Dean of Academic Affairs.

14. Daughdrill, letter to Downing, 28 January 1980, Office of the Dean of Academic Affairs.

15. *The Bulletin of Southwestern at Memphis, 1969–70* (Memphis: Southwestern at Memphis, 1969), 54. The Man course was counted as credit in "Biblical Studies," "Theological Studies," and "History of Religion." (124). Thus, it met the stated degree requirements of two courses in "Biblical Studies" and two courses in "Theology/History of Religion." Although not explicitly stated in these terms, it appears that a similar reckoning applied to the degree requirements stated in the 1968–69 catalogue.

16. Robert R. Llewellyn, Douglas Hatfield, Bernice White, David Y. Jeter, "Recommendations for a Reform of the Curriculum and Related Academic Programs," 25 July 1980, Morgan Archives.

17. Quite coincidentally, the new syllabus for the Man course in 1980–1981, the twelfth edition, was published with the "Man is the measure" cover.

18. "Recommendations," 42.

19. "Recommendations," 40–41.

20. "Deed of Trust," 13.

21. Wade also served as chair of the board's committee on faculty and educational program.

22. The suggestion for interdisciplinary natural and social science courses echoed Diehl's intentions for the college's curriculum during the founding era of the Man course. See chapter 1.

23. Report to the Faculty from the Committee on Curriculum, Standards and Standing, 8 January 1981, Morgan Archives.

24. Minutes of the 14 January 1981 meeting of the Southwestern faculty, Morgan Archives.

25. Fred W. Neal, memorandum to Dean Gerald Duff, 18 June 1981, Memphis, Tenn. Whitaker recalled one aspect of this first workshop (e-mail message to author, 21 June 1995) : "I remember Granville Davis telling us that presentation of a Man text is a three-step process: what does it say, what does it mean, what does it mean to us? Dr. Davis also said that he had often wished to be a pipe smoker so that he would have something to chew on while he waited for students to think up answers to his questions. That notion of sitting on silence is probably very important to the discussion aspect of Search."

26. "90% of Students Surveyed Want Man Alternative," *Sou'wester,* 13 February 1981.

27. Minutes of the 23 April 1981 and 7 May 1981 meetings of the Curriculum, Standards, and Standing Committee, Morgan Archives.

28. Neal had reiterated this point in his narrative statement about the religious dimensions of the Man course. His point was not included in the version that accompanied the 28 January letter.

29. *The Bulletin of Southwestern at Memphis, 1981–82* (Memphis: Southwestern at Memphis, 1981), 94.

30. "'Man' description creates controversy," *Sou'wester,* 30 April 1981.

31. The Man Staff, "Statement of Concern," n.d., and reported in the *Sou'wester* article.

32. Daughdrill, internal office memorandum, 23 June 1981, Office of the Dean of Academic Affairs.

33. Downing, letter to Daughdrill, 22 July 1981, Office of Dean of Academic Affairs.

34. Minutes of the 28 July 1981 meeting of the Executive Committee, The Board of Trustees, Southwestern at Memphis.

35. "Man council drafting description of course," *Sou'wester,* 9 October 1981.

36. Annually, the Man staff had presented the Shewmaker Award to the student named by the staff as the outstanding student in that year. The award consisted of a stipend to purchase books of the student's choice in the humanities. A second award was created in 1982–1983 and, in 1985, was named to honor Fred W. Neal.

37. "Man council drafting description of course."

38. Minutes of the 6 October 1981 and 27 October 1981 meetings of the Man Administrative Committee.

39. Llewellyn, memorandum to Neal and the Man Staff, 25 September and 2 October 1981, based on telephone conversations with Arant and Sears.

40. Minutes of the October 1981 meeting of the Board of Trustees, Southwestern at Memphis.

41. "Board discusses 'Man' description," *Sou'wester*, 30 October 1981.

42. "A Change," *Sou'wester,* 30 October 30 1981.

43. Daughdrill, letter to Downing, 4 October 1982; and Downing, letter to Daughdrill, 23 November 1982, Office of Dean of Academic Affairs.

44. Rhodes was present at the announcement of the name change in July 1984. He died in November 1984.

45. Minutes of the 4 December 1981 meeting of the Man staff; also see course description for Humanities 101–102, 201–202 in *The Bulletin of Southwestern at Memphis, 1982–83* (Memphis: Southwestern at Memphis, 1982), 97.

46. Report on the 5 January 1984 meeting of the Man Administrative Council.

47. In addition to Clark, Whitaker, and White, the women faculty members who from time to time were members of the Man staff in the period 1975–1985 were Diane Sachs from the anthropology and sociology department and Sharon Welch, Janet Everts, and Valarie Ziegler from the religious studies department. Ziegler chaired the committee that eventually dealt with the issue of an appropriate name for the Man course. See chapter 4.

48. Fred W. Neal, interview by author, 28 June 1995, Memphis, Tenn.

49. Fred W. Neal, James W. Jobes, Douglas W. Hatfield, Elaine E. Whitaker, eds, *Man in the Light of History and Religion, A Syllabus for Humanities 201–202,* 12th ed. (Memphis, Tenn.: Rhodes College, 1980, revised 1984). The preface continued: "Those who would insist that it is time we include readings concerning women may be gratified to see that we have incorporated selections from Simone de Beauvoir's *The Second Sex.*"

50. This problem was reflected in an item recorded by Hatfield in the minutes of the Man Staff 16 February 1982 meeting: "In response to Prof. Neal's comment that some departments were not making sufficient allowance in course load for Professors who are engaged in teaching the Man course, Prof. Jobes asserted that the Man Staff should 'fuss moderately much' on behalf of members of the staff who will be teaching Man as an overload."

51. Fred W. Neal, memorandum to Dean Gerald Duff, 5 April 1982, Memphis, Tenn. Neal always maintained that even those faculty members who would normally teach in only one year of the course—either the freshman or the sophomore year—should have the experience of teaching both years at least once. Only in this way would the faculty appreciate, and thus enable students to appreciate, the interdisciplinary nature of the Man course.

52. Robert Amy, professor of biology, letter to James M. Vest, Memphis, Tenn., 1 November 1994.

53. Elaine Whitaker, e-mail message to author, 21 June 1995.

54. Fred W. Neal, interview by author, 28 June 1995, Memphis, Tenn.

55. Elaine Whitaker, e-mail to author, 21 June 1995. As Neal's associate director, Whitaker was directly involved in editing the syllabus in which the gender issue regarding the course title was addressed.

56. Mary Elizabeth Walker began discussions with development officers for the college in August 1984. She expressed interest in honoring Neal since she had enjoyed the Man course, taught through a special continuing education program. Mrs. Walker agreed to an idea proposed by the academic dean that an endowment be established to honor Fred Neal and Granville Davis, the two faculty members responsible for the continuing education version of the Man course. The document announcing the endowment (November 1985) states: "The gift creating the Douglass Faculty Seminars for Interdisciplinary Teaching will establish a permanent endowment to prepare faculty to teach the 'Man in the Light of History and Religion course. The seminars will be in memory of Memphis attorney George Porter Douglass, father of Mary Elizabeth Douglass Walker, '41, and they will honor Dr. Fred W. Neal and Dr. Granville D. Davis, two members of the College faculty who have recently provided the major leadership for the [Man] course." Neal reported that both he and Davis were surprised and pleased by the gift.

57. "Dr. Neal Says Farewell to Man," *Sou'wester*, 26 April 1985. See also note 51 above.

58. The second year of the course continued to follow the ninety-minute Tuesday-Thursday format until the "track" system was adopted. See chapter 4.

59. "Dr. Neal says Farewell to Man."

60. Neal's publishing responsibilities for the Man course made him an ideal user of computer-assisted word processing. From the very first, when word-processing support was made available at the college, Neal lobbied for equipment and became one of the first users of this technology. Whitaker reported (e-mail to author, 21 June 1995) that special precautions had to be exercised in Neal's office because the orange shag rug had a tendency to produce static charges that threatened the computer's electronic circuitry. Vest had joined the Man staff in 1984.

61. Fred W. Neal, interview by author, 28 June 1995; and "Dr. Neal says Farewell to Man."

62. Ibid.

63. Fred W. Neal, memorandum to Dean Gerald Duff, 30 August 1984.

64. Ibid. For his own teaching Neal was given the college's Clarence Day Award for Teaching in 1985, an award that annually recognizes Rhodes's most outstanding teacher.

65. Fred W. Neal, final lecture to the sophomore Man class, 28 March 1985.

66. John Gladney, Rhodes class of 1974, interview by author, October 1994. Gladney is a surgeon in Louisiana. In 1995 he recognized eleven faculty members, six of

whom taught in the Man course, with a substantial gift to the college in memory of his mother and of his family's ties with Rhodes over a sixty-year period.

Chapter 4

1. Special thanks are due to the following people who made contributions to this chapter beyond the instances mentioned below: Christopher M. Caldwell, Annette B. Cates, Harmon C. Dunathan, Janice M. Herbert, Larry Lacy, Glenn W. Munson, Fred W. Neal, Cecelia M. Vest, Nancy F. Vest. The data on SAT scores were supplied by David Wottle, the college's dean of admissions, in September 1995. *U.S. News and World Report* publishes its annual college guide every October.

2. Fred Neal, interview by James Vest, 1 May 1995.

3. Douglas Hatfield, interview by James Vest, 1 May 1995.

4. Robert R. Llewellyn, in a memorandum nominating Douglas Hatfield for the college's Charles E. Diehl Award for Faculty Service, September 1994. Observations in this paragraph are based on that document and on the comments of Search staff members.

5. John Searle, *The Campus War: A Sympathetic Look at the University in Agony* (New York: World Publishing Company, 1971), 175.

6. Ibid., 176.

7. Material in this paragraph is drawn from Douglas Hatfield, Annual Report to the Dean of Academic Affairs, 1987–88.

8. A balanced account of this conflict can be found in David Bromwich, *Politics by Other Means* (New Haven, Conn.: Yale University Press, 1992).

9. Hatfield, Annual Report, 1989–90, 2.

10. Comments reported to the authors by Valarie Ziegler.

11. See Carol P. Christ and Judith Plaskow, eds., *Womanspirit Rising* (New York: Harper Collins, 1992). Rhodes established an interdisciplinary Women's Studies Program, which first offered a minor in the 1990–1991 academic year.

12. Material in this section based on an e-mail communication to the authors from Valarie Ziegler, December 15, 1994.

13. Alumnus Christopher M. Caldwell, who was a sophomore in the course at the time, remembers the "Man Wall" in the refectory: "Many suggestions for names appeared, and some other suggestions as well: one disgruntled student wrote: 'Why not call it what it is . . . *Useless!*'" (interview by James Vest, January 1995).

14. Information in this paragraph taken from e-mail communications to the authors from Hatfield, 26 Oct. 1994 and 12 May 1995 and from Llewellyn, 15 May 1995.

15. See *The Will to Power*, trans. Walter Kaufman and R. J. Hollingale (New York: Vintage Books, 1967), sec. 972, 979.

16. Robert Watson, interview by James Vest, September 19, 1994.

17. Gail Streete, e-mail communication to the authors, February 3, 1995.

18. Linda Nelson, Peggy Harlow, and Chesley Dickinson, interview by James Vest, May 11–18, 1995.

19. Hatfield, Annual Report, 1991–92 and 1992–93.

20. Harmon Dunathan, interviews by the authors, 28 September –12 December 1994.

21. Robert Llewellyn, interviews by the authors, 28–29 September and 5 October 1994.

22. Hatfield, Annual Report, 1990–91, 5.

23. Hatfield, Annual Report, 1988–89, 1.

24. E-mail communication to the authors, 27 October 1994.

25. Hatfield, Annual Report, 1991–92, 2–3, 5–8.

26. Recommendations of the SACS committee headed and cited by Bill Berg, director of institutional research, in a memo to department heads, 25 February 1991.

27. Departmental mission statements, Rhodes College, 11 March 1991.

28. Memo from Bill Berg to department heads, 16 October 1990.

29. See, for example, student comments recorded in Hatfield, Annual report, 1990–91, appendix.

30. Hatfield, Annual Report, 1993–94, 5–6.

31. By 1995–1996, there were three sections of the history track, three of literature, two of philosophy, and two of religion. Two politics tracks were added in 1996–1997.

32. Portions of this section are adapted from Llewellyn's memorandum nominating Hatfield for the college's Charles E. Diehl Award, September 1994.

33. Hatfield, Annual Report, 1989–90, 1.

34. Material in this paragraph adapted from memos sent by Douglas Hatfield to Dean Gerald Duff, 1 May 1985 and 20 Sept. 1985, and from the anonymous evaluations of the workshop conducted 26–30 Aug. 1985.

35. "The George Porter Douglass Faculty Seminars for Interdisciplinary Teaching"; cf. a letter dated 8 November 1985, from Douglas Hatfield to Mary Elizabeth (Mrs. David T.) Walker, thanking her for establishing the seminars.

36. Hatfield, Letter to Mrs. David T. Walker, 8 November 1985.

37. John Bruhwiler, interview by the authors, 3 November 1994.

38. Ibid.

39. Robert Watson, interview by James Vest, 21 September 1994.

40. Richard Wood, communication to James Vest, 12 October 1994.

Chapter 5

1. For a discussion of this phenomenon and its implications, see Robert F. Davidson, "Trends in the Humanities in General Education," in *The Humanities in General Education,* ed. Earl J. McGrath (Dubuque, Iowa: W. C. Brown Co., 1949), 289–308.

2. McGrath, ed. *Humanities in General Education,* preface, v.

3. The first quotation is from J. Glenn Gray, "The Humanities at Haverford College," in McGrath, ed., *Humanities in General Education,* 1, the second from the editorial statement of purpose in the first issue of *The Christian Scholar* (March 1953), 3, and the third is the title of an address by Everett M. Dirksen, rpt. in *Christian Education: A Journal of Christian Higher Education* 32 (June 1949), 187ff.

4. Cf. the titles of numerous articles on this subject in the late 1940s and early 1950s in *Christian Education* and *The Christian Scholar*—e.g., "Saving Religion in Colleges," "Religion in Liberal Arts Education," and "The Christian College in a Secular Society." An early discussion of these issues appeared in Robert F. Davidson, "Program for the Christian College," in *The Christian Century* (24 Sept. 1941), 1174–76, in which Davidson expressed the view that "genuine and intelligent Christian character provides the surest undergirding of our democratic way of life" (1175).

5. Information in this and the preceding paragraph is based on interviews by the author with E. Ashby Johnson, September 1994–February 1995, and with Robert Meacham, Leslie Bullock, and Fred Neal, February–April 1995, as well as on details supplied the author by Diana Sanderson of the Presbyterian Historical Foundation, Montreat, N.C., and Elizabeth Kesler, archivist at Rhodes College.

6. The Presbyterian Education Association South was founded by the Southern Presbyterian Church in 1914 to foster discussion of values and the relation of religion to higher education. The Faculty Christian Fellowship advanced similar goals in an interdenominational context. Fred Neal characterized Blakely as a quiet individual who "made things happen" (interview by the author April 1995). According to Leslie Bullock, who founded the Christianity and Culture curriculum at St. Andrews, Blakely had a rare talent for bringing people together. Neal and Bullock agree that Blakely's efforts were a catalyst for much of what is described in this chapter.

7. "Danforth Associates: Statement of Purpose," rpt. 1980. Members of that organization who taught in the Search course include Ray Allen, Robert Amy, W. Taylor Reveley, and James Vest.

8. Materials in this paragraph are drawn from the author's conversations and correspondence with humanities course directors Daniel D. Rhodes, E. Ashby Johnson, Fred Neal, and Leslie Bullock, September 1994–April 1995. The first quote is from Rhodes, the second from Bullock and the third from historian William Wilbur of Eckerd College, in his address "Prolegomena to a History of FPC/Eckerd College," 18 April 1994.

9. Robert F. Davidson, *Adventures in Ideas and Values* (Laurinburg, N.C.: St. Andrews Press, 1984), 106. According to Leslie Bullock the problems were both financial and conceptual, and centered on the issue of whether the synod should continue to fund preparatory schools and junior colleges or concentrate on four-year coeducational colleges (conversation with the author, 7 April 1995).

10. "The Church and Higher Education: The Educational Institutions Survey Report by the Committee on Educational Institutions to the Synod of North Carolina, Presbyterian Church in the United States," July 1955. The commission that produced the seventy-two page report was headed by Dean Francis Rosecrance of New York University and included Sara Blanding, president of Vassar College, Thomas Spragens, president of Stephens College, John O. Gross, executive secretary, General Board of Education of the Methodist Church, and John D. Millett, president of Miami University.

11. The original intent was to include Peace College in Raleigh in the merger as well, but Peace supporters rallied to the cause and kept the college intact.

12. Information supplied by Leslie Bullock in a conversation with the author 7 April 1995.

13. Information in this section adapted from Davidson, *Adventures*, 107–9. Davidson specifies that, as with the curriculum, the special planning for the physical plant, which was unusual at the time, was envisioned and executed as an integral part of the institution's Christian commitment to make education available to all.

14. Davidson, *Adventures*, 108.

15. Ibid., 109.

16. Leslie Bullock, conversation with the author, 7 April 1995.

17. Jameson Jones, interview by the author and Donald W. Tucker, October 10, 1994.

18. This and all subsequent quotes in this paragraph are from "Curriculum Suggested by Panel of Educators for Consolidated Presbyterian College, Laurinburg, N.C., Under a Grant from the Fund for the Advancement of Education," 6–15. William Taeusch, dean of the College of Wooster, chaired the panel, which met daily 5–31 August 1957. Other participants included Ruth Eckerd, professor of higher education at the University of Minnesota, Sidney French, dean of Rollins College, Price Gwynn, Jr., dean of Flora Macdonald, and Rene Williamson, professor of political science at Louisiana State University.

19. Comments in this and the following paragraph by Bullock and by Professor of English Emeritus Carl D. Bennett are from conversations with the author, 16 December 1994, and 7 April 1995.

20. Material in this section is based on information supplied by St. Andrews professors W. M. Alexander, Carl Bennett, Leslie Bullock, Rodger W. Decker, and Carl Walters; Vice-President for Academic Affairs Lawrence E. Schulz; and Librarian Elizabeth Holmes.

21. Davidson, *Adventures,* 111–112.

22. *Learning for Tomorrow: The Role of the Future in Education* (New York: Vintage, 1974), 368–371, in an Appendix compiled by Billy Rojas and H. Wentworth Eldredge entitled "Sample Syllabi and Directory of Futures Studies" listing models for those inter-

ested in constructing future-oriented course offerings. Course requirements for Christianity and Culture 402 included two papers to be presented and defended before the class, one a research paper dealing with topics such as "What is the future for democracy?" and "Will belief in God continue to be a possibility?" and the other a position paper "in which the student takes a moral stand" (369).

23. *Eight Hundred Colleges Face the Future*, ed. Manning Pattillo and Donald Mackenzie (St. Louis: Danforth Foundation, 1965), 62–63. Two innovations singled out by the report as "highly significant" in establishing "a reasoned framework of belief" were the Christianity and Culture Program at St. Andrews, "which is the backbone of liberal education at that institution" and the Christian Culture Program at St. Mary's College, Notre Dame, Indiana.

24. "Science at St. Andrews: Mix Well and Call it Interdisciplinary," *College Management* 3 (April 1968), 11–16. This article highlights the conceptualization, floor-plans, and "interdisciplinary lab furniture" of the "barrierless" science building at St. Andrews, and describes the STMS program.

25. Richard Prust, letter to the author, 26 April 1995.

26. Carl Walters, conversation with the author, 19 December 1994.

27. Catalog copy written by SAGE Chair Richard Prust and supplied to the author, April 1995.

28. These details and others in the following paragraphs, as well as quotes from E. Ashby Johnson, are based on the interviews by the author and Donald W. Tucker, June 1994–April 1995.

29. Quotations in this paragraph are from A. J. Carlson, "Thirtysomething: Interdisciplinary Study at Austin College," in *ACknowledge* [the alumni magazine of Austin College] (Fall 1988), 8–9.

30. Ibid., 8.

31. Ibid., 8–9.

32. Material in this section was supplied the author by Austin College's Vice President for Academic Affairs and Dean of the Faculty, David W. Jordan, and by Carlson.

33. Quotes in this section from John M. Bevan are from interviews by the author, 3 March and 20 May 1995. According to Bevan, Blakely saw this as an opportunity to combine resources in a cooperative way, and although the road was sometimes rocky, the idea of creating something innovative and important eventually prevailed. Professor of History Emeritus William Wilbur adds that Blakely was instrumental in inviting Fay Campbell, his counterpart in the Northern Presbyterian Church, and Rev. Clem Bininger of Ft. Lauderdale, the head of its governing board, to help initiate this joint effort. Cf. Wilbur's "Prolegomena to a History of FPC/Eckerd College," an address delivered at Eckerd, April 18, 1994 (7, 10–11).

34. Fred Neal, interview by the author, 16 February 1995. Cf. Davidson, *Adventures*, 101–103, 110n.

35. Information supplied by William Wilbur in a letter to the author, 26 April 1995.

36. Ibid.

37. Bette Ackerman, interview by and e-mail communication to the author, 27 October 1994.

38. Bradford Pendley, memo to the author, 21 October 1994.

39. Material in this paragraph taken from conversations by the author with Thomas Oberhofer, director of the Core Program at Eckerd, 31 October and 4 November 1994.

40. Oberhofer, interview by the author, 31 October 1994.

41. These details and others in the following paragraphs, as well as quotes from Daniel Rhodes, are taken from answers prepared by him during the summer of 1994 in response to a series of questions by the author or from interviews by the author, September 1994—May 1995.

42. Information supplied to the author by Daniel Rhodes and by Max Polley, another longtime participant in Davidson's Humanities program, who sees this as a major step in the process of exploring educational alternatives that led Davidson in the late 1960s to a thoroughgoing curriculum reform known as the "Blue Sky" initiative.

43. According to Max Polley, who was part of the founding staff of the program, the motion was discussed at a faculty retreat at Montreat, and the proposal passed by a single vote (interview by the author, 19 March 1995).

44. From the author's conversations with Polley and with Leslie Bullock, April 1995.

45. This and subsequent quotations in this paragraph are taken from "The Western Tradition to the Renaissance," Syllabus 1962–63, Introduction, iii–v.

46. This and subsequent quotes from Polley are from a conversation with the author, 24 April 1995.

47. Information in this paragraph is based on material supplied to the author by Max Polley and Daniel Rhodes. The final quotation is an allusion to the third-century theologian Tertullian's famous rhetorical question: "What indeed has Athens to do with Jerusalem?" In other words, what has reason to do with faith?

48. Information in these paragraphs was supplied by Brian Shaw in an interview by the author, 24 October 1994.

49. Quotes from Manning in this and the following paragraph are taken from the *Davidson Journal* (Spring 1995), p. 37, and from an interview by the author, 22 May 1995.

50. Information in this section is based on communications to the author from Brinkley, classics; Simpson, English; and Norment, religion; as well as from Dean of the Faculty J. Scott Colley and program director Patrick Wilson, September 1994–May 1995.

51. Information in this and the following paragraphs supplied to the author by Robert Padgett and Tom Jolly.

52. "The Heritage Program" brochure, prepared by Padgett, 1969, 3.

53. Information and quotations in this and the following paragraph are taken from a letter to the author from Padgett, 11 May 1995.

54. Comments from David Davis in this section are taken from an interview by the author, 3 November 1994.

55. Information in this section is based on communications to the author from Patterson during the summer of 1994 and also on reports of the Interdisciplinary Humanities Program Planning Group, which Patterson headed, and an account written for this study by Patterson and Pamela Royston Macfie of the Department of English, who chaired the interdisciplinary program from 1992 to 1995.

56. Report of the Curriculum and Academic Policy Committee to the College Faculty, 23 April 1990.

57. Interdisciplinary Humanities Program: Detailed Description and Reading List, 7 February 1992.

58. "Final Report" of the Interdisciplinary Humanities Program Planning Group, College of Arts and Sciences, The University of the South, 4.

59. Report to Dean Robert L. Keele, Provost Frederick Croom, and Vice-Chancellor Samuel R. Williamson, 31 October 1994.

60. The author is indebted to Donald W. Tucker and Michael Nelson for their assistance in the formulation of this section.

61. Fred Neal, conversation with the author, 9 February 1995.

62. From introductory comments to a Search lecture on Plato and Aristotle presented at Rhodes College, 10 February 1995 by guest lecturer Aristide Tessitore, associate professor of political science, Furman University. Other points in this section are based on remarks by Fred Neal in conversation with the author, 9 February 1995, and on comments by Michael Nelson.

63. Special appreciation is due to the following individuals, without whose assistance this chapter could not have been written: Albert E. Dimmock, Rex Enoch, Jesse B. Garner, Elizbeth G. Kesler, W. Larry Lacy, Frank Laney, Robert R. Llewellyn, Glenn W. Munson, Fred W. Neal, Diana Sanderson, Sally Thomason, Donald W. Tucker, Nancy F. Vest.

64. Material in this section based on a December 1994 report, " 'Man's Search for Meaning . . .' and the Center for Adult Education," prepared from materials in the archives of the Meeman Center for Special Studies at Rhodes College by the center's director, Sally Thomason.

65. Thomason, memo to the author, 9 January 1994.

66. Robert Watson, interview by the author, 19 September 1994.

67. Comments by Cullen in this section are from e-mail communications to the author, 13 February 1995.

68. Leigh MacQueen, interview by the author, 23 September 1994.

69. James Russell, interview by the author, 21 September 1994.

70. Robert Llewellyn, e-mail communications with the author, 3–4 November 1994.

Chapter 7

1. Gilbert Allardyce, "The Rise and Fall of the Western Civilization Course," *American Historical Review* 87 (1982), 695–725.

2. William J. Bennett, *To Reclaim a Legacy: A Report on the Humanities in Higher Education* (Washington, D.C.: National Endowment for the Humanities, 1984).

3. Allan Bloom, *The Closing of the American Mind: How Higher Education Has Failed Democracy and Impoverished the Souls of Today's Students* (New York: Simon and Schuster, 1987).

4. Gerald Graff, "Academic Writing and the Uses of Bad Publicity," *South Atlantic Quarterly* 91 (1992), 5–17.

5. George Levine et al., *Speaking for the Humanities*, Occasional Paper No. 7 (Washington, D.C.: American Council of Learned Societies, 1989); Darryl J. Gless and Barbara Herrnstein Smith, eds., *The Politics of Liberal Education* (Durham, N.C.: Duke University Press, 1992); Roger Kimball, *Tenured Radicals: How Politics Has Corrupted Our Higher Education* (New York: Harper and Row, 1990); and Dinesh D'Souza, *Illiberal Education: The Politics of Race and Sex on Campus* (New York: Free Press, 1991).

6. John Searle, "Storm Over the University," *New York Review of Books*, 6 December 1990, 34–42. Searle is describing the critics' views in the quoted passage, not his own.

7. In a section called "Biblical Studies at Rhodes," the college's catalogue annually offers a fuller statement of how the Search course satisfies the Bellingrath-Morse requirement. The entire first year, including the long Greco-Roman unit, explores the various roots of Christianity. In addition, all of the units of the second year treat the influence of biblical religion on the Western world. "Biblical Studies at Rhodes," *Rhodes College Catalogue, 1995–1996* (Memphis: Rhodes College, 1995), 76–78. The program "Life: Then and Now," which students may take instead of Search, also satisfies the Bellingrath-Morse requirement.

8. David Damrosch, *We Scholars: Changing the Culture of the University* (Cambridge, Mass.: Harvard University Press, 1995), 111–122.

9. As a way of dealing with intellectual disagreements among faculty, decentralizing teaching is the opposite of Gerald Graff's much discussed proposal to "teach the conflicts." Graff urges faculty to bring the issues of interpretation that divide them into the classroom. But unless one assumes, as he does, that the conflicts that excite professors are of interest to students, no approach could be more dreary. Graff's own examples are not encouraging in this regard: "The administrative distinction between Creative Writing and orthodox literary study has always veiled divergent attitudes toward literature; con-

fronting the antagonism as an explicit theme would enhance both kinds of study. The tension between vocational courses (like basic composition) and liberal humanistic studies is inevitable—why not make something of it?" Graff and William E. Cain, "Peace Plan for the Canon Wars," *Nation* (6 March 1989), 310–313. See also Graff, *Beyond the Culture Wars: How Teaching the Conflicts Can Revitalize American Education* (New York: Norton, 1992).

David Bromwich offers an additional criticism of the teaching-the-conflicts approach. "The timely books and articles that take a position on the conflicts are not built to last; there will be another debate, with different books and articles, for the early 1990s and the late. When a pedagogy like this has been tried, in the more arid tracts of the social sciences, it cuts down the generations of students to blocks of five or six years, and one generation is forced to talk with the last about the fraying ends of a half-dead quarrel." Bromwich, *Politics By Other Means: Higher Education and Group Thinking* (New Haven, Conn.: Yale University Press, 1992), 127.

10. See chapters 2 and 3. I was able to find no faculty member who could explain why the miniseminars were abandoned. All remember them as having been successful.

11. Donald Kagan, *On the Origins of War and the Preservation of Peace* (New York: Doubleday, 1995).

12. As this book was going to press, plans were being laid to treat Islam in the religion track of second-year Search, beginning in the 1996–1997 academic year.

13. Bromwich, *Politics By Other Means*, 107.

14. Bill Berg, Rhodes director of institutional research, memorandum to author, September 1995.

15. Sven Birkerts, *The Gutenberg Elegies: The Fate of Reading in an Electronic Age* (Boston: Faber and Faber, 1994), 15, 3.

16. Jay David Bolter, *Writing Space: The Computer, Hypertext, and the History of Writing* (Hillsdale, N.J.: Erlbaum, 1991), 2.

17. Richard A. Lanham, *The Electronic Word: Democracy, Technology, and the Arts* (Chicago: University of Chicago Press, 1993), 3.

18. Ibid., 17, 99.

19. Bolter, *Writing Space*, 59.

20. Richard A. Lanham, "The Extraordinary Convergence: Democracy, Technology, Theory, and the University Curriculum," in Gless and Smith, *The Politics of Liberal Education*, 39. For all his professions of concern for teaching traditional material in new ways, Lanham cannot seem to resist attaching the epithet "dubious classic" to every "great book" he mentions.

21. Birkerts, *Gutenberg Elegies*, 136–38.

22. Quoted in Jay David Bolter, "Topographic Writing and the Electronic Writing

Space," in Paul Delany and George P. Landow, eds., *Hypermedia and Literary Studies* (Cambridge, Mass.: MIT Press, 1991), 105.

23. Myron Tuman, *Word Perfect: Literacy in the Computer Age* (Pittsburgh, Pa.: University of Pittsburgh Press, 1992), 73.

24. Lanham, *The Electronic Word*, 7.

25. Tuman, *Word Perfect*, 80. In unguarded moments, some critics of the Western tradition who experienced and rejected the "great books" approach during their own college years bemoan the ignorance of their students, who have not read enough to understand what the criticism is all about.

Contributors

ELLEN T. ARMOUR is assistant professor of religious studies at Rhodes College. She earned her Ph.D. in theology from Vanderbilt University and has written several articles on deconstruction, feminism, and religion. Her current book is called *Deconstruction, Feminist Theology and the Problem of Difference: Subverting the Race/Gender Divide*. She has taught at Rhodes since 1991.

DANIEL E. CULLEN received his Ph.D. in political science from Boston College. He has taught at Bentley College, Acadia University, Vanderbilt University, and, since 1988, at Rhodes College, where he is associate professor and chair of political science. He is the author of *Freedom in the Political Philosophy of Rousseau* and is currently writing *Rousseau's America*.

JEAN BETHKE ELSHTAIN, the Laura Spelman Rockefeller Professor of Social and Political ethics at the University of Chicago, is the author of hundreds of essays and book reviews in scholarly journals and journals of civic opinion. She has also written or edited twelve books, including *Public Man, Private Woman: Women in Political and Social Thought, Women and War, Democracy on Trial,* and, most recently, *Augustine and the Limits of Politics.*

DOUGLAS W. HATFIELD is the J. J. McComb Professor of History at Rhodes College, where he has taught since 1965. He earned his Ph.D. from the University of Kentucky and has written articles on religion and politics in nineteenth century Germany for the *Journal of Church and State* and the *Red River Valley Historical Journal.* Since 1986, he has been the director of the Search course.

JAMES JOBES, professor of philosophy at Rhodes College, earned his Ph.D. in philosophy at the University of Virginia. He has taught at Rhodes since 1964, and has written for the *British Journal of Aesthetics* and *Canadian Philosophical Reviews.*

LARRY LACY is professor of philosophy at Rhodes College, where he studied as an undergraduate and has taught since 1962. He earned his Ph.D. at the University of Virginia and has written articles for the *Southern Journal of Philosophy* and *Christian Scholar's Review*. His current book is called *Christian Eschatology and the Problem of Evil*.

ROBERT R. LLEWELLYN received his Ph.D. in philosophy from Vanderbilt University and has taught at Rhodes College since 1969. He has written articles on Whitehead's structure of space and time and Plato's *Republic*. From 1978 to 1991, he served as associate dean and, for a time, as acting dean at Rhodes.

KENNETH MORRELL received his Ph.D. in classical philology from Harvard University. He joined the Rhodes faculty as assistant professor of Greek and Roman studies in 1993, after teaching at St. Olaf College, and is a member of the development team for Perseus 1.0, a database for the study of ancient Greece.

FRED W. NEAL is the R. A. Webb Professor Emeritus of Religious Studies at Rhodes College. After earning his Ph.D. in church history from the University of Chicago, he inaugurated studies in philosophy and religion at Mississippi State College. He joined the Rhodes faculty in 1958 and served for many years as the director of the Search (then Man) course. He was senior editor of several editions of the course's syllabus and books of readings.

MICHAEL NELSON joined the faculty of Rhodes College as professor of political science in 1991, after receiving his Ph.D. in political science from Johns Hopkins University and teaching for twelve years at Vanderbilt University. His books include *Presidents, Politics, and Policy* and *The American Presidency: Origins and Development, 1776–1993*, which won the Benjamin Franklin Award. A former editor of the *Washington Monthly*, he has written for publications ranging from the *Public Interest* and *Political Science Quarterly* to *Newsweek* and the *New York Times*. More than forty of his articles have been reprinted in anthologies of political science, history, sports, and English composition.

GAIL CORRINGTON STREETE is associate professor of religious studies and director of the Women's Studies program at Rhodes College. She received her Ph.D. in biblical studies from Drew University and holds a master's degree in classical studies from the State University of New York at Buffalo. Before coming to Rhodes in 1990, she taught at Harvard Divinity School, the College of William and Mary, and elsewhere. She is the author of *The "Divine Man," Her Image of Salvation: Female Saviors and Formative Christianity*, and (in progress) *The Strange Woman: Female Adultery and Autonomy in Biblical Literature*.

DAVID WELCH SUGGS, JR., was graduated from Rhodes College in 1995, where he was editor of the *Sou'wester*, a four-time conference champion in track and field, and a member of Phi Beta Kappa. He is currently enrolled at the University of Missouri journalism school.

JAMES W. TURNER was graduated from Rhodes College in 1995. While there, he was an officer of the Honor Council, a member of the Student Assembly, and a columnist for the *Sou'wester*. After graduating, he was commissioned as an officer in the U.S. Navy.

JAMES M. VEST is professor of French at Rhodes College, where he has taught since 1973. His books include *The French Face of Ophelia from Belleforest to Baudelaire* and *The Poetic Works of Maurice de Guerin*. He has written more than a dozen articles on nineteenth-century French authors, as well as a study of Shakespearean themes in Alfred Hitchcock's *Vertigo*. He earned his Ph.D. at Duke University.

Index

Bold-face numerals indicate illustrations.

CELEBRATING THE HUMANITIES

was composed electronically using Bembo text and display types.
The book was printed on acid-free, Glatfelter Supple Opaque Recycled Natural paper,
Smyth sewn and bound over 88-point binder's boards cased in Roxite B grade cloth
and with covers printed in four colors by Thomson-Shore, Inc.
Book and cover designs are the work of Gary Gore.
Published by Vanderbilt University Press
Nashville, Tennessee 37235.